CISTERCIAN STUDIES SERIES: NUMBER FORTY-TWO

THE MESSAGE OF THOMAS MERTON

Woodcut by Lavrans Nielsen
Edited by Brother Patrick Hart

CISTERCIAN STUDIES SERIES: NUMBER FORTY-TWO

The Message of Thomas Merton

edited by

Brother Patrick Hart

CISTERCIAN PUBLICATIONS

Kalamazoo, Michigan

1981

Typeset by the Carmelites of Indianapolis

Library of Congress Cataloging in Publication Data
Main entry under title:
The Message of Thomas Merton.
    (Cistercian studies series; no. 42)
    Bibliography: p. 211
    1. Merton, Thomas, 1915-1968—Addresses, essays, lectures. I. Hart, Patrick, Brother. II. Series.
    BX4705.M542M4   271'.125'024   80-23637
    ISBN 0-87907-842-1

TO THE MEMORY OF
THOMAS MERTON
1915 – 1968

Contents

vii

Acknowledgments

Grateful acknowledgements are made to the editors and publishers of a number of journals in which some of these essays first appeared, although in considerably different form. Archbishop Jean Jadot's *Preface*, Abbot Flavian Burns' address, and Monsignor William Shannon's paper were first published in *Cistercian Studies* (1979). E. Glenn Hinson's contribution originally appeared in *Religion in Life* (Copyright © 1979, Abingdon), and Victor Kramer's study was printed in *Studia Mystica* (1980). The Epilogue by James Douglass, 'Merton's Glimpse of the Kingdom' was first published in *The Agitator* (December 1979).

We are indebted to the Trustees of the Merton Legacy Trust for their permission to quote from several unpublished manuscripts of Thomas Merton, including *The Inner Experience, Cold War Letters, Prayer as Worship and Experience* and *Ascetical and Mystical Theology Notes.*

Foreword

THE FIRST DECADE has passed since the death of Thomas Merton by accidental electrocution in Bangkok, Thailand, following his address to Eastern monastic leaders on 10 December 1968. Among the many celebrations commemorating the event throughout the world was a two-week Merton Commemoration at Columbia University in New York from 26 November to 10 December 1978. Merton had done his undergraduate as well as graduate studies there (his Master's thesis was on William Blake and he had commenced his doctoral work on the poetry of the English Jesuit, Gerard Manley Hopkins.) It was singularly appropriate that his *alma mater* should honor his memory in this way.

During the course of the commemoration a Merton Center for Religious Studies was established at Columbia University with the Reverend Paul Dinter as its first director. It was he who first suggested this volume and encouraged me to edit it for publication. The majority of the presentations and papers delivered during the Columbia Symposium are gathered here in an effort to make available to a wider audience the essential message of Thomas Merton as it emerged.

In addition to the Columbia Merton Commemoration papers, this volume contains a representative selection of contributions from several other programs beginning with the Vancouver School of Theology's Merton Symposium and People's Festival in May of 1978 to Bellarmine College's Merton Week in early December of the same year. The Preface by Archbishop Jean Jadot, former Apostolic Delegate to the United States (he had been Papal Nuncio in Thailand a decade earlier and was present at Merton's Funeral Liturgy in Bangkok), was originally addressed to the Community at Gethsemani Abbey on 10 December 1978, during the memorial

Concelebrated High Mass at which the Archbishop was principal celebrant. This again was fitting because Archbishop Jadot had several meetings with Merton in Bangkok shortly before his death and had discussed his interests in the Eastern religions, which he developed in the course of his talk.

Abbot Flavian Burns' opening address to the Merton Week at Bellarmine College, sponsored by the Thomas Merton Studies Center, speaks of Merton's message, which all the following essays elucidate or develop in one way or another. Rather than a sharing of personal reminiscences, which a previous volume attempted to do (see *Thomas Merton/Monk: A Monastic Tribute*, Doubleday Image Books), the present volume explores Merton's message for us today, and interprets that message in terms of the present moment in history. Hence, the essays taken as a whole tend to be an assessment of Merton's achievement and a critical evaluation of that contribution.

During the decade since Thomas Merton's death nearly a hundred doctoral dissertations, magisterial theses and serious studies have been made, or are in progress, on Merton or some aspect of his life and writings. His own books have been republished in new editions, both in this country and in translations abroad. More critical studies are beginning to appear on his many-sided interests, from his social concern to contemplative prayer, from incarnational poetry to ecumenism. As I reflect on the growing influence of Thomas Merton, I have come to the conclusion that it is in large measure the result of his remarkable ability to articulate something of his christian contemplative vision in such a personal way as to allow the reader to identify easily with him and his search for meaning in life.

Finally, I would like to express my gratitude to all those who have so generously contributed to this volume dedicated to Thomas Merton's memory. May his message of hope encourage us all on our journey to the Father.

P.H.

Preface

Archbishop Jean Jadot, D.D.

Archbishop Jean Jadot, a native of Belgium and former Apostolic Delegate to the United States, had been Papal Nuncio in the Far East in 1968, and had several conversations with Thomas Merton in Bangkok, Thailand, shortly before the latter's death. He assisted at Merton's funeral liturgy in Bangkok along with many Asian monastic and religious leaders and participants in the congress. His words, which form the Preface to this volume, were delivered to the Community at the Abbey of Gethsemani on 10 December 1978, at the Memorial Concelebrated Mass at which he presided. He also participated in the Merton Commoration at the Cathedral of the Assumption in Louisville, Kentucky, on the eve of the anniversary.

FATHER LOUIS (Thomas Merton) was just returning from his visit to India when I met him in Bangkok. He had been greatly impressed by the profoundly religious character of the Indian culture. He noticed above all the emphasis placed on contemplation.

The attraction of contemplation remains something of a mystery to the Western mind. We are more ordered to doing, caught up as we are in the present age of science and technology. Consumerism continues to expand under the pressure of high-powered advertising campaigns. All around us we see that Western society is taken up with possessions. The 'good things of life' are those which are tangible, measurable. The short range goal of so many today is to seek greater comfort. The long range goal is to make more money and to secure social status.

Fortunately, we can see at the same time a reversal of this trend. More and more people are discovering that what one does must be a means both of self-fulfillment and service to others. Action, then, not only helps one 'to have'; it also enables one to become a responsible person, 'to be'.

The contemplation which so strongly impressed Thomas Merton is above all a way of 'becoming oneself'—of 'being'. Thus, contemplation treats 'having more' with disinterest. The accent is on detachment. Speaking about Indian spirituality, Thomas Merton told me of the lasting impression he kept of detachment from material goods. This was manifested even in the midst of a level of poverty which is difficult for us to conceive. We are accustomed to having the bare necessities of life—and often a great deal more than what is necessary—readily available. Detachment is practised there in other ways as well. There is the detachment from social support: celibacy, the eremitical life or, if total isolation is not possible because of the visits of pilgrims or the curious, there is the semi-eremitical life implying long periods of silence.

Even those who are not hermits practise detachment in making a concerted effort to ignore or at least to curb their desires, personal preferences, and tastes, for example, in the moderate use of food, clothing, entertainment, and possessions. In the end, such detachment leads to a kind of dissolution of the primary psychologcial personality. By that I mean a sort of 'non-being', often called 'nirvana'. This opens up a greater communion with the universe, the totality of reality. In a word, there could be, as we Westeners say, the temptation of a form of pantheism where God alone exists and where each one is like a part of this Whole.

My encounter with Thomas Merton in Bangkok on the day before his death and again just a few hours before his fatal accident, left me with three strong convictions.

First of all, there is the need to stress 'being' rather than 'having'. 'Being' in this context means becoming a little more each day a human person, a creature of God. 'Having' refers to the possession of material goods, cultural wealth, the self-righteous

attitude toward virtues manifested by the Pharisees of the gospels.
Time does not permit us to pursue this point in depth. Suffice it to
say that placing 'being' over 'having' calls for the detachment from
self and, *at the same time*, the cultivation of the fundamental riches
of my personality. The goal is to become more what God wants
me to be. While awaiting the Lord Jesus I must work hard for the
coming of the Kingdom of God.

Merton and I did not discuss the gospel as such. But the words
and parables of Jesus formed a silent background enlightening the
entire conversation. Ringing in my mind are texts such as: 'If anyone wants to be a follower of mine, let him renounce himself and
take up his cross and follow me. For anyone who wants to save his
life will lose it; but anyone who loses his life for my sake will find
it. What, then will a man gain if he wins the whole world and
ruins his life.'[1] Or again: 'Unless a grain of wheat falls on the
ground and dies, it remains only a single grain.'[2] And finally: 'You
did not choose me, no, I chose you and I commissioned you to go
out and to bear fruit, fruit that will last.'[3]

The second conviction which my encounter with Thomas Merton reinforced is the importance of heeding the call to an interior
life. This goes beyond simple obedience to laws, moral norms, and
social rules. Such a life demands that we personally engage ourselves, giving ourselves to God without any reserve, sharing with
him that which is most intimate in our heart of hearts. I saw in
Thomas Merton a distrust of certain psychological methods which
fabricate a cheapened life of the spirit (perhaps close to what we
call today 'cultism'—I say 'perhaps' because the real nature of this
cultism still need to be studied with care). Man can develop his
psychological faculties without necessarily becoming a more
spiritual person. St Paul has already explained the distance that
separates the *psyche* from the *pneuma*.

Thomas Merton was able to appreciate the positive elements
which may be found in various ideologies. His conference in
Bangkok three hours before his death dealt with Marxism. He was
very conscious of the danger for the future of humanity of a world
enthralled by ideologies which are completely secular, be they
atheistic or agnostic. These pacify psychological anxieties, fears,

guilt complexes, frustrations brought on by loneliness and being misunderstood. But at the same time, they kill the fear of the Lord, in the biblical sense, the radical dread within the human spirit (*l'angoisse métaphysique*), all the impulse toward a transcendent God, toward the Father of our Lord Jesus Christ, the King of Glory who is to become all in all.

Once again I am getting into an area that deserves more attention than we are able to give it. Permit me at least to emphasize the responsibility this places before us who make up the Church. There is today in the world a thirst for God, an aspiring toward purity of life and the insatiable brotherhood of mankind. After all, by the grace of faith and baptism we have received the Spirit of God who remains in our midst as a source of living water for the world.

The third conviction I have to relay after visiting with Thomas Merton is the importance of returning to the old tradition of the spiritual master. Merton was struck by the role played by the guru in Indian religious life. The guru is the sage, the man of God, the holy person who teaches by his way of life and by his words how to live or—to return to my first point—the guru teaches what one must do 'to be'.

In India, people go hundreds of miles to find one of these sages. They may hope only to see him or to listen to him speak even for a moment, in order to receive an enlightening or encouraging word. All of this is close to the Judeo-Christian tradition. Individuals and groups of people sought Jesus out to receive his counsel, to listen to him speak. Think, for example, of those who came and said, 'Master, we know that you are an honest man and teach the way of God in an honest way and that you are not afraid of anyone because a man's rank means nothing to you. Tell us your opinion, then . . . '.[4] Similarly, the gospel according to St Mark describes how a man ran up, knelt before Jesus and asked, 'Good Master, what must I do to inherit eternal life?'.[5]

From generation to generation, the role of the spiritual master has been carried on in the Church. In fact, our history has produced a wealth of men and women whose writings remain to this day valuable resources for those who give and those who seek spiritual guidance. Among these are John Cassian and the Fathers of the Desert. Along with Benedict, Gregory, Bernard, Thomas, and Bonaventure, there are Catherine of Siena and Teresa of Avila.

In his little book on *Spiritual Direction and Meditation*, Father Louis notes that 'Those who have years of experience in the religious life are presumably able to direct themselves—but even they sometimes need to consult a wise spiritual guide. No religious should assume that he has absolutely no need, at any time, of spiritual direction.'[6] We can all benefit from such wise counsel.

By way of conclusion, I wish to share with you a classic description of the spiritual master from the *Introduction to the Devout Life*.

'A faithful friend is a strong defense... the medicine of life and immortality. Those who fear the Lord find him' (Sirach 6:14-16).... For this purpose choose one out of a thousand, as John of Avila says. For my part, I say one out of ten thousand for there are fewer men than we realize who are capable of this task. He must be full of charity, knowledge and prudence. If any of these three qualities is lacking, there is danger. (1,4)

I am sure you will agree that St Francis de Sales captures what Thomas Merton has been for so many of us even following his death ten years ago.

NOTES

1. Mt 16:26
2. Jn 12:24
3. Jn 15:15
4. Mt 22:16
5. Mk 10:17
6. Collegeville, Minnesota: The Liturgical Press, 1969, p. 16

Introduction

Brother Patrick Hart

BORN OF ARTIST PARENTS (a New Zealander father and an American mother) on 31 January 1915, in the French Pyrenees, the young Thomas Merton was educated in France, England, and America. After a soul-searching conversion experience while at Columbia University, he entered the Catholic Church and several years later (10 December 1941) entered the cistercian novitiate at the Abbey of Gethsemani near Bardstown, Kentucky. The early monastic training of Father Louis (his monastic name) and his study of the cistercian heritage together with his love of the Scriptures and the liturgy of the Church, led him deeply into the heart of the christian mystery. Merton was a poet, an artist, and a writer who was thoroughly steeped in the rich christian literature of the past and present. An example of this was his great admiration for the 'French prophets', such as Bernanos, Bloy, Claudel, Mauriac, and Peguy, who were to have such a profound influence on his life and later writings.

Thomas Merton's concept of the contemplative life, which developed early in his monastic life, must be seen as a full-flowering of the christian life in the Church.[1] As a result of his conversion experience, which he articulated eloquently in *The Seven Storey Mountain*, he was saturated with the thought of the gratuitous love of God for him personally. He never ceased extolling that fact during his life, and everything was a response to God's initiative. If he perhaps stressed too romantically the contemplative ideal in his early monastic life, he was more realistic in his later years. In an interesting passage from an unpublished manuscript entitled *The Inner Experi-*

1

ence Merton laid down a few basic notes on contemplation which bear quoting: 'The first thing that you have to do before you start thinking about such a thing as contemplation is to try to recover your basic natural unity, to reintegrate your compartmentalized being into a coordinated and simple whole, and learn to live as a unified human person. This means that you have to bring back together the fragments of your distracted existence so that when you say "I" there is really something present to support the pronoun you have uttered.'[2]

Therefore, we must know who we are, from whom we originated, and where we are going. In Merton's words: 'Before we can realize who we really are, we must become conscious of the fact that the person we think we are, here and now, is at best an imposter and a stranger.'[3] The false self, or the empirical ego, as Merton refers to it, is illusory, a mask for our true identity, our true self, which is the deepest self in which we stand naked before God's love and mercy. Solitude and prayer help strip us of this false self, since there is no need of such a fabrication before God, the one who knows us through and through.

Merton emphasized in his writings the fundamental duty of the Christian to orientate his entire being and life to God as a 'Pilgrim of the Absolute' to borrow Leon Bloy's apt phrase. Merton saw the great tendency today of orientating one's being and life, not to God, but to one's neighbor in the so-called horizonal theology of social concern, or to one's own self-fulfillment and self-realization. For Merton, however, the spiritual life was not primarily our work, but rather the work of *God in us*. Hence, our moral and ethical life must lead to something beyond itself; it must lead to an experience of our union with God and to our transformation in him.

Every Christian is called in some way or other to an ultimate union with God in Christ, as Merton wrote in *Life and Holiness*, describing sanctity as the ultimate perfection of the spiritual life, which is constituted 'first of all by an ontological union with God in Christ'.[4] This sums up in a few words the essence of Merton's christian and contemplative vision, which we will explore in greater detail in these pages: 'Sanctity consists in a perfect union of the mind and will with God.'[5]

Although it is true that genuine holiness is impossible without some concern for moral and ethical values, we must be careful to distinguish between a pseudo-spirituality of activism and a true spirituality of christian action guided by the Spirit of Christ. Merton's view of holiness was a call to sharing in the transcendence of God, as he wrote in *Life and Holiness*: 'We must first be transformed interiorly into new men, and then act according to the Spirit given us by God, the Spirit of our new life, the Spirit of Christ' (p. 57). Merton's social concern flowed from this vision.

For Merton, as for all Christians, being must take precedence over doing (and having). 'We must first be sons of the heavenly Father', as Merton expressed it in an essay on the monastic vocation. But this refers as well to every christian vocation, and not only to monks and nuns. This inward-looking spirituality has been referred to as a 'spirituality of being'. Yet it is a spirituality intended to give direction and meaning not only to our understanding of God and the mystery of our salvation in Christ, but also to our neighbor and our involvement in history, and above all, a spirituality of being must give a new dimension to our own life and work. All genuine social action must be grounded in this vision of reality.

Hence, we can say that the focus of Merton's spirituality consists in revealing the double-experience we all must continually undergo in the spiritual life. First, the experience of ourselves and our own destitution apart from God and his mercy. And then the experience of God whose mercy gives salvation to us in Christ: 'mercy within mercy within mercy'. As Merton wrote so movingly in *Thoughts in Solitude*6 wherein he describes what the discovery of the spiritual life really is: 'It is the silence of our whole being in compunction and adoration before God, in the habitual realization that He is everything and we are nothing, that He is the Center to which all things tend, and to Whom all our actions must be directed.'

The Christian, then, in Merton's view, must become acutely aware of the presence and action of God in his life, and must also enter into an intimate relationship with him. But this presupposes a true knowledge of self. In this respect an in others, Merton was following a solid monastic tradition. St Bernard of Clairvaux, in his *Degrees of Humility*, stressed the essential need of self-knowledge as the first degree of truth, before one could be compassionate or merciful to one's neighbor, or really to experience the presence of the living God in one's life.

We must recognize our dignity as the object of God's redemption and then transcend ourselves in an intimate relationship with God. Merton expressed this very well in his posthumously published volume, *Contemplative Prayer*:[7] 'we know him (God) insofar as we become aware of ourselves as known through and through by him'. Hence, the continuity between self-knowledge and the awareness of God. And this knowledge is affective in Merton's spirituality: we are made essentially for a loving knowledge of God. Our whole being, including thought and feeling, must be brought into communication and ultimately into communion with God.

Merton firmly believed that every Christian should ideally have some experience of God as a living and personal reality in his life. For a fully integrated christian life, our contact with God must be such that we experience a union with him as well as a transformation of consciousness. These two principles underlie Merton's spirituality and are closely related, as we shall see in the pages that follow.

Our one goal in life, according to the teaching of Thomas Merton, is to realize the end for which we were created, that is, a personal and intimate union with God in Christ by love. In *Zen and the Birds of Appetite*[8] Merton expressed this well: 'Paradise is not the final goal of the spiritual life...the ultimate end is the Kingdom of God.'

'Man is the image of God, not His shadow,' wrote Merton in his book, *Conjectures of a Guilty Bystander*.[9] Merton believed, with the Fathers, that the image of God is the summit of spiritual consciousness in us, the highest peak of self-realization. Following St Gregory of Nyssa, who in turn had influenced St Bernard of Clairvaux, Merton was absorbed in the thought that the divine image in man is especially constituted by his freedom. According to St Augustine God is sought in the most intimate depths of one's own spirit. 'At the summit of his own self-realization, which he calls the *memoria*, Augustine finds not only himself but the light by which he sees himself as he really is. And in this light, he is aware of God from whom the light comes. His awareness of God instantly broadens out into love. Charity springs up in the illumination of his soul's depths and carries him out of himself and beyond himself to the God who is enthroned in the very summit of his own personal being: the *apex mentis* or the "spark" of the soul.'

These lines are quoted from *The New Man*,[10] a work of Thomas Merton which manifests a turning point in his thought. The idea of transformation of consciousness became one of his favorite themes. In fact, it was to be a preoccupation for him all during his latter years, especially in his studies of Eastern philosophies and religions.

Very early in his writings, Merton expressed his views on the subject of freedom, although it appears in an unpublished part of the manuscript of *The Seven Storey Mountain*: 'The freedom that is in our nature is our ability to love something, someone besides ourselves, and for the sake, not of ourselves, but of the one we love. There is in the human will an innate tendency, an inborn capacity for disinterested love. This power to love another for his own sake is one of the things that makes us like God, because this power is the one thing in us that is free from all determination. It is a power which transcends and escapes the inevitability of self-love.'[11]

In a later book, *New Seeds of Contemplation*, Merton spells out this idea further: 'To say that I am made in the image of God is to say that love is the reason for my existence, for God is love' (p. 60). Writing an introduction to *The Monastic Theology of Aelred of Rievaulx* in 1968, shortly before his death, Merton again speaks of the image theme in these words: 'The image of God in man—the openness to love, the capacity for total consent to God in Himself and in others—remains indestructible. But it can be buried and imprisoned under selfishness. The image of God in man is not destroyed by sin but utterly disfigured by it. To be exact, the image of God in man becomes self-contradictory when its openness closes upon itself, when it ceases to be a capacity for love and becomes simply an appetite for domination or possession: when it ceases to give and seeks only to get. . . . In monastic terms: the inclination to love, which is at the core of man's very nature as a free being, is turned in on itself as its own object and ceases to be love.'[12]

Man has, in Merton's words, 'become alienated from his inner self which is the image of God'. Thus, Merton speaks, in *Life and Holiness*, of sin as essentially a refusal 'to be what we are, a rejection of our mysterious, contingent, spiritual reality hidden in the very mystery of God. Sin is our refusal to be what we were created to be . . . images of God' (p. 12). In a word, sin is a refusal to grow.

Our alienation from God, the result of sin through Adam's fall, has been rectified in the Incarnation of the Son of God, Christ Jesus. This great mystery is central to Merton's theology, as he himself expressed it in *The Ascent to Truth*: 'For although like all other mysteries it flows from the highest of all, the mystery of the Trinity, yet with regard to us the Incarnation is the most important of all because it is through Christ that we are incorporated into the life of the three Divine Persons and receive into our souls the Holy Spirit, the bond of perfection, Who unites us to God with the same Love which unites the Father and the Son' (p. 313).

Merton saw this mystery as essentially a re-creation or restoration of the divine likeness and freedom in man, as John Higgins has shown in his study *Merton's Theology of Prayer*.[13] 'Having lost his capacity for realizing his union with God to the extent that the divine image in him has been distorted, man now recovers the original perfection intended for human nature by God. Christ, Merton holds, has now "restored man to his original existential communion with God, the source of life." '

In *The New Man* Merton defines our supernatural union with God in Christ an 'an immediate union with the Triune God as the source of the grace and virtues in our spirit' (p. 85). This implies an actualization of the divine image in us and our basic orientation towards God. In this new re-creation God's love is further revealed and concretized in the love of Jesus Christ. It is through him that the divine likeness is restored. We thus become a new creature, sharing in God's supernatural life through our incorporation into Christ.

Merton describes this union in *New Seeds of Contemplation* as a spiritual union in which Christ mystically identifies his members with himself by giving us his Holy Spirit: 'A "new being" is brought into existence. I become a "new man" and this "new man", spiritually and mystically one identity, is at once Christ and myself. . . . This spiritual union of my being with Christ in one "new man" is the work of the Holy Spirit, the Spirit of Love, the Spirit of Christ' (p. 158).

Our whole work in life, according to Thomas Merton, is to seek the perfect possession of God in Christ. This was really the secret of his spirituality, and such an ideal is meant not only for monks, to whom St Benedict in his *Rule* singles out the seeking of God as the one requirement for the novice in the monastic way. Since God is present in the depths of our being, 'the ground of our being', we must find ourselves, become conscious of our true selves. This search consists in a double-movement, in Merton's theology: our entering into the deepest center of ourselves and then, having passed through that center, to go out of ourselves to God.

The first thing we must remember in our search for God is that we are in some way already possessed by God in the inmost depths of our being. This is why Merton could write in *The Silent Life*:[14] 'In the end, no one can seek God unless he has already begun to find Him. No one can find God without having first been found by Him.' In *Life and Holiness*, he says the same thing with a slightly different nuance: 'our seeking of God is not a matter of our finding Him by means of certain ascetic techniques. It is rather a quieting and ordering of our whole life by self-denial, prayer and good works, so that God Himself, Who seeks us more than we seek Him, can "find us" and "take possession of us"' (p. 29).

We will never reach the realization that we are possessed by God unless we first realize our own nothingness and emptiness. This requires completely surrendering our exterior self, the empirical ego, to God's love and so forgetting ourselves as the object of reflection that we lose everything that is centered on our illusory and superficial selves and thus gain the truer and deeper self that is the image of God within us. God's love will then fill the emptiness, and we will be one with him. Thus, there is a fullness in our nothingness, as Merton writes in *Zen and the Birds of Appetite*: 'It is in so far as "emptiness" and "nakedness" are also pure gift that in Christian terms they equal fullness' (p. 137). So we lose ourselves in order that there may be 'no self' but that God becomes the highest and most perfect self-realization.

This *kenosis*, or self-emptying, is essential to Merton's thinking. Writing in *New Seeds of Contemplation* he again stresses the fact 'that a man cannot enter into the deepest center of himself and pass through that center into God, unless he is able to pass entirely out of himself and empty himself and give himself to other people, in the purity of a selfless love' (p. 64).

Towards the end of his life, in *Faith and Violence*,[15] Merton formulated our problem today as the failure of many Christians to realize the truth that 'the infinite God is dwelling within them, so that He is in them and they are in Him. They remain unaware of the presence of the infinite source of being right in the midst of the world and of men... What is required of Christians is that they develop a completely modern and contemporary *consciousness* in which their experience as men of our century is integrated with their experience as children of God redeemed by Christ.'

The idea of consciousness then is very important in seeking a solution to the problem of our search for union with God. We are enabled by means of it to undertake the double movement of which we spoke above—entering into ourselves and then transcending ourselves. It is in reality a self-awareness, and Merton explained this in detail in *Zen and the Birds of Appetite*: 'Modern consciousness then tends to create this solipsistic bubble of awareness—an ego-self imprisoned in its own consciousness, isolated and out of touch with other such selves in so far as they are all "things" rather than persons' (p. 22). In this type of cartesian self-awareness, man becomes so preoccupied with his own self as subject that awareness of self becomes all important.

In contrast to this cartesian self-awareness, Merton proposes a type of consciousness which is an immediate experience of being in which the subject as such disappears; and yet, at the same time, this consciousness goes beyond all reflexive awareness of one's ego-self since man becomes preoccupied with a pursuit for his own transcendent self.[16] In *Conjectures of a Guilty Bystander*, he writes: 'One who has experienced what it means to *be* has in that very act experienced something of the presence of God. For God is present to me in the act of my own being, an act which proceeds directly from His will and is His gift. My act of being is a direct participation in the Being of God' (p. 221).

Merton contrasts this kind of consciousness with the cartesian consciousness: 'It starts not from the thinking and self-aware subject but from Being ontologically seen to be beyond, and prior to the subject-object division. Underlying the subjective experience of the individual self there is an immediate experience of Being. This is totally different from an experience of self-consciousness . . . It is not "consciousness of" but *pure consciousness*, in which the subject as such disappears.'[17]

When the self has arrived at this dissolution, it has entered into the very center of its being where it is totally empty and naked. Only now is it capable of going beyond itself by becoming filled with the presence of God. A real 'transformation of consciousness' occurs in the individual subject from an awareness of his false self, or empirical ego, to the true self or the person. Now the individual is no longer conscious of himself as an isolated ego, but sees himself in his inmost ground of being as dependent on Another, as formed through relationships, particularly his relationship with God. By forgetting himself both as subject and as an object of reflection, man finds his real self hidden with Christ in God. And so, as his self-consciousness changes, the individual is transformed; his self is no longer its own center; it is now centered on God. This entire theme is wonderfully developed in a chapter of *Zen and the Birds of Appetite* entitled 'The New Consciousness'.

We must begin to take the first step in our transformation by being what we actually are at the moment and recognize our present alienation. In Merton's words in *New Seeds of Contemplation*: 'Everyone of us is shadowed by a false self. This is the man I want myself to be but who cannot exist, because God does not know anything about him. And to be unknown to God is altogether too much privacy. My false and private self is the one who wants to exist outside the reach of God's will and God's love—outside of reality and outside of life. And such a self cannot help but be an illusion' (p. 33).

That precisely is the great danger today, according to Merton:

we settle for living our illusory lives and yield to a superficial personalism which identifies the 'person' with this external or empirical ego and devote too much effort to the cultivation of this false self. When pursued, it leads only to frustrations of all kinds because we become alienated from our deepest self which is the image of God. The result of this, only too apparent in our day, is evidenced by the rugged individualism where the individual ego becomes the center of all our endeavors. Unbridled selfishness, greed, and injustices of all kinds ensue.

Speaking of this rugged individualism in society, Merton wrote with great precision in *Disputed Questions*: 'Individualism is nothing but the social atomism that has led to our present inertia, passivism and spiritual decay. Yet it is individualism which has really been the apparent ideal of our western society for the past two or three hundred years. This individualism primarily an economic concept with a pseudospiritual and moral facade, is in fact mere irresponsibility. It is, and has always been, not an affirmation of genuine human values but a flight from the obligations from which these values are inseparable. And first of all a flight from the obligation to *love*.'18

The discovery of the true self, in Merton's thought, is also a discovery of one's responsibility to other such selves, all our brothers and sisters in Christ. The real force that holds together our union with God in Christ is charity. He expresses this eloquently in *The New Man* where he writes: 'And the charity of Christ, which springs from the Father as from its hidden and infinite source, goes out through us to those who have not yet known Him, and unites them, through Christ in us, to the Father' (p. 111).

In *No Man Is an Island*, Merton asserts that 'all charity comes to a focus in Christ, because charity is His life in us. He draws us to Himself, unites us to one another in His Holy Spirit, and raises us up with Himself to union with the Father.'19 Because charity is synonymous with Christ's life in us, the person who lives perfectly in him must also be able to reach out to others in genuine friendship and love. To achieve this ideal we must plunge ourselves ever more deeply into the mystery of God's love for all of us. We must learn to identify spiritually with everyone to the extent that we no longer regard others as 'objects' but rather try to become the person we love. In a word, we must try to see the other person as another self, as one also deeply loved by Christ. Thus, we slowly learn to love others in and for God.

It is no easy thing to love others with disinterested love. A kind of death of one's own being is involved, a sacrifice of one's self. Yet, as Merton emphasized so often, this is really a part of the self-emptying that is required in our search for union with God: we cannot enter into the deepest center of ourselves and pass through that center into God unless we are able to pass entirely out of ourselves and empty ourselves and give ourselves to other persons in the purity of a selfless love. In view of this conviction Merton wrote in a too little-known article, 'Notes on Love', towards the end of his life: 'Love alone gives us the true dimensions of our own reality. For we are created in the image and likeness of God, Who is Love, and therefore, the union with God that we are searching for must ultimately be a question of love.' And the love of others is imperative if we are to transcend ourselves and grow without illusions in this true love of God, for 'it is by loving Him . . . that we grow in our capacity to love others', as Merton wrote in *The Living Bread*.[20]

Thomas Merton was greatly influenced by the early Cistercian Fathers, especially St Bernard of Clairvaux's *De diligendo Deo*, in wrestling with the problem of love of God and neighbor. It was one of themes most often discussed by the Fathers. Commenting on this in *Conjectures of a Guilty Bystander*, Merton could write: 'The demands of the Law of Love are progressive. We begin by loving life itself, by loving survival at any price. Hence, we must first of all love ourselves. But as we grow we must love others. We must love them as our own fulfillment. Then we must come to love them in order to fulfill them, to develop their capacity to love, and finally we must love others and ourselves in and for God' (p. 121). This is essentially what St Bernard of Clairvaux taught his monks in the twelfth century, and it is just as appropriate for us today as when it was written.

By way of conclusion, we can say with Thomas Merton that it is our privilege and our christian duty ever to strive for an awareness of our union with God in Christ. Our life must be a continuous search for God as we come to realize that we are already possessed and loved by God. And God will be discovered only insofar as we can find him within ourselves, for our God is Christ within us. Merton said this beautifully in *New Seeds of Contemplation*: 'Therefore when you and I become what we are really meant to be, we will discover not only that we love one another perfectly but that we are both living in Christ and Christ in us, and we are all One Christ. We will see that it is He Who loves in us' (p. 65).

The Christian who has thus found his true self is the one who has become intensely aware of his life in Christ as well as the need, the vital necessity, of love in his life. His life becomes one of self-transcendence and of communion. So, in the end, we can say with Merton that it is not really a matter of either God or man, but rather of finding God by loving others and discovering the true meaning of the person in our love for God. Actually neither is possible without the other.

This thought was expressed well in a letter written by Thomas Merton in response to a request from Pope Paul VI in 1967 for a 'message of contemplatives' just a year before Merton's death in Bangkok, Thailand. It was later published in *Cistercian Studies* and is included in a volume of monastic texts by Merton recently published. Thomas Merton came to the conclusion that:

> we exist solely for this, to be the place He has chosen for His presence, His manifestation in the world, His epiphany . . . if we once began to recognize, humbly but truly, the real value of our own self, we would see that this value was the sign of God in our being, the signature of God upon our being. Fortunately, the love of our fellow man is given us as the way of realizing this . . . It is the love of my lover, my brother or my child that sees God in me, makes God credible to myself in me. And it is my love for my lover, my child, my brother, that enables me to show God to him or her in himself or herself. Love is the epiphany of God in our poverty.[20]

The entire life of Thomas Merton can be summed up as the living out of a great desire for solitude and a contemplative experience of the living God. From this flowed the practical consequences of the gospel message in christian action. His tremendous gift from God, his personal charism, was to articulate something of that ineffable experience, something of the reality of the mystery of God, to all of us. Thousands of readers have drawn strength from his words as well as the witness of his life, which was essentially a contemplative vision. May his words and his life guide us on our journey through life, so that one day we may all be united in the splendor of God's glory.

NOTES

1. For a more thorough assessment of Merton as 'contemplative' see *Thomas Merton/Monk, A Monastic Tribute*, edited by Brother Patrick Hart (New York: Doubleday Image Books) pp. 125-140.

2. This manuscript cannot be published as a book, according to the Merton Legacy Trust, but may be viewed and quoted by students of his work. It is available at the Merton Studies Center, Bellarmine College, Louisville, Ky.

3. *New Seeds of Contemplation* (New York: New Directions) p. 33.

4. *Life and Holiness* (St. Louis: Herder and Herder) p. 57.

5. *The Ascent to Truth* (New York: Harcourt Brace) p. 187.

6. *Thoughts in Solitude* (New York: Farrar Straus) p. 52.

7. *The Climate of Monastic Prayer* (Kalamazoo: Cistercian Publications) p. 113.

8. *Zen and the Birds of Appetite* (New Directions) p. 131.

9. *Conjectures of a Guilty Bystander* (New York: Doubleday) p. 149.

10. *The New Man* (Farrar Straus) pp. 60-61.

11. See *A Thomas Merton Reader*, edited by Thomas P. McDonnell for the complete text. (Doubleday Image Books brought out an updated edition in 1974.)

12. See Merton's Introduction to *The Monastic Theology of Aelred of Rievaulx* (Cistercian Publications, 1969) p. x.

13. John J. Higgins, SJ, *Merton's Theology of Prayer* (Cistercian Publications 1971) p. 11. Later published as *Thomas Merton on Prayer* by Doubleday.

14. *The Silent Life* (Farrar Straus) p. vii.

15. *Faith and Violence* (University of Notre Dame Press) p. 222.

16. See particularly, *Mystics and Zen Masters* (Farrar Straus) p. 21.

17. *Zen and the Birds of Appetite*, pp. 23-4.

18. *Disputed Questions* (Farrar Straus) p. x.

19. *No Man Is an Island* (Harcourt Brace) p. 134 (also published by Doubleday Image Books in a paperback edition.)

20. *The Living Bread* (Farrar Straus) p. 147.

21. *The Monastic Journey*, edited by Brother Patrick Hart, Doubleday Image Books, see appendix.

The Consciousness of God
and His Purpose in the Life
and Writings of Thomas Merton

Flavian Burns ocso

Abbot Flavian Burns, ocso, entered the Abbey of Gethsemani in 1951, and after his ordination to the priesthood studied Canon Law in Rome at the Gregorian University for two years. Following Abbot James Fox's resignation in 1968, he was elected abbot by the community of Gethsemani and was superior at the time of Merton's death. He retired in 1973 and returned to his hermitage at Gethsemani until 1980, when he was appointed superior of the cistercian community of Holy Cross at Berryville, Virginia. His contribution to this volume was an address given at the opening of the Merton Week at Bellarmine College on 3 December 1978, sponsored by the Thomas Merton Studies Center.

IT WOULD BE TEMPTING to indulge in reminiscences of that fatal day ten years ago, when we first received news of Father's death, and perhaps interesting to you, but frankly my personal sense of loss is still too acute for anything like that, strange as it may seem, and then, of course, I also believe that his memory would be better served by using this opportunity to continue to speak his message—at least, as I understand it. It is for this reason that I have chosen as the subject for my talk and our reflections here today: 'the consciousness of God and his purpose in the life and writings of Thomas Merton'; for I believe that such a consciousness was, and is, at the heart of Thomas Merton's message, and was very much a part of his personal life.

As it happens, there is a most fitting starting place for our reflections in the statement that Father Louis wrote on the occasion of the inauguration of the Merton Collection at Bellarmine on 10 November 1963. The enclosure for monks was more strict in those days than it is today, so Father Louis asked his very dear friend, Dan Walsh, to read the statement for him. Now, I intend to get in on the act, so to speak, by re-reading a part of this same statement to you here today.

> First of all, it is more than strange that the man who will read these words to you, Dan Walsh, is the one who first told me of the Abbey of Gethsemani. It is he, therefore, who first turned my thoughts in this direction. It is partly due to him that I came to this diocese and this state twenty-two years ago. But he is no more a native Kentuckian than I am, and if he is here now, it is partly because of me. I am quite sure that neither he nor I were ever able to forsee that he would one day be speaking here, on such an occasion as this. One of the awesome things about this event, then, is that it indicates to me that when Dan and I were talking together over a couple of glasses of beer in a New York hotel, years ago, God was present there and was doing His work in us.[1]

That, to my mind, is a very explicit and moving expression of a consciousness on the part of Father Louis of both God and his purpose active in his life! And I must add that I who read these words to you today, 15 years later, am also no native Kentuckian and, more importantly, that my own personal life and vocation, (and that of so many, many others) was also being influenced by the action of God taking place as those two men talked over a couple of beers in a New York hotel years ago! In fact, my standing before you here today must, in all honesty, be considered part of that influence. Father Louis' statement continued with the thought:

> Therefore, we can trust He still continues to be just as present, and just as active here, in all of us now! This is a momentous consideration. . . .[2]

It was precisely this *consideration* that dominated the personal thinking and doing of Father Louis Merton! The autobiographical nature of so much of his writing is not due to a man all wrapped up in himself and in his own subjective view of the universe. It stems, rather, from the man's consciousness of himself as a being called into personal existence by God for a purpose—a purpose that transcends all the immediate and pragmatic purposes people tend to let preoccupy their private thoughts and ambitions—a purpose which actually pertains to God himself and his all-pervading purpose for creation. For Father Louis, the whole point of every quest was the discovery of, and the personal entering into, this purpose of God.

In an intriguing passage from his novel, *My Argument with the Gestapo*, written before his entrance into the monastery but only published after his death, Father Louis has his hero say: 'But if you want to identify me, ask me not where I live, or what I like to eat, or how I comb my hair, but ask me what I think I'm living for, in detail, and ask me what I think is keeping me from living fully for the thing I want to live for. Between these two answers you can determine the identity of any person. The better answer he has, the more of a person he is.'[3]

'What I think I'm living for'—the purpose and 'in detail'! 'And what is keeping me from living fully for the thing I want to live for', that is to say, all that goes to make purposeful living a struggle and perhaps even seemingly impossible, and the answers to those two questions determine the identity of the person. Now that is what I call self-scrutiny! And when the answers to these questions are hidden in God's own mysterious purpose, we realize very quickly that there is no true self-knowledge apart from our experience and knowledge of him and his purpose.

But the answers to these questions are not the kind that can be found by mental inquiry alone—nor even by prayer alone. They must be found in the living out of personal life. As Father has his hero go on to say:

> I am all the time trying to make out the answer, as I go on living. I live out the answer to my own two questions myself and the answer may not be complete, even when my life is ended: I may go on working out the answer for a long time after my death, but at last it will be resolved, and there will be no further question, for with God's mercy I shall possess not only the answer but the reality that the answer was about.

This sentiment, expressed so early in his career as a writer, seems to me to be constant throughout all his life. It is what I am now referring to as a consciousness of God and his purpose, as it pertains, in detail, to one's personal life.

What do we know of God's purpose? In the statement read by Dan Walsh, from which I have already quoted, Father Louis also says: 'Whatever I may have written, I think it all can be reduced in the end to this one root truth: that God calls human persons to union with Himself and with one another in Christ . . .'.

That echos pretty well what St John and St Paul preached to the early Church, how God's plan is to make us all into that one temple, with Christ as the cornerstone, a dwelling place for God in the Spirit where God would—eventually—be All in All!

God's purpose, therefore, is known to us through faith in his revelation in Christ, but it is not known to us in detail—not on the day to day basis in which we have to live. For this, as Jesus Christ himself taught us, we must learn the habit of *watching* and *listening*, that is to say, attending to God's living Word, and docility to his Spirit living and active in our daily lives; in other words, having a consciousness of God and his purpose in our daily lives.

I submit that this kind of consciousness or attention is not, as a matter of fact, all that common—even among pious and well-meaning people. Too often, I'm afraid, we fall into the error of attending only to abstract goods and ideals—abstractions formed admittedly after mature and sober thought, but abstractions nonetheless! And while we pursue our abstract good we all too often become insensitive to the possibility that God may have something else in mind. For example, we strive for justice, or peace, or food for the hungry—all very good ideals in themselves—but in the process we often neglect the consideration of how these things relate, here and now, to God's purpose!

This, unfortunately, is a very grave, and often costly, mistake, the consequences of which are many and mostly bad. For if and when our abstract ideal runs into trouble, especially from other obviously well-meaning people, with other and perhaps somewhat contrary abstract ideals or methods of achieving them, we may very well be led into situations and attitudes not quite compatible with or conducive to, the spirit of the gospel message. So much wasted energy and fruitless good will can result from good people struggling against one another. And this, as we know, is a great source of discouragement and disillusionment to all involved—a prelude to cynicism and despair.

Attending to God's purpose with docility to the message of the moment can help to free us. We have hints of this even in the life of Christ himself: for example, when he was twelve years old and stayed behind in the temple. It seems, from the account we have received, that he was of the opinion that it was fairly obvious that he was where he was supposed to be: 'How is it that you sought me? Did you not know that I must be about my Father's business?' But then, without any answer from Mary or Joseph to these questions, he receives the answer from his Father—perhaps only through the disconcerted looks of Mary and Joseph—that his Father's business is back in Nazareth, and that for a lot more years to come!

And when that time actually did come, it seems that Christ himself did not know it, but once again learned it only by reason of his docility to the will and purpose of his Father as revealed to him through the words and actions of others: 'And Mary said: "They have no wine". But he replied: "What is that to you or me? My hour has not yet come."' But then at Mary's words to the waiters that they should do whatever he tells them, his hour does come and he works that first sign, changing water into wine, which would prove so decisive to his disciples and his public work and message. Somehow he had heard the word from his Father that yes, the time had come! The kind of receptivity to the message and inspiration of God that he shows in these incidents only comes to those who are open and sensitive. As Jesus so often said in his own preaching: 'He who has ears to hear, let him hear'. The implication is that there are those without ears to hear—or, if having ears to hear as a rule, may not now be attentive. Once more I will say that it is precisely this kind of attentiveness to God that I mean by the expression 'consciousness of God and his purpose'.

As we all know, a good part of Father Louis' writing had to do with prayer and contemplative living. The heart of his message pertains precisely to this kind of attending to God: prayer as listening rather than as speaking. He would agree, I'm sure, with Karl

Rahner's designation of the human person as a 'Hearer of the Word'. And he would also agree with what Father Rahner says in the introduction to his book of that title, where he answers the perhaps unspoken objection: 'But what if there is no word from God? What if God is silent?' Father Rahner answers: 'Should God, of his free choice, wish not to reveal himself but to remain silent, man would attain the ultimate and highest self-perfection of his spiritual and religious existence by listening to the silence of God.'[4]

The point here is that what matters is our being in the state of hearers, listening and attentive to God. Even divine words are not as important in practice as our listening. As it is, the world is full of God's word, sounding loud and clear in many and diverse ways, but an awful lot of it is falling on unresponsive ears—and this not only because of indifference or disbelief or sinful desires, but also because all too often otherwise good and generous people are too sure that they have already heard God's word and are busy now with trying to do it, or get it done, with the unfortunate consequence that they lose their hearing ability in the process.

Prayer as listening and being attentive to God, a consciousness always of him and his unfolding purpose, is something that must be part of our daily lives, even moment to moment, as far as possible. I know that you will say that this is all well and good for those who live in cloistered monasteries or in hermitages! I admit that it is easier there, though not necessarily always done! But I sincerely believe that it is possible and necessary in every way of life. After all, to paraphrase the Lord's words: What good is it for a person to accomplish all things, if he fails to fulfil the purpose for which he personally was created?

I believe that the writings of Father Louis on prayer and contemplative living give much practical aid and inspiration for improved attentiveness to God applicable to any way of life. If our way of life is too busy or too filled to permit our being a hearer of God's Word, then let's face it: our way of life is too busy and too filled. Not to have room for attention to God is pragmatic unbelief!

Another aspect of the teaching of Father Louis about attending to God and his purpose is the importance of humility and reverence to the mystery of personal life, both our own and that of others. To think that we, as baptized and believing Christians, have the answers to life's questions once and for all, is a terrible and much too common mistake. Questions always remain, and this is right and proper.

Just recently some of the monks and I were discussing a passage from Father Louis' writings on the monastic vocation where he makes this point himself explicitly. He says:

> But the monastic vocation is a mystery. Therefore it cannot be completely expressed in a clear succinct formula. It is a gift of God and we do not understand it as soon as we receive it, for all God's gifts, especially His spiritual gifts, share in His own hiddenness and in His own mystery. God will reveal Himself to us in the gift of our vocation, but He will do this only gradually. We can expect to spend our whole lives as monks entering deeper and deeper into the mystery of our monastic vocation . . . If we are really monks, we are constantly rediscovering what it means to be a monk, and yet we never exhaust the full meaning of our vocation.[5]

This, I'm sure, can be said with equal truth of any vocation, and every human person has a personal vocation. In reading these words about God speaking to us in the mystery of our vocation, we can't help but be reminded of those earlier quotations from Father Louis' novel about the questions and answers that go to make up our identity as persons.

A contemporary scholar and author has written a very moving passage on the crucial nature of the question we live and are, and how it is often a cause of profound unease. 'To be uneasy in this regard', he says, means to be uncertain of one's own center, to be an enigma to oneself, to be a wearisome and laborious question; but in addition, it also signals the need for transcendence. It is the existential self which grasps its identity as a metaphysical question, and thus encounters self-hood; the questioner is not only the questioned, but the very question itself.'[6]

We have all heard the story, I'm sure, of Gertrude Stein on her death bed asking her companions: 'What is the answer?' And when no reply was forthcoming: 'Well, then what is the question?'[7] Those were her last words, and, who knows, perhaps her salvation.

There is therefore no one once-and-for-all answer, applicable to all. Parents know this by their own experience for they usually try to hand on to their children the answers they have found. But, for the most part, it doesn't work; each person has his or her own question to answer, and other people's answers, though we may be able to learn something useful from them, will never perfectly satisfy our own needs and situation. When parents or teachers fail to understand this they often spoil their ability to be helpful, for then the young people leave off their own quest for answers and spend their energies uselessly, merely making objections to other people's answers.

They do this, of course, to some extent in understandable self-defense, but unfortunately defensiveness and the putting up of defenses are not the best means of coming to personally meaningful answers. For this we need the opposite: openness of mind and receptivity, even eagerness and readiness to hear. God does give answers, in his own time and in his own way, to the questions he has so knowingly set before us in our personal life and destiny. But we must have patience and a lack of avarice—even spiritual avarice—for God respects the nature of the life he has created and so must we. Finding the answers to the question we are is a matter of growth and takes a lifetime—perhaps even more. To paraphrase the Lord once more: Sufficient for the day are both the questions and the answers thereof.

In the Epilogue to his excellent book on Thomas Merton, George Woodcock quotes Father Louis as saying: 'I do not have clear answers to current questions. I do have questions.' And then Woodcock goes on to say: 'There is indeed a sense in which one can regard his whole life as a question, for the contemplative does not ask questions only of men and of the world; his quest leads him to the very heart of existence within himself, and if he is a Christian he awaits there an even deeper answer.'[8]

What Thomas Merton's message has to offer us is not the answer to our questions, but only some friendly and fraternal adivce on a way of being conscious and attentive to God, so that we may hear the answers when they are spoken to us.

NOTES

1. *The Thomas Merton Studies Center*, by Thomas Merton, John Howard Griffin, and Monsignor Alfred Horrigan (Santa Barbara: Unicorn Press, 1971) pp. 13-14.

2. *Ibid.*, p. 14.

3. As quoted by George Woodcock, *Thomas Merton: Monk and Poet*, pp. 32-33, from *My Argument with the Gestapo* (New Directions, paperback edition).

4. Karl Rahner, *Hearers of the Word* (Herder and Herder, 1969) p. 16.

5. Thomas Merton, *The Monastic Journey*, edited by Brother Patrick Hart (Sheed Andrews & McMeel, 1977) pp. 12-13.

6. Thomas M. Tomasic, 'William of St. Thierry against Peter Abelard: A Dispute on the Meaning of Being a Person,' *Analecta Cisterciensia* 28 (1972) pp. 13-14.

7. Elizabeth Sprigge, *Gertrude Stein: Her Life and Work* (New York: Harper & Bros., 1957) p. 265.

8. George Woodcock, *Thomas Merton: Monk and Poet* (New York: Farrar Straus and Giroux, 1978) p. 183.

Merton's Published Journals: The Paradox of Writing as a Step Toward Contemplation

Victor A. Kramer

Victor A. Kramer, Associate Professor of English at Georgia State University in Atlanta, teaches courses in American literature and literary criticism. He has written James Agee *(Twayne, 1975) and is co-editor of* Olmsted South *(Greenwood, 1979). His forthcoming volume on Thomas Merton will appear in the Twayne United States Authors Series. In addition, he has contributed numerous articles and reviews to journals such as* Texas Quarterly, Renaescence, The Southern Review, Journal of the American Academy of Religion, Commonweal, Library Journal, Journal of Aesthetics and Art Criticism *and* Modern Fiction Studies. *The paper included in this volume was prepared for the Merton Commemoration at Columbia University.*

MERTON'S LITERARY CAREER developed as it did in large part because he sought to ignore that he even had such a career. We now understand that he apparently needed to write—just as other men breathe—but that writing was always part of his movement toward solitude. Through his almost constant writing, Merton defined a relationship to God and celebrated the mystery of living. His constant writing did not make it easier to provide answers about the mystery of life; indeed, it made it harder. Yet if answers became more oblique, Merton's questions became increasingly more intriguing. Journals written throughout his career provide a map of both his spiritual and his literary movements, movements which were often not what the writer himself might have expected. The lesson, however, is a simple one; Merton called it a paradox in his autobiography:

> . . . a paradox that lies in the very heart of human existence [to] be apprehended before any lasting happiness is possible in the soul of man. The paradox is this: man's nature, by itself, can do little or nothing to settle his most important problems. If we follow nothing but our natures, our own philosophies, our own level of ethics, we will end up in hell.[1]

Correspondingly, a careful reading of Merton's writing reveals the fact that he learned to give up a consciousness of himself through the exercise of writing. Of course, Merton's writing is often an analysis of self, but such analysis (paradoxically) leads to an awareness of the unimportance of self and to an awareness of one's relationship to others, and to the mystery of the universe as a whole. To forget self through focus on self seems improbable; but such self-forgetfulness is Merton's continual accomplishment through his writing, and especially in his journals. They are the record of an artist who strives to go beyond mere artistry. Still another paradox, however, is the fact that these journals are successful as works of art.

Merton's journals are significant as crafted works of art and as inspirations to readers, but this prose is also evidence of how his artistic and spiritual interests developed. The journals provide significant information about this writer's changing interests and abilities. He was truly a contemplative, but also a man who retained all of the instincts of a literary person, and one who was never unaware of basic questions about the uses of his literary talent. His journals were, of course, his working ground, a testing place and foundation for his ideas and spiritual development. In a paradoxical way, therefore, it seems to have been necessary for Merton to write so that he could become more quiet. His journals are the record of an artist-contemplative who never forgot that language was his most valuable instrument; unlike some literary artists, however, Merton realized that writing (and perhaps especially his journals) was only a means, not an end.

Merton's vocation as writer was clear to him already while he was a student at Columbia, and one of the best indications of that fact is the correspondence exchanged between him and Mark Van Doren, an exchange which began in 1938 and continued for three decades. Significantly, Van Doren was instrumental in seeing that Merton's early poetry found a publisher. Perhaps in an unconscious way the young writer realized that Van Doren would recognize the value of his literary production. It was to Van Doren that Merton hurriedly sent a considerable amount of manuscript on the day before he left to enter the monastery. It is not the purpose of this paper to trace the literary friendship between Merton and his teacher, but I would like to mention that study of their correspondence reveals two continuing patterns: one, of course, is that Van Doren and Merton remained close over the entire thirty year period; and secondly, Merton sometimes came to rely on Van Doren's judgment about literary matters.

A note of Merton's, 9 December 1941, indicates this and would bear investigation in relation to his subsequent career.[2] While it is often lamented that Merton destroyed most of his fiction before he became a monk, it is clear that he systematically saw to it that acquaintances (especially Van Doren and Robert Lax) were aware of what he had written. Subsequent letters to Van Doren indicate that Merton continued to be concerned about the fate of his early manuscripts. He realized that some of his poems, his secular journal, and a novel in the form of a journal which he had written during the years before he entered the Cistercians had value as a record of his spiritual development. He could not therefore, suppress completely his wish to see those materials in print. They reveal a spiritual journey made possible because of the interests of an aspiring writer.

Within Merton's *Secular Journal*, which covers the period from October 1939 to late November 1941, he provides us with a record of his concerns about the vocation of writer; at one point he jokingly comments about an unpublished novel:

The Labyrinth has just been rejected by Macmillan. Since then it has been to Viking, Knopf, Harcourt Brace, then to the agent Curtis Brown, who sent it to Modern Age, Atlantic Monthly Books, McBride, and now Carrick and Evans' 'No' has not yet reached me.
So many bad books get printed, why can't my bad book get printed?[3]

Within the context of the *Secular Journal* the entry is significant because it clearly reveals Merton's wish to be recognized as a writer. Of course, his entire literary career might be described as a mode of combining a gift for a literary vocation along with a contemplative life. Thus a significant value of the *Secular Journal* is that it allows us to see early aspects in the development of Merton's dual vocation, a vocation which remained a combination of the contemplative and the active by means of the writing. His final entries in this volume are especially revealing:

November 24, 1941
St. Bonaventure

I got back from New York by the night train, having spent the night wedged into various positions in the hard green seats of the Erie daycoach. I am not physically tired, just filled with a deep, vague undefined sense of spiritual distress, as if I had a deep wound running inside me and it had to be stanched. As if I ought to go back to the chapel, or try to say something in a poem. The wound is only another aspect of the fact that we are exiles on this earth.[4]

Merton notes that he was in such distress he felt he should *either* return to prayer in the chapel or attempt a poem. This is interesting in relation to similar insights recorded in other places (letters, journals, essays) where he acknowledges how writing helps him to clarify things. If we look carefully at this entry we begin to see how Merton's attention to matters he had immediately experienced brought him to a better understanding of his spiritual life. This is a two page entry. Beyond its opening sentences, already quoted, Merton records his feelings as he returned to the peace of St Bonaventure's and, as well, his conviction that he must go beyond that kind of peacefulness:

[a] quietness which does not belong to me, and cannot. For a moment I get the illusion that the peace here is real, but it is not. It is merely the

absence of trouble, not the peace of poverty and sacrifice. This 'peace' cannot be enough for me any more.[5]

To go beyond meant finally to commit himself to life in the Abbey of Gethsemani. But Merton was clearly the type of person who seemed to think best with a pen or pencil in hand; and to some degree what happened when he became a cloistered monk was that his need to write was accentuated. This became a way of praising God. His prodigious production grew out of the somewhat strange situation of continuing as a writer by virtue of the vow of obedience, not because of any direct decision to do so.

Merton retrospectively understood that his vocation was primarily that of a christian writer—a Christian striving to find God through language. Thus his experience as a cloistered monk seemed to be, in a fundamental way, paradoxical. By accepting the silence of the monastery he became one of the most vocal priest-poets in the history of the Church. Merton himself realized the peculiarity of such a career. In the author's preface for *A Merton Reader* he noted:

> I have had to accept the fact that my life is almost totally paradoxical. I have also had to learn gradually to get along without apologizing for the fact, even to myself. . . . I have become convinced that the very contradictions in my life are in some ways signs of God's mercy to me: if only because someone so complicated and so prone to confusion and self-defeat could hardly survive for long without special mercy.[6]

What Merton as mature writer seems to be implying is that God chose to place him in a monastery, but since he apparently was a writer first, and a monk second, he was allowed to work his way closer to God by means of the writing. Such insight clarifies the 24 November 1941 entry of the *Secular Journal* referred to earlier. Already in 1941 Merton realized that it was impossible to plan one's career; he wrote on 27 November that 'If God wants me to write I can write anywhere'.

Clearly, Merton never fully wanted to give up being a writer, but significant also is the fact that he was willing to do so if that appeared to be God's will. Reflecting upon his career, Merton realized that in a strange sort of way it had become possible both to have one's writing and to give it up. He realized that writing remained his most important gift, the one thing he could give, and in so giving, gain. We can see how his mind works and why he saw value in his own journals from additional remarks which he included in the preface to his *Reader*. Writing was something to give away:

> When a thought is done with, let go of it. When something has been written, publish it, and go on to something else. . . . No one need have a compulsion to be utterly and perfectly 'original' in every word he writes. All that matters is that the old be recovered on a new plane and be, itself, a new reality. . . .
>
> In other words I have tried to learn in my writing a monastic lesson I could probably not have learned otherwise: to let go of my idea myself, to take myself with more than one grain of salt. If the monastic life is a life of hardship and sacrifice, I would say that for me most of the hardship has come in connection with writing. It is possible to doubt whether I have become a monk (a doubt I have to live with), but it is not possible to doubt that I am a writer, that I was born one and will probably die as one. Disconcerting, disedifying as it is, this seems to be my lot and vocation. It is what God has given me in order that I might give it back to Him.[7]

All his writing was a way for Thomas Merton to strengthen his relationship to God, and it is also a way to lead others on the same journey.

It might be good to think of all of Merton's journals as journeys. This is still another paradox to be recognized—for when one agrees to stay put (the vow of stability) one can really begin to travel. Merton's writing finally allowed him to move beyond a concern just with self, yet the only way to do this was to begin with an examination of self. Just like Thoreau's apology within the opening pages of *Walden* for the subject matter he knows best, himself, Merton's strategy builds on paradox.

Merton's *Secular Journal* is a record of events which led up to his entrance into Gethsemani; he himself realized the book had value precisely because of its immaturity. It is a document sometimes almost arrogant in tone, yet it is a record of Merton's raising of fundamental questions, and his acceptance of the vocation of writer. He realized to be a good writer is to be 'tuned in' to the universe. One of the fundamental realizations reflected in the *Secu-*

lar Journal is an understanding that a good poet must see beyond the immediate. For such reasons he was attracted to the poetry of William Blake, and Blake is mentioned early in the journal. Blake has insisted 'that all good poetry was poetry dictated by the angels'.[8] If you believe in angels, as did Blake, and if you believe in divine Providence, as did Merton, then you begin to understand that what a good poet does is never done alone.

What Merton often focuses on in his *Secular Journal* is a world where things so often seem to be taken out of context. His entry about the Art Exhibit at the World's Fair of New York in 1939 reveals his pleasure in looking at paintings of Fra Angelico ('The Temptation of St Anthony') and Breughel ('The Wedding-dance'). Yet he writes about the misconceptions he often heard expressed by viewers, misconceptions which derived from their assuming that a painting was to be learned or understood. Merton stresses about his appreciation of both paintings that they suggest worlds beyond language, while modern man is so given to affixing labels and expressing opinions that it has become impossible for him even to appreciate that there are whole areas of experience beyond the apparently measurable.

In the *Secular Journal* we also see this young writer literally sorting out what was of importance for him. And we also see him laughing at a society which has not yet got to such a level of insight. His fascination with language remains fundamental. More precisely, he is concerned with the abuse of language. On 18 April 1940, he meditates about a society which has lost its respect for traditional values, a society which is 'worshipping frustration and barrenness'. Especially in Germany and Italy, he notes, there is so much talk about peace, life, and fertility, but, he says,

> The people who yell loudest about all these things are clearly responsible for the worst war that was ever heard of and are also busy putting out of existence in lethal chambers everybody that has gone crazy as a result of this kind of thinking (gone crazy, that is, without getting into the government).[9]

It was related concerns with abuses of thinking and language that brought Merton to the composition of an imaginary journal which remains today as his only extant novel.

The novel, written in 1941, is *My Argument with the Gestapo*; it is an imagined journey to the England and France which Merton had known during the preceding ten years. This journal is Merton's way of examining the complexity of modern life and the changes which had taken place in his own lifetime. He sees London and England in two ways—as they had been—and as they are now.

The impression made by Merton's journey-journal is that the writer-hero (who is suspect because he is a writer) has seen beyond the superficiality and veneer of civilization. To explain this, however, he must first return to the reality so full of superficiality so that he can begin to explain what is beyond. So much of life in England, for Merton, seems to have been a void filled by activities, activities which he realized in retrospect were often meaningless. Yet what happens, he questions, if enormous numbers of people, British and German, are willing to fight to the death for such triviality and meaninglessness? Could it be that the English

> are fighting for Cadbury's chocolate, for Woodbines, for the London County Council, for the Gasworks, for the Doulton Pottery at Lambeth, and for the broken span in the middle of the Waterloo Bridge . . . for Lord Nelson's blind eye, his last words ('Kiss me, Hardy'), and his notorious mistress, Lady Hamilton, as portrayed in our films by Vivien Leigh.[10]

Apparently it is for such triviality that many men act.

But why imagine such things in a novel-journal? Merton's writer is interrogated by two men who observe him writing:

'Who are you working for?'

'How will you find out by writing?'

The answers provided—that one is working for oneself and that one may not find out anything by writing—are disconcerting at best! But in the process is recognized the craziness of a world where everything seems acceptable. The writer further attempts to answer the question of why he is manufacturing this book.

> 'I will keep putting things down until they become clear.'
> 'And if they do not become clear?'
> 'I will have a hundred books, full of symbols, full of everything I ever knew or even thought.'[11]

Which is to say, perhaps one can never understand, but one can take some steps toward acceptance.

One of the craziest incidents in this novel occurs when its poet-hero is apprehended by French police who try to understand his journal. Of course, they can make little sense of it. The resultant interrogations are hilarious, primarily because it is assumed that if anything is written, it must be of a political nature. To face the fact that the journal is a private memoir is more than the French authorities are able to do.

At the end of this book the writer entrusts his manuscript to a Mr R., who has been asked to deliver it to an agent in America. Mr R. assumes it must be a pornographic novel. He, too, cannot understand a book which is apparently neither pro-British nor pro-German.

My Argument is a narrative, but more important it is a record of a writer asking fundamental questions about how language is used, and why. These themes are the ones which reveal Merton's interest in the nature of language and the responsibilities of the writer. What he often reports (about English, French and German events) is a perverse misuse of language. More often than not when language is used in the book, it is tied only to the immediate or to man's attempt to control the immediate. But the writer of Merton's journal seems to be moving toward the conclusion that the reasons for keeping a journal—for any kind of writing?—are to see that one's relationship to others (something more than the mundane and trivial activities of day-by-day-living) can lead to something beyond visible life. The ending of Merton's novel with another reference to Blake is, I think, symbolic of a method he relied upon throughout his career. Little has been accomplished within this novel; yet the writing of it has been a help. Then, the text tells us, the manuscript is entrusted to 'the hands of a maniac who believes he understands world affairs, political rights and wrongs'. What Merton seems to mean is that he entrusts his book to us, but the book (any book) cannot provide definitive answers, only hints:

> Yet here is the typewriter and a pile of new paper, white, untouched. I think suddenly of Blake, filling paper with words, so that the words flew

about the room for the angels to read, and after that, what if the paper was
lost or destroyed?
That is the only reason for wanting to write, Blake's reason.[12]

We might say that for similar reasons Merton realized the value of
keeping a journal. Writing was a way (at least temporarily) of putting himself in contact with the supernatural, with things beyond
the realm of mere men. Such is a legitimate way of approaching
The Sign of Jonas, the journal which chronicles the years of Merton's life beyond *The Seven Storey Mountain*, into the late
nineteen-forties after ordination.

The Sign of Jonas is a valuable book because, while a record of
many of Merton's activities during the years when he was study-
ing to be a priest, it also treats (sometimes indirectly) the question
of literary vocation. Merton's questions about what it means to be
a writer are crucial, and *Jonas* is a documentation of his working
out an accomodation with the vocation of writer.

Merton at first thought that it might have been more advan-
tageous for him had he not been forced to write, but he was also
fast coming to the realization during those years that his 'lamenta-
tions' about his obligatory writing job had been foolish. He noted
that:

at the moment, the writing is one thing that gives me access to some real
silence and solitude. Also I find that it helps me to pray, because when I
pause at my work I find that the mirror inside me is surprisingly clean and
deep and serene and God shines there and is immediately found, without
hunting, as if He had come close to me while I was writing and I had not
observed His coming.[13]

Other entries in *Jonas* indicate that Merton thought that he
needed to cease writing. He felt that he might be a better contemplative without the distractions of preparing books for the
press. Yet he had been told to go on writing, and he eventually
came to understand that it was good to 'go on trying to learn to
write under the strange conditions imposed by Cistercian life'. But
we also note that he remained ambitious to be a good writer. Thus
he was dissatisfied with his book about Mother Berchmans
because it was too verbose:

I have no objection, I know that I talk too much. It is a vice Cistercian writers have—at least modern Cistercian writers. It means that we do not really know the meaning of silence and that we have not discovered the secret of the contemplative life.[14]

In other places in *Jonas* it is clear why Merton admires successful writers; without a doubt he wants to write well. The fact that he includes such references within the published journal indicates that he felt he had not attained the level of artistic proficiency he desired. References to T. S. Eliot, Rilke, and Dylan Thomas are typical of such self-criticism:

Thomas's integrity as a poet makes me very ashamed of the verse I have been writing. We who say we love God: why are we not as anxious to be perfect in our art as we pretend we want to be in our service of God? If we do not try to be perfect in what we write, perhaps it is because we are not writing for God after all. In any case it is depressing that those who serve God and love Him sometimes write so badly, when those who do not believe in Him take pains to write so well.

He goes on to say:

I am not talking about grammar and syntax, but about having something to say and saying it in sentences that are not half dead. Saint Paul and Saint Ignatius Martyr did not bother about grammar but they certainly knew how to write.
Imperfection is the penalty of rushing into print.[15]

What he is saying is that he himself needs to find ways to be more concerned about his literary production, and less concerned about his public. He knows, as he puts it a few pages later, 'the chief thing that has struck me today is that I still have my fingers too much in the running of my own life'.[16] Later, he reports he even caught himself dreaming about the possibility of *The Seven Storey Mountain* being made into a movie:

If they make it into a movie, will Gary Cooper be the hero? Or maybe there is no Gary Cooper. But anyway that is the kind of folly I have to look out for now. . . . Here is the book I couldn't make a go of ten years ago—now it is a success just when I am at Gethsemani and Gethsemani needs the money. . . .[17]

Merton notes that he must remember souls are dependent upon his writing. What the writing brings the writer must be quite secondary.

The Sign of Jonas is a curious book, and mostly so because it is clearly the work of a writer. He uses this journal as a way of showing that he has found his vocation as contemplative but he clearly never ceases to be concerned about his responsibilities as writer. The result, therefore, is a journal which documents how Merton found his way toward God through the writing.

There are many levels of concern in *Jonas*. Merton realizes that any writer can focus on different kinds of reality; and one of the most important facts of *The Sign of Jonas* is how it reveals its writer sorting out possibilities. Sometimes this is explicit: For instance Merton describes three levels of depth and concern:

[1] the slightly troubled surface of the sea...
[2] the darkness that comes when I close my eyes...
[3] ...[the] positive life swimming in the rich darkness which is no longer thick like water but pure, like air.

He believed that God intended him to write about the second level, not the first:

I abandon all problems to their own unsatisfactory solutions: including the problem of 'monastic spirituality'. ...God in me is not measured by your ascetic theory and God in you is not to be weighed in the scales of my doctrine. He is not to be weighed at all.[18]

Merton focused on his second level, the depth of darkness that comes when one closes one's eyes to the troubles apparent on the surface. His epilogue, 'Fire Watch, July 4, 1952', is an example of such focus.

As Merton developed as a writer, the simplicity of 'levels' of depth, an illusion of life separated into strands, became much less satisfying to Merton the writer. Later, he assumed a responsibility to draw connections between the quiet of the monastery and the troubled surface of the world he chose earlier to ignore. Later journal entries re-enforce the connections which he saw. What sets the journal *Conjectures of a Guilty Bystander* apart from *The Sign of Jonas* is its systematic concern with contemporary problems. In *Conjectures*, we see Merton making connections between what he observes in the contemporary world and in his art, and we also see him making many more overt judgments about secular values in relation to Christianity. Strangely, this need to speak out provides still another way toward meditating.

Conjectures is the product of a writer at ease with himself, but no longer at ease with not choosing to speak out. To speak out, however, sometimes means to demonstrate how it is sometimes best to be silent. *Conjectures* is a record of someone who has found that, in many ways, it is best to remain silent; but it is the record of a writer who sees that he has a responsibility in the world. Thus the text seems to function paradoxically; Merton is drawn into the world, yet he also values the silence of the cloister and what he has learned in that silence, values that cannot easily be passed on to others. *Conjectures* is a book which comes out of silence, but it leads the reader (as has been the case for Merton himself) directly back to the world. His entry about the city of Paris as *the* city is important in this regard; Merton writes:

> Paris means in many ways less to me than some other cities, since I never spent more than a few days there at one time . . . . Yet there is one thing I may say about it: I came into this world because of Paris . . . .

And Merton knows that Paris is more than the Louvre and light on the Seine or bookstores on the Boulevard St. Michel. He begins to provide some explanations and his paragraphs explode:

> Paris is to a great extent the Dionysian legend, and Dionysius means the *Divine Names* and the *Mystical Theology* . . . set the Middle Ages on its ear. Dionysius links Paris with Cologne.
> Paris also means St Bonaventure, Duns Scotus . . . . Paris means St Louis, whose name was given me in religion . . . . It means Pascal, whom I like, and Descartes, whom I don't.
> It means Baudelaire . . . Valéry, Péguy . . . . It means Manet and Monet, Renoir . . . once you start this litany there is no end to it. Through these words, plays, paintings, and poems Paris has kept reaching out and grabbing hold of me in London, in Cambridge, in Rome, in New York, and in the monastery lost in Kentucky.[19]

Such a listing seems to be mostly preoccupied with raising questions, not with providing answers. Merton himself says as much elsewhere when he writes an entry in *Conjectures* about a 'pleasant breezy note' which he had received requesting an article on 'the

Holiness of the Church'.[20] He was annoyed, but admits that the
conviction some people have that he secretes articles like perspira-
tion is more his fault than theirs; he also notes that if readers were
ready to read his articles carefully they 'might not take it for
granted that I could simply reach into the back of my mind for a
dish of ready-to-serve Catholic answers about everything under
the sun'. In this same section further reflections about his role as
writer suggest what Merton felt he had accomplished:

> It seems to me that one of the reasons why my writing appeals to many
> people is precisely that I am not so sure of myself and do not claim to have
> all the answers. In fact, I often wonder quite openly about these 'answers',
> and about the habit of always having them ready. The best I can do is look
> for some of the questions.

Of course, such questioning is what provides the value of *Conjectures*, and it is also what led to writing so many other works. From
its many entries we see how the habit of keeping a journal provided fuel for Merton's writing of essays on myriads of subjects. Entries which are meditations about technological progress, the
responsibilities of western democracy, racial discord, urbanism,
mercantilism, and 'primitive' civilization hold the book together,
and through this journal we have a record of Merton's evaluation
of the culture which surrounds him.[21]

   Conjectures stands as a meditation about our contemporary
needs. It is also, sometimes, the raw material which will be
fashioned into later essays and poems. Note, for instance, these
words within the section 'The Night Spirit and the Dawn Air':

> At every moment we are sent north, south, east and west by the angels of
> business and art, poetry and politics, science and war to the four corners of
> the universe to decide something, to sign something, to buy and sell. We
> fly in all directions to sell ourselves, thus justifying the absolute nothing-
> ness of our lives.[22]

Merton's words are a capsule version of his long poem *The
Geography of Lograire*.
   It should be emphasized that as Merton became more interested
in the intricacy of the world, he simultaneously became less interest-

ed in castigation. His report of a moment he experienced in downtown Louisville is, I think, characteristic of changes in attitude:

> I was suddenly overwhelmed with the realization that I loved all those people, that they were mine and I theirs, that we could not be alien to one another even though we were total strangers. It was like waking from a dream of separateness....[23]

It is a commonplace now to assert that Merton became more compassionate as he matured in his role as contemplative and writer. The value of a book like *Conjectures* is that it demonstrates how he was learning to make the best of embracing the world while remaining aloof from aspects of it: He writes:

> To leave things alone at the right time: this is the right way to 'stop' and the right way to 'go on'.
> [or]
> It is essential to experience all the times and moods of one good place. No one will ever be able to say how essential, how truly part of a genuine life this is....
> [or]
> Even though one may not be able to halt the race toward death, one must *nevertheless choose life* and the things that favor life....
> [or]
> The Christian does not struggle to 'make an adjustment'.... He accepts 'yes' with complete joy, docility and abandon....[24]

Merton recognized his task as writer as one where he would speak for many 'even when I seem to be speaking out only for myself'. He saw his role as a monk and writer as part of a chain of events that was begun with his decision first to come to Kentucky. Each day which followed was a link in the chain. He also realized that through an attentiveness to the particularities of each day it was becoming possible for him to be much less concerned about the succession of historical or political events; the pattern of a particular day then becomes

> more and more woven into the great pattern of the whole experience of man, and even something quite beyond all experience. I am less and less aware of myself simply as this individual who is a monk and a writer, and who, as monk and writer, sees this, or writes that.[25]

Which is to say, Merton learned to lead readers to an awareness of how one might find one's true self through a forgetting of self. His essay 'The Day of a Stranger' illustrates this point.

'The Day of a Stranger' is a very simple piece. It is significant that it is designed to read like a journal. The effect is to reassure the reader that Merton had found peace day by day.

Fundamental to 'The Day of a Stranger' is the fact that Merton must confront questions about *his* relationship to the world. It seems significant that he would do so by structuring the essay like a journal. What he is implying is that we must pay attention to the way every day develops in its special rhythm. The quiet of the 'Day of a Stranger' establishes an important tone, and especially as it relates to other kinds of writing done by Merton during this same period. (The essay 'Rain and the Rhinoceros' in *Raids on the Unspeakable* functions in a similar manner.) His message is one of learning how to live in harmony with each day's rhythm:

> I exist under trees. I walk in the woods out of necessity. I am both a
> prisoner and an escaped prisoner. . . . I know the birds in fact very well,
> for there are precise pairs of birds. I share this particular place with them:
> we form an ecological balance. This harmony gives the idea of 'place' a
> new configuration.[26]

He assures us that he is learning how to live, and by providing an account hour by hour, we sense the rhythm that he has come to feel. A similar feeling is experienced with Merton's final journal, a record of his trip to Asia.

The Asian Journal, while only a working manuscript reveals the exuberance of a writer who was looking ever wider for ways to connect his belief with aspects of the world. This journal is clearly the meditation of a contemplative, but also of someone who knows that he can no longer rest assured in the complacency of routines, even in a hermitage.

The Asian Journal of Thomas Merton is not a finished work. It was constructed by editors from three different notebooks, yet it is of great value because it collects a large number of meditations by Merton made during a relatively short period. Quotations from readings, impressions of cities, private meditations, poetry—all combine to make us aware of how aware he was of interrelatedness. This final journal reveals how the writer's mind worked, and how he jotted down material which might be of use later. We can see, above all, that the contemplative life was nurtured by the real world. Thus, Merton quotes Murti on Madhyamika about the need to be part of the interrelatedness of the empirical world:

> After reading Murti on Madhyamika, a reflection on the unconscious content and inner contradiction of my own drama. There I was riding through Lower Dharamsala, up to the mountain, through McLeod Ganj, in the Dalai Lama's jeep, wearing a snow-white Cistercian robe and black scapular. Smiles of all the Tibetans recognizing the jeep. Namaste gestures (palms raised together before the nose), stares of Indians. Am I part of it? Trying to fit into an interrelation, but on my own terms? Trying to find a dogmatic solution to this contradiction? Learning to accept the contradiction?[27]

There are certainly no solutions in this book, but we are provided with a working document which is of value precisely because it gives a picture of Merton in the process of working out his daily living. *The Asian Journal* is, therefore, more documentation of a writer working his way toward interrelatedness.

What is most striking about the *Asian Journal* is Merton's exuberance not just about the trip, but about the many avenues which his mind and spirit were exploring. Everywhere he looked he saw evidence that the entire world was sacramental. Whether he writes of the fun and confusion of travel; of the faces of 'men worn out by a dirty system'; an idea for editing still another book, or of dawn in New Delhi, his procedure is the same.[28] He is always looking carefully at what is right in front of him at that particular time. What he teaches us is that the sacramentality of our world is always there to be observed and honored in its immediacy.

The importance of the entries throughout Merton's published journals is that they give us such a detailed listing of the sacramentality of the world as observed. All, lived and observed, has meaning, and in retrospect that meaning can sometimes become clearer than when it is actually experienced. What the journals as a whole suggest is that we must be more attentive to the details of our lives, for it is through such details that God speaks.

Cumulatively, these journals are Merton's record of his encounter with God's world. It is through the appreciation of the
everyday experiences that we begin to learn how to apprehend our
harmony with all of creation. The journals are insights, fragments,
prayers, notes, phrases which can lead us to see the divine plan,
the completeness, the wholeness which is sometimes hidden. We
are each part of that wholeness. Merton's job as a writer is to help
us appreciate this fact as he himself had begun to do so.

Through the word one is united with others. It is not far-fetched
to maintain that Merton's writing was most often done in moods
which reflect a constant awareness of his responsibility as a member of the christian family. Just as the 'Eucharist is a *convivium*, a
sacred banquet [at which] the Church, rejoices together at a common table with the Apostles and all the saints and all believers',
Merton's writing is executed as something to be shared because it
can nurture others. It was in his book *The Living Bread* that he
wrote of communion as a *sacrum convivium:*

> Communion is something that we share with one another. And this sharing
> is not merely psychological, it is one of the objective spiritual points of the
> Sacrament. The Eucharist is the sacrament of charity, the *sacramentum unita-
> tis*, the Sacrament of our union in Christ. Consciousness of this unity, of this
> sharing of the life of Christ, is necessary if the Eucharist is to fulfill its func-
> tion as a perfect sacrifice of praise for the honor and glory of God.[29]

In a related manner, Merton's writing functions as a means of
bringing man closer to a realization that God is to be recognized in
relation to everything man experiences. Merton wrote in the belief
that it was a 'paradox' 'that we are taken "out of this world"
while remaining in the world'. Man's 'journey' is then a journey
not 'in space, but a journey in the spirit'. Further, a life in the
spirit and truth 'does not diminish our appreciation for the reality
of creation with which God has surrounded us. It makes it more
real for us, because we now see all ordinary created things in a new
light'.[30] This is what Merton accomplished in his journals.

These journals are not therefore an escape from a world of evil,
but a record of an escape from an illusory self which makes it difficult to see the good that surrounds man in everything he does.

The published journals are the record of a born writer's movement toward a clear appreciation of how we might all come to wholeness if we could come to see what surrounds us moment by moment. In his earlier books what was perhaps most obvious about Merton's insights was a constant disapproval of the way man has apparently lost his ability to see. His later journals cease such condemnation. They are, instead, the record of how one man saw beyond seeing by looking carefully.

NOTES

1. *The Seven Storey Mountain* (New York: Harcourt, Brace, and Co., 1948) p. 169.
2. Thomas Merton to Mark Van Doren, 9 Dec. 1941, Columbia University Library.
3. *The Secular Journal* (New York: Farrar, Straus and Cudahy, 1959) p. 159.
4. *Ibid.*, p. 264.
5. *Ibid.*, p. 265.
6. *A Thomas Merton Reader* (New York: Doubleday, 1974) p. 16.
7. *Ibid.*, p. 16-17.
8. *The Secular Journal*, p. 5.
9. *Ibid.*, p. 89.
10. *My Argument With the Gestapo* (New York: Doubleday, 1969) p. 22.
11. *Ibid.*, p. 52-53.
12. *Ibid.*, 259.
13. *The Sign of Jonas* (New York: Harcourt, Brace and Co., 1953) p. 207.
14. *Ibid.*, p. 54.
15. *Ibid.*, p. 59.
16. *Ibid.*, p. 76.
17. *Ibid.*, p.110.
18. *Ibid.*, p. 338-339.
19. *Conjectures of a Guilty Bystander* (New York: Doubleday, 1968) p. 181.
20. *Ibid.*, p. 49.
21. *Ibid.*, p. 73, 89, 112, 137, 196, and 306.
22. *Ibid.*, p. 196.
23. *Ibid.*, p. 156.
24. *Ibid.*, p. 176, 179, 219, and 267.
25. *Ibid.*, p. 245.
26. *A Thomas Merton Reader*, p. 432.
27. *The Asian Journal* (New York: New Directions, 1973) p. 116.
28. *Ibid.*, pp. 9, 10, 31 and 56.
29. *The Living Bread* (New York: Farrar, Straus and Cudahy, 1956) pp. 129-130.
30. *Ibid.*, p. 96.

Thomas Merton and the Possibilities of Religious Imagination

Elena Malits, CSC

Elena Malits, CSC, *is a Holy Cross Sister who teaches a Merton Seminar each semester at the combined theology departments of St. Mary's College and the University of Notre Dame. She did her doctoral work at Fordham University on "Journey into the Unknown: Thomas Merton's Continuing Conversion" in 1974. She has published articles and reviews in many literary and scholarly journals. Harper and Row has published her recent study on Thomas Merton entitled :* The Solitary Explorer *(1980). Her contribution to this volume was given at the Merton Commemoration at Columbia; she also presented to the Merton Session of the Cistercian Conference held at Western Michigan University in May of 1978 a paper on "Merton's Metaphors: Signs and Sources of Spiritual Growth" which was subsequently published in* Cistercian Studies.

FROM BEGINNING TO END, Thomas Merton's life was deeply affected by visual images he encountered and the verbal images, the metaphors, he constructed to articulate the meaning of his experience. In *The Seven Storey Mountain*, Merton's relatively early autobiography, he recalled several 'mental pictures' from his boyhood which were impressed upon him, and to which he returned in writing his lifestory. These became for the autobiographer highly-charged symbols, bearing much more than the young Merton could have grasped at the time of the experience. In retrospect, however, Merton the writer could interpret those visual impressions as images of his sinful, rootless, searching life prior to his religious conversion.

Thus the memory of Tom Merton and his boyhood friends refusing to let his little brother play with them became a symbol of all sin as the rejection of love:

> When I think now of that part of my childhood, the pciture I get of my brother John Paul is this: standing in a field. . .this little perplexed five-year old kid. . .as insulted as he is saddened, and his eyes full of indignation and sorrow. . . . And his tremendous desire to be with us and to do what we are doing will not permit him to go away. . . . Many times it was like that. And in a sense, this terrible situation is the pattern and prototype of all sin: the deliberate and formal will to reject disinterested love for us for the purely arbitrary reason that we simply do not want it.[1]

Likewise, Merton's many Atlantic crossings in his youth, and especially his memory of the fateful one which eventually led him to Gethsemani, provided the autobiographer with an image of God's providence working through the wanderer's own purposelessness.[2]

But there is one particular visual image that Merton associated with his first 'conversion' experience. In *The Seven Storey Mountain* he described how at age eighteen, while on holidays in Rome, he chanced upon the old churches and discovered the byzantine mosaics of Christ the Pantocrator. That artistic rendering of the Lord of Glory profoundly affected the youthful Merton. It yielded his first real insight into Christianity:

> And now for the first time in my life I began to find out something of Who this Person was that men called Christ. It was obscure, but it was a true knowledge of Him, in some sense, truer than I knew and truer than I would admit. It was there I first saw Him, Whom I now serve as my God and my King, and Who owns and rules my life. It is the Christ of the Apocalypse, the Christ of the Martyrs, the Christ of the Fathers. It is the Christ of St John, and of St Paul, and of St Augustine and St Jerome and all the Fathers—and of the Desert Fathers. It is Christ God, Christ King. . . .[3]

It is not accidental, I think, that what one might call Merton's first religious awakening was mediated by an aesthetic experience. He insisted that it was the art of the ancient roman churches which attracted him and imperceptibly led him to a response which he could not have anticipated. 'After all the vapid, boring, semi-pornographic statuary of the Empire, what a thing it was to come upon the genius of an art full of spiritual vitality and earnestness and power—an art that was tremendously serious and alive and eloquent and urgent in all it had to say.'[4] Merton's attention was captured by a compelling iconography—but that engendered a process of reflection which led to a change of heart. He began to spend time in the churches and slipped into an attitude which was as close as the somewhat jaded young man had ever come to prayer. He took up reading the Gospels. The image of the byzantine Christ prodded Merton to an authentic, though short-lived, feeling of compunction. It was not yet a full-fledged religious conversion, but an incipient one. And a powerful aesthetic experience had triggered it.[5]

If Thomas Merton's initial religious experience was occasioned by an artistic image, so was his final one. Just a few days before he died, the monk encountered some superb statues of the Buddha in a garden in Ceylon. Again, an aesthetic illumination led Merton to his culminating spiritual insight. In language close to that of buddhist enlightenment, yet full of overtones from the christian mystical tradition he had so well appropriated, Merton described his moment of vision, his ultimate breakthrough:

> I am able to approach the Buddhas barefoot and undisturbed, my feet in wet grass, wet sand. Then the silence of the extraordinary faces. The great smiles. Huge and yet subtle. Filled with every possibility, questioning nothing, knowing everything, rejecting nothing. . . . I was knocked over with a rush of relief and thankfulness at the *obvious* clarity of the figures, the clarity and fluidity of shape and line, the design of the monumental bodies composed into the rock shape and landscape, figure, rock and tree. . . . Looking at these figures I was suddenly, almost forcibly jerked clean out of the habitual, half-tied vision of things, and an inner clearness, clarity, as if exploding from the rocks themselves, became evident and obvious. . . . The thing about all this is that there is no puzzle, no problem, and really no 'mystery'. All problems are resolved and everything is clear, simply because what matters is clear. The rock, all matter, all life, is charged

with dharmakaya... everything is emptiness and everything is compassion. I don't know when in my life I have ever had such a sense of beauty and spriritual validity running together in one aesthetic illumination. Surely, with Mahabalipuram and Polonnaruwa my Asian pilgrimage has come clear and purified itself. I mean, I know and have seen what I was obscurely looking for. I don't know what else remains but I have now seen and have pierced through the surface and have got beyond the shadow and the disguise.[6]

Thomas Merton's development as a religious person is framed by these two aesthetic experiences wherein a new understanding is made available to him through artistic images which embody a tradition's most profound insights. In the case of the byzantine Christ, Merton was confronted by an image of the risen Jesus as Lord of all creation and Judge of the world. That image released in Merton a recognition of his own deepest yearnings and invited the youth to review and repent of his disordered life. In the case of the Buddhas of Polonnaruwa, the image of fully enlightened human peace confirmed the intuition garnered by Merton's experience of christian mysticism through the years and, more recently, of eastern meditation techniques: the extraordinary character of the ordinary and the charged presence of the divine in everything that is.

One could cite many examples throughout Merton's life of the creative impact of visual images on the development of his religious sensibilities. The sight of woods and lakes around the monastery was utterly essential to Merton's ability to pray. His serious experimenting with photography in the 1960s was a way of learning to see with the inner eye and an exercise in contemplation.[7] It seems evident that Thomas Merton was shaped by the images he discovered in nature and art.

He was also himself a shaper of images. Merton was, indeed, receptive to images offered him by the God of nature or artists of genius and cultures inspired by authentic human values. He was no passive receiver, however; he always dialogued with the images which he found (or, as he would be inclined to say, which found him). The monk knew how to let images speak to him. He could learn from good images because he was open to whatever message they had to give. And he could appropriate natural or genuinely artistic images because he was able actively to interpret them in relation to his own life.

Thomas Merton possessed, moreover, the gift of constructing images. He composed photographs which imaged his inner vision of a tree, some rocks, an arrangement of nails on an old board. He delighted in playing spontaneously with Zen calligraphy and in sketching all sorts of faces and movements and scenes, with either piercing irony or serene compassion. He was the son of a painter, and from him the monk inherited 'his way of looking at things and some of his integrity'.[8] But Thomas Merton was not primarily an artist; he was a writer and a poet, someone who traded in verbal images.

My own view (which I have argued in other papers and articles)[9] is that Merton's poetic genius expressed itself more poignantly and powerfully in his prose than in his poetry *per se*. That is a moot point which I do not wish to pursue right now. What I do want to claim is that Merton's gift for creating rich metaphors showed itself forcefully in his autobiographical writings—and many of his books and essays fall into that generic category.

The Seven Storey Mountain, written during his early years in Gethsemani, is dominated by the metaphor of Merton's life as the upwards journey of purification. Drawing on Dante, whose *Comedia* had so entranced him in college, Merton fitted his personal story of conversion and the discovery of a monastic vocation into a framework of christian spirituality which resonated with overtones of biblical, ascetical, and mystical theology. He used the image of the transforming quest to signify both his sinful past and the monk's ongoing repentance. Merton interpreted his life before his religious conversion at Columbia as a restless search which would have remained fruitless but for a beneficient providence which was leading him by strange paths. And he understood his monastic vocation as a commitment to a conscious and freely-accepted quest which would progressively burn away all the dross until he was ready for the vision of God. This image of Merton's life as a continuing journey of transformation not only provided literary coherence for the autobiography; it served to unify the man's very life. The metaphor functioned as a mirror in which Thomas Merton could recognize his true self: a redeemed sinner, a man who would find God in the measure to which he remained faithful to an ongoing search, a monk called to an open-ended process of growth. The metaphor of the journey captured all the tensiveness embodied in the paradox of the human situation as Merton experienced it, and it bespoke his religious understanding of his own unique story.

Merton's journal of his 'young adulthood' in the monastery was entitled *The Sign of Jonas*. He longed for contemplative stillness and undisturbed prayer, yet found himself impelled to write. He was assigned that task under monastic obedience and his own compulsions forced him to it as a psychic necessity. A side of Thomas Merton nonetheless wanted to give up writing entirely as a condition for contemplation. 'Jonas' was an apt metaphor for himself during this period of his life. 'Like the prophet Jonas', wrote Merton, 'I found myself with an almost uncontrollable desire to go in the opposite direction. God pointed one way and all my "ideals" pointed in the other.'[10]

A decade later, in the midst of different struggles, Merton came up with a new metaphor for himself. He called the journal published in 1965, *Conjectures of a Guilty Bystander*. Merton was now passionately involved in writing about issues of violence, war, racial injustice, the consumer society. He was commenting on what he saw as essentially spiritual problems in the society, but he was still something of an outsider and not in the front lines of battle. Merton did not pronounce himself 'guilty' because he chose to remain in the monastery. Indeed, he made a strong case that the common good of society required that some individuals retain a 'critical distance' on the problems. He felt himself guilty because his own spiritual transformation was so very incomplete; he remained an accomplice in the world's evils. 'Though I often differ strongly from that "world", I think I can be said to respond to it,' the bystander said; but 'I do not delude myself that I am not still part of it.'[11]

Since Merton's last journal was published posthumously we do not know what he would have named it—but certainly nothing so prosaic as *The Asian Journal of Thomas Merton*. Surely, in characteristic style, he would have discovered a pregnant metaphor to express the self undergoing new growth through his experiences in the Orient. In the talks he gave while traveling in the east, Merton spoke of himself variously as a 'marginal man',[12] 'a pilgrim' seeking 'to drink from ancient sources of monastic vision and experience',[13] as one who had to confront the question sparked by the story of Tibetan monks fleeing the Communist takeover, 'are we planning for the next twenty years to be traveling with a train of yaks?'[14] He might have used any of those images for himself in the title of the *Asian Journal*. My own hunch is that Thomas Merton might have appropriated as a metaphor for himself after his encounter with the East, the Zen saying he quoted in the last conference before he died in Bangkok: '"Where do you go from the top of a thirty-foot pole?"'[15] Perhaps Merton would have modified the image to fit the paradox of his personal situation more directly: 'Where do you go from the top of a seven storey mountain?'

I have considered but a few of the many autobiographical metaphors which Merton used to articulate to himself and to communicate to us who he understood himself to be as he progressed on his monastic journey. In finding the appropriate image for himself at a given stage of development, I think that Merton was enabled to identify where he was coming from, where he was presently standing, and where his life might be going. The metaphors which the writer created for himself actually helped the man take hold of his life and move responsibly in certain directions. The shaping of images of himself, then, functioned to intensify Merton's religious consciousness and to press upon him the critical task of discernment.

It was primarily Thomas Merton's experience as a man who grasped and valued the role of images and imaginative activity in his own religious search which led him to help others take them seriously. He was instrumental in getting some of the rules of monastic enclosure changed at Gethsemani in order to allow the monks time in the woods. Merton insisted that a contemplative needed to be in touch with nature and to nurture his prayer with the rich, creative images drawn from contact with woods, sea, sky, mountains, fields, desert. He also strongly stressed the importance of good art in the life of a contemplative. Merton did everything possible as Master of Novices to expose the young monks in his charge to the work of great artists and artistic traditions. He played a key role in getting the monastic church at Gethsemani completely redone. Its style of stark simplicity and spare beauty betrays Merton's influence: the remodelled church suggests the strong romanesque features of cistercian origins blended with a contemporary feel for the use of space and fidelity to the quality of materials. Merton was similarly insistent about the need for a strong literary education for monks. When it was not possible for them to be reading novels, Merton gave his novices conferences on literary topics. There was a whole series on Faulkner and Camus, for instance.

Merton summed up his view of the significance of natural, artistic, and literary images in the development of the religious personality this way:

> The lack of qualitative judgment, of taste, of personal discrimination, of openness to new possibilities, is bound up with one great defect—a failure of imagination. Our prayer itself is poor in imagination. The pragmatic and legalistic approach to the religious life in general, and to the contemplative life in particular, has resulted in a dreadful banality. Creativity has not been desired, imagination has been discouraged, and emphasis has been on submission of will, accepting the incomprehensible stupidity of a mechanical existence instead of thinking of a realistic way of improving things. But the solution is not in changing observances and practices, or in changing the laws. The solution lies deeper, in the life of prayer. If what goes on inside our minds and hearts is banal, trivial, petty, and unimaginative, we cannot be creative in our outer works. So much that is new and experimental is proving to be a frightful letdown because it is so second-rate, so superficial, so imitative. And so much of it is in the worst possible taste—as many of our old pieties were also in the worst taste.[16]

For Merton, the cultivation of a person's imaginative capacities is not a luxury or in any way extraneous to the christian life. It is a task at the very heart of the religious endeavor. Both prayer and authentic action require, in some measure, a spontaneous and a disciplined imagination. Merton was adamant that when imagination is not constructively developed and employed, it works destructively. We will be victimized by futile distractions at prayer unless we know how to respond to images—consciously drawing on creative ones to enlarge our prayer, and able to deal with impoverished ones.[17] We will also be tyrannized by images forced upon us in the consumer society unless our imaginations have been exercised to criticize these images and to replace them with liberating ones.[18]

In order to understand ourselves and our world, in order to escape the imposition of somebody else's definition of what matters, in order to be free to see rightly and respond fully, Merton argued, we need to know how to exercise our imaginative skills. That is the key to growth in understanding and responsibility:

> Imagination is the creative task of making symbols, joining things together in such a way that they throw new light on each other and on everything around them. The imagination is a discovering faculty, a faculty for seeing relationships, for seeing meanings that are special and even quite new. The imagination is something which enables us to discover unique present meaning in a given moment of our life. Without imagination the contemplative life can be extremely dull and fruitless.[19]

As much as Thomas Merton emphasized the importance of imaginative activity in prayer and christian action in the world, he did not neglect its role in regard to thought. If for Paul Ricoeur 'the symbol gives rise to thought',[20] for Merton the image is both the beginning and end of thinking. Critical reflection begins by being confronted with an image which we examine, analyze, and either affirm or displace. And the judicious assessment of images does not terminate merely in abstract concepts; rather, this process should generate more adequate, more truthful, images. Images which are the fruit of analysis and judgment will then stimulate further inquiry. It is a continuing process.

A good example of the way in which Merton thought by examining images and suggesting more fruitful ones can be seen in his essay, 'Is the Contemplative Life Finished?':

> What do we think the contemplative life is? How do we conceive it? As a life of withdrawal, tranquility, retirement, silence? Do we keep ourselves from action and change in order to learn techniques for entering into a kind of static present reality which is there and which we have to learn how to penetrate? Is contemplation an objective static 'thing', like a building, for which there is a key? Do you hunt for this key, find it, then

unlock the door and enter? Well, that is a valid image from a certain point of view, but it isn't the only image. The contemplative life isn't something objective that is 'there' and to which, after fumbling around, you finally gain access. The contemplative life is a dimension of our subjective existence. Discovering the contemplative life is a new self-discovery. One might say that it is the flowering of a deeper identity on an entirely different plane from a mere psychological discovery, a paradoxical new identity that is found only in loss of self. To find one's self by losing one's self; that is part of 'contemplation'.[21]

Merton astutely criticizes the static image of contemplation as a 'key' and replaces it with the dynamic one of 'self-discovery'. The 'flowering of a deeper identity' is Merton's metaphorical reformulation of the nature of contemplation which invokes a psychological idiom, but avoids mere psychologizing. This image, in fact, possesses something of the power of the gospel paradox of 'finding oneself by losing oneself', while appealing to the contemporary interest in identity.

As another example of the way Merton's metaphors represent the development of his understanding and enable us to grasp new theological meaning, compare the two sets of images he used for the monastic vocation in two very different stages of his own living out of that call. In the late 1940s, he described the monastic life this way:

It takes a man above the terrors and sorrows of modern life as well as above its passing satisfactions. It elevates life to a superhuman level to the peace of the spiritual stratosphere where the storms of human existence become a distant echo and do not disturb the center of the soul. . . .[22]

By the middle of the 1960s, Merton articulated the perception of his monastic vocation in radically changed terms:

My own peculiar task in my Church and in my world has been that of the solitary explorer who, instead of jumping on all the latest bandwagons at once, is bound to search the existential depths of faith in its silences, its ambiguities, and in those certainties which lie deeper than the bottom of anxiety. In these depths there are no easy answers, no pat solutions to anything. It is a kind of submarine life in which faith, sometimes mysteriously, takes on the aspect of doubt when, in fact, one has to doubt and reject conventional and superstitious surrogates that have taken the place of faith.[23]

The mature Thomas Merton inhabited the 'existential depths' instead of the 'spiritual stratosphere'. His obligation 'to search' in a
'kind of submarine life' expressed a grasp of the monastic life precisely related to the human situation, whereas the early image of it
being 'above the terrors and sorrows of modern life' could only
suggest an escapist view. What we have in Merton's later images
for his monastic vocation is the fruit of nearly twenty years of living the life to the best of his ability, of critical reflection upon that
life, and of his constructive effort to discover metaphors which
could express the insights born of thoughtful experience.

Thomas Merton was ahead of his time on almost every front:
religious renewal, the relationship of action and contemplation in
the christian life, ecumenism in the broadest terms, the importance
of narrative for theology. In large measure, his ground-breaking
role was due to his imaginative gifts. Merton was able to sum up a
situation by hitting on an image which expressed it. That gave him
a foothold for critical evaluation and led him to create new images
which would suggest a direction for change. As Merton envisioned new metaphors for himself in different situations and while
undergoing change, so could he offer us images of ourselves as
Christians, particularly Catholics, in the 1940s, the 1950s, and the
1960s.

Was Thomas Merton's capacity to do that a particular genius?
In part, yes, of course. But it was also the result of a discipline
which helped him to trust the accuracy of his perceptions by sub-
mitting them to the kind of critical insight which practice brings to
theory. Last winter as I listened to eminent philosophers, theologians, literary theorists, and other intellectuals at the University of
Chicago's special conference, 'Metaphor: the Conceptual Leap', I
kept wondering what Thomas Merton might have added to that
erudite discussion. Surely he would have agreed with David Tracy
that 'the study of metaphor may well provide a central clue to a
better understanding of that elusive and perplexing phenomenon
our culture calls religion'.[24] Merton appreciated that metaphor
represents a conceptual leap which takes us into new intellectual
territory. But he also would have insisted that metaphors have
something to do with the very form, the existential shape, of one's

life. Fruitful metaphors for one's self, for one's world, for the God one worships, are rooted in the religious tradition one appropriates, and new images will emerge from the quality of life consciously related to that tradition as *living*. Merton said it like this:

> Our very existence, our life itself contains an implicit pretention to meaning, since all our free acts are implicit commitments, selections of 'meanings' which we seem to find confronting us. Our very existence is 'speech' interpreting reality.[25]

The imaginative activity of Thomas Merton was able to select certain meanings and to interpret reality as radically open to transcendence because, I think, he fully and freely committed himself to a continuous journey in faith. The possibilities of religious imagination for him were realized in that ongoing quest for transformation which the title of his autobiography suggested. Near the end of his life Merton nicely brought together the traditional metaphor of the christian life as a journey and his own characteristic concern for discovering one's true identity:

> Our task now is to learn that if we can voyage to the ends of the earth and there find *ourselves* in the aborigine who most differs from ourselves, we will have made a fruitful pilgrimage. That is why pilgrimage is necessary, in some shape or other. Mere sitting at home and meditating on the divine presence is not enough in our time. We have to come to the end of a long journey and see that the stranger we meet there is no other than ourselves —which is the same as saying that we find Christ in him.[26]

Redolent with images from the Gospels, such writing is nonetheless characteristically Thomas Merton's: the images are rooted in a tradition, but reinterpreted, personalized, made contemporary, and given a new twist. As always, Merton's imaginative activity was taking him somewhere—and he beckons us to follow.

NOTES

1. *The Seven Storey Mountain* (New York: Signet Books, 1948) pp. 28-29.
2. *Ibid.*, p. 132.
3. *Ibid.*, p. 112.

4. *Ibid.*, p. 111.

5. *Ibid.*, pp. 113-116.

6. *The Asian Journal of Thomas Merton* (New York: New Directions Books, 1973) pp. 233-236.

7. John Howard Griffin, *A Hidden Wholeness: the Visual World of Thomas Merton* (Boston: Houghton Mifflin Company, 1970) pp. 3-4.

8. *The Seven Storey Mountain*, p. 10.

9. See my 'To Be What I Am: Thomas Merton as a Spiritual Writer', in *In the Belly of a Paradox*, ed. Gerald Twomey (New York: Paulist Press, 1978); 'Merton's Metaphors: a Monk's Signs and Sources of Spiritual Growth', in *Cistercian Studies*, 1 (1979); 'Thomas Merton: Symbol and Synthesis of Contemporary Catholicism', *The Critic* (Spring, 1977); review of *The Collected Poems of Thomas Merton* in *The Notre Dame English Journal* (Fall, 1978); 'Conjectures of a Guilty Participant: Reflections on Reading Thomas Merton', *Sisters Today* (December, 1978).

10. *The Sign of Jonas* (New York: Image Books, 1956) p. 20.

11. *Conjectures of a Guilty Bystander* (New York: Image Books, 1968) p. 7.

12. *Asian Journal*, p. 305.

13. *Ibid.*, pp. 312-313.

14. *Ibid.*, p. 339.

15. *Ibid.*, p. 338.

16. *Contemplation in a World of Action* (New York: Image Books, 1973) p. 355.

17. *Ibid.*, p. 356.

18. *Ibid.*, p. 358.

19. *Ibid.*, p. 357.

20. Paul Ricoeur, *The Symbolism of Evil*, (New York: Harper & Row, 1967) p. 347.

21. *Contemplation in a World*, p. 352.

22. *The Waters of Siloe* (New York: Image Books, 1949) p. 28.

23. *Faith and Violence* (Notre Dame, Indiana: University of Notre Dame Press, 1968) p. 213.

24. David Tracy, 'Metaphor and Religion: the Test Case of Christian Texts', in *Critical Inquiry: Special Issue on Metaphor* 1-6.

25. *Seeds of Destruction* (New York: Macmillan, 1967) p. 162.

26. *Mystics and Zen Masters* (New York: Delta Books, 1967) p. 112.

Expansive Catholicism:
Ecumenical Perceptions of
Thomas Merton

E. Glenn Hinson

E. Glenn Hinson is the David T. Porter Professor of Church History at the Southern Baptist Theological Seminary in Louisville, Ky. His numerous published writings include Seekers after Mature Faith, *a guide to the Christian devotional classics,* A Serious Call to a Contemplative Life-style, The Integrity of the Church, *and* Jesus Christ, *a study in Christian origins. He also introduced and edited* The Doubleday Devotional Classics, *a three-volume collection of Protestant devotional writings. He has written numerous articles for scholarly periodicals including* Review and Expositor, Religion in Life, Journal of Ecumenical Studies, Cistercian Studies *and* Revue de Qumran. *Dr Hinson's contribution to this volume was originally delivered at the Vancouver School of Theology's Merton Symposium in May 1978.*

THOMAS MERTON cannot be classified as an ecumenist in any of the customary senses of the word. So far as I have discovered, he published little directly on the subject of ecumenical relations of Roman Catholics with other Christians. His writings on other subjects contain relatively few comments on ecumenism. When he did make reference to the ecumenical movement in the last decade of his life, he was not intent on propagandizing for it.

Nevertheless, despite its secondary place in his thinking and activities, I believe Merton was making a significant contribution to ecumenical dialogue from the background of the contemplative tradition and was himself unusually well equipped to do so. Indeed, he came to envision a 'quite momentous' part for the christian contemplative to play in any dialogue involving the world's religions. Difficulties posed by monastic seclusion notwithstanding, he thought the contemplative could bring a special element to the dialogue, namely, religious experience.[1] Merton would have approved readily the conviction articulated by Abraham Joshua Heschel in an address delivered at Union Theological Seminary in New York in 1965, about the same time Merton wrote 'Contemplation and Dialogue'.

> I suggest that the most significant basis for meeting of men of different religious traditions is the level of fear and trembling, of humility and contrition, where our individual moments of faith are mere waves in the endless ocean of mankind's reaching out for God, where all formulations and articulations appear as understatements, where our souls are swept away by the awareness of the urgency of answering God's commandment, while stripped of pretension and conceit we sense the tragic insufficiency of human faith.[2]

Heschel summed up exactly the *mature* Merton's ecumenical perspective.

I emphasize the word 'mature', for Thomas Merton's Catholicism underwent a vast evolution from his early period as an overzealous convert to his last days as a fully formed Catholic. What I would argue is that his ecumenism was really an aspect, an outgrowth, a product, of both his 'Catholicism' and his contemplation. By the late 60s he had laid hold of an expansive view of Catholicism which, in accordance with more recent trends in Protestant as well as Roman Catholic ecumenism, looked beyond the unity of Christians with one another to their unity with humankind. Though it is his Catholicism which will explain the rather surprising breadth of his ecumenism, it is probably the monastic

tradition to which we must trace an evident low-key interest in a
structural and institutional approach to unity. Like the cistercian
tradition that nurtured him, he was not 'uptight' about the Reformation or the realignment of institutions so long as these did not become barriers to the true monastic or christian calling. The authentic union of all Christians, nay, of all persons, would be personal.

As we carry forward the ecumenical quest in which Thomas
Merton led us, there is much that we can learn from what he
said—but much more from what he was and what he did. His
own spirituality played a pivotal role in equipping him for ecumenical dialogue. It shaped in him that thread of charity which, as
he put it, sews our neighbor's soul and our own soul 'together in
one Christ'.[3] It fine-tuned him to meet people of East and West,
North and South, wealth and poverty, culture and ignorance,
devotion and secularity.

A process of maturation is clearly discernible in Merton's attitude toward other Christians, toward other religions, and toward
nonbelievers. This process seems to have kept pace with or possibly a step ahead of official changes in the Roman Catholic
Church's attitude. What I suspect is that he experienced a personal
liberation during a period of sustained physical and emotional
struggle between 1949 and 1951 and afterward eagerly snatched
at every encouragement from the church's pronouncements to expand his ecumenical horizons. His growing concern about the
future of humanity kept stretching those horizons farther and farther as he searched in universal human experience for answers to
the gripping problems of Western civilization.

The growth of Merton's Catholicism is clearly evident in a
change of attitude toward Protestantism. As would be expected of
a recent convert, in *The Seven Storey Mountain* he weighed his
Quaker and Episcopal experiences and found them wanting. At
times he came very close to panning them. Recollection of his own
inadequate religious instruction caused him to be 'overwhelmed at
the thought of the tremendous weight of moral responsibility that
Catholic parents accumulate upon their shoulders by not sending
their children to Catholic schools'. Spiritual direction his father ar-

ranged for him to get from a protestant minister was 'practically useless'.[4] The best he could obtain from Anglican church school instruction at Ripley Court School was 'a little natural faith', for the Church of England 'is a class religion, the cult of a special society and group, not even a whole nation, but of a ruling minority in a nation'.[5] He was impressed with Protestant Professor Jean Héring, whom he met in Strassburg when he was fifteen, but he suspected that Héring's piety had rubbed off from his contact with the church fathers. After visiting a Quaker meeting in Flushing, New York, Merton commented that he liked the silence but decided: 'They are like all the rest. In other churches it is the minister who hands out the commonplaces, and here it is liable to be just anybody.' Though he conceded that there might be 'much earnest and pure and humble worship of God and much sincere worship among the Quakers', such as one might find in every religion, he did not expect them ever to be 'anything more than what they claim to be—a "Society of Friends".'[6] In the Roman Catholic Church, by way of contrast, he was awed

> to discover so many ordinary people in a place together; more conscious of God than of one another: not there to show off their hats or their clothes, but to pray, or at least to fulfil a religious obligation, not a human one. For even those who might have been there for no better motive than that they were obliged to be, were at least free from any of the self-conscious and human constraint which is never absent from a Protestant church where people are definitely gathering together as people, as neighbors, and always have at least half an eye for one another, if not all of both eyes.[7]

By the 1960s Merton reviewed such statements as these with much embarrassment. In a personal letter to me, written in 1965, he lamented his early narrowness and rejoiced that he had learned much from contacts with other Christians. From about 1960 on, he had met with ministers and seminarians of various denominations on a regular basis, but a change of perception preceded this. One is tempted to connect this change with the enthronement of John XXIII in 1958 and the breath of new air he brought to the ecumenical climate. However, while I am ready to concede this with reference to Merton's formal contacts with non-Catholics, I believe Merton's change came at an earlier date.[8]

The 'new' Merton was clearly visible when he composed *No Man Is an Island*, published in 1955. After trying to lock the 'world' out of his heart when he entered Gethsemani in 1942, he rediscovered it in a new way, and, at the same time, he discovered a much larger Catholicism than he had known before. He was still very much a Catholic, but now he was a Catholic with a difference. 'I do not intend to divorce myself at any point from Catholic tradition,' he wrote. 'But neither do I intend to accept points of that tradition blindly, and without understanding, and without making them really my own.' He proceeded to affirm his identification with humankind, something he had tried earlier to disown. 'Every other man is a piece of myself,' he reasoned, 'for I am a part and a member of mankind. Every Christian is part of my own body, because we are members of Christ. What I do is also done for them and with them and by them. What they do is done in me and by me and for me. But each one of us remains responsible for his share in the life of the whole body.'[9]

Merton welcomed the Johannine era and the Council and moved on apace at the head of the stream. In an article which he wrote on "The Council and Religious Life" in 1965 he noted with approval that the church had recognized for the first time "openly and officially" that there was a good reason for the Protestant Reformation. Ironically, he remarked, recognition of this was so new that a new word had to be adopted 'which ought to mean the same as Catholicism but which in fact implies a note of universality which the word Catholic has imperceptibly lost'. The 'new' word was 'ecumenism'.[10]

The mature Catholicism of Merton came to expression in *Conjectures of a Guilty Bystander*, which he completed in November 1965. Though he rejected the label of 'professional ecumenism' and characterized the book as 'personal and monastic reflections', this book reveals more of his ecumenical perspective than any other writing. In contrast to the brash convert twenty years before, Merton now refused to judge Protestant claims to have freedom in the Spirit. 'I am persuaded that [a Protestant] would have greater security and clearer light if he were in my Church, but he does not see this as I do, and for this there are deeper and more complex reasons than either he or I can understand,' he wrote. 'Let us try to understand them, but meanwhile let us continue each in his own way, seeking the light with all sincerity.'[11] He praised the Shakers, with whom Cistercians have much affinity. He sided with Karl Barth and other Protestant theologians against such Catholic thinkers as Teilhard on specific issues of theology. He spoke approvingly of Orthodox views of christian unity. 'I will be a better Catholic,' he decided, 'not if I can *refute* every shade of Protestantism, but if I can affirm the truth in it and still go further.'[12] Wrestling with a definition of Catholicism as he had come to perceive it by this time, he echoed the apostle Paul's mission formula. 'To be truly Catholic is not merely to be correct according to an abstractly universal standard of truth, but also and above all to be able to enter into the problems and joys of all, to understand all, to be all things to all men.'[13]

The growth of Merton's ecumenical perceptions stands out in bas-relief in his appreciation of other religions. It was in this dialogue, obviously, that he envisioned contemplatives like himself making their most significant contributions. Before he converted to Catholicism, as is well known, he had a keen interest in Eastern religions which, surprisingly, seemed to make him at times more appreciative of them than of Protestantism. During the 40s and 50s, it is true, he regularly criticized Eastern religions with the stock charges of 'pantheism', 'immanentism', and 'absorptionism'. In *The Seven Storey Mountain* he concluded that Oriental mysticism, with which he had flirted in 1937 and 1938, belonged 'purely in the natural order' and, while not *per se* evil, was 'more or less useless, except when it is mixed up with elements that are strictly diabolical'.[14] He was, however, impressed with Bramachari, who directed him to Augustine's *Confessions* and *The Imitation of Christ*, and a new Hindu religious order founded by him.[15]

It is not surprising, then, that Merton turned up the burner again in his study of Oriental religions. The Second Vatican Council's publication of the Declaration on the Relationship of the Church to Non-Christian Religions in October 1965, probably reassured him in the boldness with which he turned East, but, again, it did not provide the occasion for his revival of interest. What prompted him, rather, was a growing conviction that Western society had a fatal flaw which the wisdom of the Orient might help to correct.

In an essay written in 1961, entitled 'Christian Culture Needs Oriental Wisdom', he constructed an unequivocating apologia for the study of Eastern religions in the West. The study of humanities in the West, he insisted, 'absolutely' must introduce an element of contemplation as well as wise action. This cannot be achieved simply by going back over european and christian cultural traditions. 'We have to gain new perspectives, and on this our spiritual and even our physical survival may depend.' This is not to suggest that Christianity is inherently deficient. Rather, it is to say that Christianity, if nothing else, can learn more about its own revelation by study of other religions. In the past it has been enriched by other traditions, for example, Greek philosophy, Roman law, and Oriental philosophy and religious thought. Westerners can no longer afford to shrug off the Eastern faiths as 'pantheistic' and 'quietistic'. These religions offer values in the realm of spiritual experience which are not unlike 'supernatural wisdom itself'. Thus, concluded Merton,

> At least this much can and must be said: the 'universality' and 'catholicity' which are essential to the Church necessarily imply an ability and a readiness to enter into dialogue with all that is pure, wise, profound and humane in every kind of culture. In this one sense at least a dialogue with Oriental wisdom becomes necessary. A Christian culture that is not capable of such a dialogue would show, by that very fact, that it lacked catholicity.[16]

In a letter to a Chinese priest in California, composed about the same time as the above statement, Merton emphasized that Westerners had much to learn from Asians and criticized earlier christian approaches to Asia. In this letter the cosmic Christology which undergirded his expansive Catholicism comes through quite clearly.

> I do not know if I have anything to offer Asians but I am convinced that I have an immense amount to learn from Asia. One of the things I would

like to share with Asians is not only Christ but Asia itself. I am convinced that a rather superficial Christianity in European dress is not enough for Asia. We have lacked depth. We have lacked the breadth of view to grasp all the wonderful breadth and richness in the Asian traditions, which were given to China, India, Japan, Korea, Burma, etc., as natural preparations for the coming of Christ. I feel that often those who finally brought Christ may have fallen short of the preparation that the Holy Spirit had provided and hence Our Lord was not seen in all his divine splendor.[17]

Merton went East, therefore, as a Catholic. Obviously he did not appreciate everything in all religions. What he wanted to get at was the stamen of the Oriental flower. That could not be done, he observed, by standing afar off and saying, 'I like this or that or that'. It could be done only by becoming *in oneself* a person who claimed those faiths, to become to the Jew a Jew, to the Buddhist a Buddhist, to the Hindu a Hindu, and so on. He adopted the same stance toward these faiths that he did toward Protestantism or Orthodoxy. As a Catholic he needed to acknowledge truth wherever he found it. 'If I affirm myself as a Catholic merely by denying all that is Muslim, Jewish, Protestant, Hindu, Buddhist, etc., in the end I will find that there is not much left for me to affirm as a Catholic: and certainly no breath of the Spirit with which to affirm it.'[18] This judgment opened the way for him to look for unitive bonds between Christianity and the others.

He felt a growing affinity for Judaism. In a letter addressed to a rabbi he called the Jews 'the great eschatological sign of the twentieth century' and insisted that there is one suffering Servant—'Christ, Israel'—and 'one wedding and one wedding feast', 'one bride', 'one mystery', and that 'the mystery of Israel and of the Church is ultimately to be revealed as One'.[19] A few years later he concluded: 'One has either got to be a Jew or stop reading the Bible. The Bible cannot make sense to anyone who is not "spiritually a Semite".' The New Testament, he went on to say, is 'never a denial of Judaism, but its affirmation. Those who consider it a denial have not understood it.'[20]

Merton, for obvious reasons, felt the closest affinity with the monastic and contemplative traditions of other faiths. Against Christopher Dawson, who wanted to hang on to Christendom, and Barth, who insisted on Christ alone, Merton saw his task as

clarifying his own living tradition, i.e., 'the tradition of wisdom
and spirit that is found not only in western Christendom but in
Orthodoxy, and also, at least analogously, in Asia and in Islam'.[21]
Though he thought Christianity and Islam had 'a deep divergence'
in their concepts of faith, he insisted in a letter to a Moslem that
'mutual comprehension between Christians and Moslems is something of vital importance today' and lamented the fact that 'it is
rare and uncertain, or else subjected to the vagaries of politics'.[22]
He appreciated especially the insights of Sufism.[23]

As most of us are aware, Merton felt very comfortable with Zen
Buddhism, comfortable enough to remark just before departing
for Bangkok, 'I see no contradiction between Buddhism and
Christianity. The future of Zen is in the West. I intend to become
as good a Buddhist as I can.'[24] Western interest in Zen was, he
observed, 'a healthy reaction of people exasperated with the
heritage of four centuries of Cartesianism'.[25] The *Asian Journal*
shows that he quaffed eagerly from the Buddhist cup in his
journey to the East, always testing by the contemplative tradition
he knew. He reveled in contacts with the Dalai Lama, placing this
above all his other experiences. What impressed him was their
ability to 'communicate with one another and share an essentially
spiritual experience of "Buddhism" which is also somehow in harmony with Christianity'.[26] On visiting the Buddhas at Polonnaruwa he enthused: 'I don't know when in my life I have ever
had such a sense of beauty and spiritual validity running together
in one aesthetic illumination.' In a 7 November entry he confessed
that in depth of spiritual experience he found among buddhist
monks 'a deeper attainment and certitude than in Catholic contemplatives', although many of the latter had an equivalent desire
for this.[27]

He seems not to have followed up his early contacts with Hinduism to any extent. But he did display an unabashed admiration
for Mahatma Gandhi. In 'A Tribute to Gandhi' published in 1961
he declared that it was irrelevant whether Gandhi 'believed in'
Jesus in the traditional christian sense or not. What matters is that
he not only understood the ethic of the gospel better than most
Christians, but that he actually 'applied Gospel principles to the

problems of a political and social existence in such a way that his approach to these problems was *inseparably* religious and political at the same time'.[28] Merton was impressed with Gandhi's principle of *satyagraha*, 'non-violent dedication to truth, a religious and spiritual force, a wisdom born of fasting and prayer'. Though Gandhi dissociated himself explicitly from Christianity, 'he built his whole life and all his activity on what he conceived to be the law of Christ'. No Christian can do better.[29]

The obvious sincerity and extent of Merton's appreciation for other faiths causes one to wonder how he avoided syncretism. Some persons, to be sure, feared he was going too far and questioned the viability of East-West dialogue. In Merton's case, however, I think that such fears fail to take into account the way in which he continually measured everything by Catholic tradition, especially the contemplative tradition. He put everything through a Catholic sieve to remove items which would not mix well with his own experience. His affinity for Zen notwithstanding, for example, he did not hesitate to warn about careless and uncritical adoption of it. There is in it, he warned, 'a very subtle and elusive quality, and, although it does have the power to sterilize spiritual illusion, it can, when badly understood, become the worst of illusions'.[30] What allowed him to pursue such an interest, despite its dangers, was the fact that it squared with the thought which he derived from christian contemplatives such as John of the Cross. Nevertheless, he was capable of drawing the lines quite precisely. Responding to a moslem correspondent who had found an affinity with John of the Cross in respect to his teaching concerning detachment and the purifying effect of aridity and helplessness in prayer, Merton at first agreed. But he went on to point out that a 'deep divergence may be found, though perhaps not as deep as I anticipate' in the christian and moslem concepts of faith.[31]

In its broadest scope Thomas Merton's Catholicism allowed him to identify with every human being 'as Christ'. In this sense he defined Catholicism and thus ecumenism in terms of christian humanism, both in the cultural and philosophical sense.

Despite cultural exposure both deep and cosmopolitan, on entrance to Gethsemani Merton wanted the gates to slam shut and never open again to the outside world. It took several years of inward struggle for him to realize that he had not properly understood the monastic *contemptus mundi*. He seems to have had in mind the outcome of this struggle when, in *No Man Is an Island*, he differentiated true and false solitude.

> Both solitudes seek to distinguish the individual from the crowd. True solitude succeeds in this, false solitude fails. True solitude separates one man from the rest in order that he may freely develop the good that is his own, and then fulfil his true destiny by putting himself at the service of everyone else. False solitude separates a man from his brothers in such a way that he can no longer effectively give them anything or receive anything from them in his own spirit.[32]

In the late 50s Merton's social concern grew, and as it did it stretched his ecumenical perceptions wider and wider. In *Conjectures* he expressed his own sense of mission to the world as it had grown to maturity. 'Solitude has its own special work: a deepening of awareness that the world needs. A struggle against alienation. True solitude is deeply aware of the world's needs. It does not hold the world at arm's length.'[33]

In the 60s Merton assailed with vigor the narrow Catholic mentality which held 'that everyone else is malicious or ignorant, and that all that is required is for everyone to listen to us and agree with us in everything from faith to table manners and taste in art. Then the world will be all right.' Such a view, he explained, naïvely assumes that we still have thirteenth-century or post-Tridentine 'Christendom'. Its holders are not 'Catholic' in the true sense of the word. Indeed, he judged that

> the 'Catholic' who is the aggressive specimen of a ghetto Catholic culture, limited, rigid, prejudiced, negative, is precisely a non-Catholic, at least in the cultural sense. Worse still, he may be anti-Catholic in the cultural sense and perhaps even, in some ways, religiously, without realizing it.[34]

This does not mean that Merton was willing to accept and approve everything which modern culture concocted. Far from it.

What he was willing to accept was that part of culture, any culture, which humanized and personalized, that is, brought the fulfillment of human existence. It had to have in it the element of true wisdom. The application of this criterion meant, in practice, that Merton could be highly critical of modern technological culture, precisely because it dehumanized and depersonalized. In itself, he admitted, technology is not evil; it is not anti-spiritual. In the way Westerners have used it, however, it 'becomes nothing more than an expensive and complicated way of cultural disintegration'. By becoming autonomous technology threatens to undo man entirely. Instead of helping him to attain freedom, it has enslaved him, made him 'an implement, a "hand," or better a "bio-physical link" between machines' or 'a mouth, a digestive system and an anus, something *through which* pass the products of his technological enjoyment'.[35]

At the same time, to look at the positive side of his application of these principles, Merton had an immense capacity to appreciate the humanizing and personalizing aspects of human culture. His models were Clement of Alexandria and Erasmus. Clement was to him a model Catholic in that he articulated the true purpose of culture, a true humanism. According to Merton,

> The purpose of a Christian humanism should be to liberate man from the mere status of *animalis homo (sarkikos)* to at least the level of *rationalis (psychicos)* and better still spiritual, or pneumatic. The spiritual man is fully man precisely because he has fulfilled his latent potentialities by life 'in the Spirit,' i.e. the Holy Spirit, the Spirit of Christ.[36]

The cultural side of Merton's Catholicism or ecumenism is seen in the vast range of his correspondents. He was eager to correspond and, where possible, to have direct contact with all persons who strove for the humanization of man. They too, whether they knew it or not, were 'in Christ'. There is an interesting confirmation of this point in a letter which Merton wrote to James Baldwin. Merton told Baldwin that he found him right on target with reference to his analysis of the racial crisis in America. He disagreed with him only in Baldwin's insistence that he did what he did as a non-Christian or anti-Christian. To the contrary, Merton insisted, what Baldwin did was 'fundamentally religious, genuinely religious, and therefore has to be against conventional religiosity'.[37] Similarly, he found the thought of an existentialist such as Camus essentially christian, despite Camus' agnosticism. And he insisted on 'the right of other nations, races, and societies to be different from us and to stay different'. Prayer for their conversion will be meaningless unless and until we *'want* their problems to be solved in much the same way as we want our own to be solved'.[38] In such comments we can discern the christological sweep of Merton's thought. In 'The Power and Meaning of Love' he exposed the axle around which this broad perspective turned: 'I must learn that my fellow man, just as he is, whether he is my friend or my enemy, my brother or a stranger from the other side of the world, whether he be wise or foolish, no matter what may be his limitations *"is Christ"*.'[39]

The expansion of Merton's ecumenical, viz., Catholic perceptions, therefore, is clearly discernible. Our remaining concern is to connect his ecumenism with his contemplative vocation.

We cannot overemphasize the fact that his own approach was highly personal and that, in agreement with his own tradition, he ascribed the 'greatest importance' to 'friendship, spontaneity, and spiritual liberty' and considered 'too much emphasis on organization. . .stupefying'.[40] His way would be the way of personal and spiritual unity. He summarized his ecumenical aim quite well in *Conjectures*:

> If I can unite *in myself* the thought and the devotion of Eastern and Western Christendom, the Greek and the Latin Fathers, the Russians with the Spanish mystics, I can prepare in myself the reunion of divided Christians. From that secret and unspoken unity in myself can eventually come a visible and manifest unity of all Christians. If we want to bring together what is divided, we can not do so by imposing one division upon the other or absorbing one division into the other. But if we do this, the union is not Christian. It is political, and doomed to further conflict. We must contain all divided worlds in ourselves and transcend them in Christ.[41]

Though the perspectives of this statement are those of a contemplative, they contain some profound insights which we should not gloss over. In notes jotted down for a paper which he was to have delivered in Calcutta in October 1968, on 'Monastic Experience and East-West Dialogue', Merton observed that 'true communication on the deepest level is more than a simple sharing of ideas, of conceptual knowledge, or formulated truth'. If authentic, it requires '"communion" beyond the level of words, a communion in authentic experience which is shared not only on a "preverbal" level but also on a "postverbal" level'. He warned against the dangers of (1) reducing dialogue to talk, (2) facile syncretism, (3) blurring of differences, (4) losing sight of the real monastic goal—'true self-transcendence and enlightenment', and (5) preoccupation with institutional structure, or monastic rule, or not paying due respect to these. 'Above all,' he concluded, 'it is important that this element of depth and integrity—this element of inner transcendent freedom—be kept intact as we grow toward the full maturity of universal man.'[42]

What I wish to call attention to before bringing these remarks to a close is the way in which the contemplative vocation equipped Merton for precisely this kind of dialogue. Those of you who knew him will recognize readily what I mean when I say that he ranked at the very top of those whom I have known who were truly prepared for dialogue. He tuned in on the wave length of others with remarkable ease and precision. His 'gift' for this has been noted by many others.[43] It is perhaps best attested in the responses he got from Buddhists on his trip to Bangkok in 1968. The Dalai Lama called him a 'Catholic geshe', which a friend interpreted as 'the highest possible praise from a Gelugpa, like an honorary doctorate!'[44] Chatral Rimpoche, a distinguished Tibetan Buddhist spiritual mentor, suggested seriously that he and Merton might attain complete spiritual Buddhahood in their next lives or 'perhaps even in this life'. He was surprised that he got on so well with a Christian, exclaiming once, 'There must be something wrong here!'[45] There is also the by now well-known story that, shortly after Merton's death, four small crocodiles came out of the water onto the grass near a walkway used by participants at the conference he addressed and devoured a small dog, an incident which Buddhists connect with the appearance of a Buddha.[46]

From whence, then, this 'gift'? The fact that Merton possessed an *unusual* ability to commune and communicate 'beyond words' would lead many to ascribe it to his peculiar genius and personality. Those who know Merton's story, however, would never stop there, as Merton himself would not, for they would know that his 'gift' was poured, molded, and refined in Merton's own search for community in the Trappist order. In the last analysis, it was contemplation which equipped him for authentic dialogue and communion with all persons everywhere.

Merton's own perceptions about the unitive role of contemplation are quite visible in *The Waters of Siloe*, an early writing on the monastic vocation, published in 1949. The monk's aim, he noted then, is love of God, who is love. This love can only be demonstrated by living for the common will, *voluntas communis*, by complete surrender, obedience in 'every smallest circumstance of the common life'. So long as a monk 'retains private ownership of any corner of his own being', he falls short of this union.[47] Contemplation in no way conflicts with the common life; rather, it prepares the monk for it, for 'the more he isolates himself in the will of God, the more he becomes one, by charity, with all the others who are united in the same love of God'. He treasures solitude and silence and even physical isolation so that he may commune with God's Spirit, 'who is the common life of the monastic community and of the whole Church of God'. Solitude, therefore, unites. 'The closer the contemplative is to God, the closer he is to other men. The more he loves God, the more he can love the men he lives with. He does not withdraw from them to shake them off, to get away from them, but in the truest sense, to *find* them. *Omnes in Christo unum sumus.*'[48] The goal of monasticism is the perfection of the person of Christ, his mystical Body.

What we can learn from Thomas Merton, then, has something to do with *preparation* for ecumenical encounter, not just of Christians with one another, but of Christians with all persons everywhere. Unless we are prepared to go beyond words and thoughts, there is little prospect of genuine union. Unless we discover, as Merton did, the cosmic Christ who precedes us in our encounters with one another, we will remain hopelessly tied to our parochial perceptions. Unless we acquire the humility which comes from communion with God, we will persist in erecting defenses and barriers which exclude other persons from ourselves. Contemplation, Merton has taught us, is an essential preparation for authentic ecumenism.

NOTES

1. 'Contemplation and Dialogue', in *Mystics and Zen Masters* (New York: Delta Publishing Co., 1967) pp. 203-14.

2. 'No Religion Is an Island', *Union Seminary Quarterly Review*, XXI (1966) 122.

3. 'The Power and Meaning of Love', in *Disputed Questions* (New York: Mentor-Omega Books, 1965) p. 100.

4. *The Seven Storey Mountain* (New York: Signet Books, 1952) p. 57.

5. *Ibid.*, pp. 68, 69.

6. *Ibid.*, p. 119.

7. *Ibid.*, pp. 204-5.

8. Patrick Hart, 'The Ecumenical Concern of Thomas Merton', *The Lamp*, (Dec., 1972) p. 21, dates the first contacts in the 50s, but if so, it was the *late* 50s, after John XXIII became pope.

9. *No Man Is an Island* (New York: Doubleday Image Books, 1967) pp. 11, 16.

10. *New Blackfriars*, 47 (Oct. 1965) 6.

11. *Conjectures of a Guilty Bystander* (New York: Doubleday Image Books, 1966) p. 90.

12. *Ibid.*, p. 144.

13. *Ibid.*, p. 185.

14. *Seven Storey Mountain*, p. 185.

15. *Ibid.*, pp. 189 ff.

16. 'Christian Culture Needs Oriental Wisdom', *Catholic World*, 195 (May, 1962) 72-79.

17. *Seeds of Destruction* (New York: Macmillan, 1967) pp. 198-99.

18. *Conjectures of a Guilty Bystander*, p. 144.

19. *Seeds of Destruction*, pp. 189-90.

20. *Conjectures of a Guilty Bystander*, p. 14.

21. *Ibid.*, p. 194.

22. In *Seeds of Destruction*, p. 207.

23. *Conjectures of a Guilty Bystander*, pp. 210-11.

24. Quoted by David Steindl-Rast, 'Recollections of Thomas Merton's Last Days in the West', *Monastic Studies* reprint, p. 10. This article was later published as a chapter in *Thomas Merton/Monk*, edited by Brother Patrick Hart (New York: Sheed and Ward, 1974, and reissued in paperback by Doubleday Image Books).

25. *Conjectures of a Guilty Bystander*, p. 285.

26. *The Asian Journal of Thomas Merton*, ed. Naomi Burton, Patrick Hart, and James Laughlin (New York: New Directions, 1968) p. 148.

27. *Ibid.*, pp. 235, 124.

28. *Seeds of Destruction*, p. 159.

29. *Ibid.*, pp. 160, 164.

30. 'Zen: Sense and Sensibility', *America*, (May 25, 1963) pp. 752-54.

31. In *Seeds of Destruction*, p. 208.

32. *No Man Is an Island*, pp. 185-86.

33. *Conjectures of A Guilty Bystander*, p. 19.

34. *Seeds of Destruction*, pp. 187-88.

35. *Conjectures of a Guilty Bystander*, pp. 76-77.

36. *Seeds of Destruction*, p. 175.

37. *Ibid.*, p. 209.

38. *Conjectures of a Guilty Bystander*, pp. 87-88.

39. In *Disputed Questions*, p. 100.

40. *Conjectures of a Guilty Bystander*, p. 315.

41. *Ibid.*, p. 21.

42. *The Asian Journal*, pp. 315, 317.

43. See my article, 'Merton's Many Faces', *Religion in Life*, 42 (1973).

44. *The Asian Journal*, p. 125.

45. *Ibid.*, p. 144.

46. John Moffitt, 'Thomas Merton—The Last Three Days', *Catholic World* (July, 1969) pp. 160-63.

47. *The Waters of Siloe (New York: Doubleday Image Books, 1962) pp. 358-59.*

48. *Ibid.*, pp. 262-63.

Syllables of the Great Song:
Merton and
Asian Religious Thought

Deba P. Patnaik

Deba P. Patnaik was born in Cuttack, India, and was educated in India, England, and the United States. He has taught literature, philosophy, religion, creative writing and photography for some years in this country. He also taught and lectured in Mexico, Europe, Scandinavia, and the USSR. He is a writer, translator, poet and critic who has been published in England, the United States, Europe, and India. His latest work on Merton's photography entitled The Geography of Holiness: Thomas Merton's Photography *was published in 1980 by Pilgrim Press. He had personal contact with Merton while teaching at the University of Louisville. His contribution to this volume was originally presented at the Columbia University Merton program in November of 1978.*

THE TITLE of this paper came to me on 10 November, through the cables of autumn birds, when I watched them raising their last and furious protest as 'the threat of winter' gleamed. 'November analyzed our bankruptcies', writes Thomas Merton in 'Two States of Prayer'.[1] And this commemoration in November, may I suggest, has for us all an appropriateness of its own. 'In my ending', sang the Trappist poet-monk, 'is my meaning'. He died in the last month of the year. The celebration is a fitting occasion for remembrance, recollection, and reflection. This is what I intend to do—to remember a rare human person; to thank publicly an abiding friend; to recollect his acts, feelings, thoughts, his struggle, hope, and achievement; and to reflect on our times and the meaning of his life; to try to understand the topography of Merton's life of faith—the human, religious, and spiritual world of the man, who, like Elias of his poem, 'becomes his own wild bird with God in the center'.[2] What emblems does he hold out for us? What signs of an apocalypse does he intimate?

Perhaps the Merton Commemorative Year, to quote from another poem of his, is 'the year of strategy'—a time to meditate on him, and to act before the 'final seizure', before our 'frozen understanding separates/ And dies in floes', as he warns in 'Ode to the Present Century'.[3]

Autumn 1968: on the University of Louisville campus, dappled leaves were whimsically tumbling down in the sunny September wind. Merton had come to the campus that afternoon to say goodbye to me before he took off on his Asian trip. We talked about several things as we walked on crunchy heaps of leaves through the trees, his hands locked behind him. I felt there was something unique about it, for in the past we had taken many walks together in the woods and on the undulating hills of Gethsemani. At one point, we stood watching two albino squirrels, permanent residents of the campus, devouring the year's last berries. We stood there for many minutes exchanging our silences and smiles. He suddenly overwhelmed me with a compliment; then, with somber passion, remarked, 'You're right, a world network of spiritual human beings will hold us together. We'll exchange notes when I get back.' He paused, gave a faraway look, and added, 'Deba, this journey is very crucial. It's a final one for me. Remember me in your thoughts. I'll be praying for you.' He embraced me as if I were his brother. Why do I say 'as if'? This is the point that struck me when I started thinking about this paper—Merton's expansiveness, his genuine and spontaneous ac-

ceptance of the other person as his very own, his profound loving-
ness and humility. Some may detect a tragic irony in what he said
—'a final one'. But the finality he meant was in terms of his spiritual consummation, because his Asian journey, to my mind, was a
culmination.

This is what he writes about his Asian journey: 'The moment of
take-off was ecstatic. . . . We left the ground—I with Christian
mantras and a great sense of destiny, of being at last on my true
way after years of waiting and wondering and fooling around.
May I not come back without having settled the great affair. And
found also the great compassion, mahakaruna. I am going home,
to the home where I have never been in this body.'[4] These
passages speak significantly and pointedly. After years of waiting
and wondering, and with 'a great sense of destiny' to settle 'the
great affair'—'my true way'—to rediscover for himself and for us
'the great compassion, mahakaruna', the only true way for all nations and peoples of the world to survive and live in this age of
technology and nuclear holocaust.

Is Japan the home? India? Sri Lanka? Thailand? Remember in
Cables to the Ace, section 87—'The surest home is pointless.' For
this journey of Merton, geography was not necessary at all. The
home he refers to is the ground of being/becoming, of mystical
contemplation, ecstatic faith, and spiritual enlightenment that the
ancient and holy cultures of these countries exemplified. Merton
died 'in a distant country', I believe, 'having become a pure cone',
as he says in section 74 of *Cables to the Ace*—a pure cone of song
and light that continues to penetrate and inspire us to our true self.
He died a free man; and 'the freeman's road has neither beginning
nor end'.[5]

Some years ago I gave a talk on Merton in a Catholic school in
New York. During the question-answer period two rather impa-
tient, I should say irate, priests pontificated that Merton was a
charlatan, a confused monk, unchristian and uncatholic. What
business had he to wander off and flirt with Oriental religion and
philosophy? Why did he have to go East? What kind of trappist
monk was he, especially when he would not keep his mouth shut
on social and temporal affairs? Many have raised such doubts and
questions, still do, only to betray their own ignorance, limitedness,

and misunderstanding. Father Louis was no charlatan, no confused, unchristian, uncatholic monk. His words, thoughts, and actions—his entire life as a monk—testify to his 'terrible honesty' (Eliot) and to his inspiring, living faith as a contemplative, a christian, and as an evolved human person. Let us not forget, St Augustine was steeped in Plotinus, as was St Thomas in Aristotle and Averroes, and Teilhard in marxian thought.

We should recognize that the Asian journey from 15 October to 10 December 1968, was both a physical fact and a psychological and spiritual actualization of a symbolic movement that started a long time ago in Merton. This incorporates two powerful and inextricable metaphors—motifs—in Merton's life; the journey and the East. Asia—the East—did not mean for Merton a geographic, spatial point; it is a trans-reality, supra-reality toward which the soul of the contemplative journeys. The eastward journey, as his 'Pilgrim's Song' says, is toward light. It is 'a whole new universe' with 'new holiness rising'.[6] The journey metaphor, therefore, acquires the meaning of renewal, transformation, and union. The life of a monk, Merton believed, is a life of journey in this temporal existence—a journey through doubts, struggles, hope, and mystery, not a static point or moment. He frequently suggests this idea in his writings. The journey is toward the very source of being, toward the eternal Present, toward oneness with the Mystery. To me, Merton's journey to, and involvement with, the East resonates with this meaning.

Merton's deep and concentrated study and knowledge of the Asian religious and philosophical thought was no flirtation or intellectual dilettantism. No attempt to let 'Christian rabbits..suddenly appear by magic',[7] out of a Hindu hat or a Taoist tuxedo. Nor did he try to establish himself as an original theologian, or an erudite commentator in comparative religion. In May of 1962 Merton asked in an article for the *Catholic World*:

Can we be content to leave the rich Asian heritage of wisdom at the level of 'comparative religion', and subject it to superficial and passing consideration, checking off concepts like 'Tao' and 'Dharma' and 'Dhyana' as a bored tourist might saunter through the Louvre vaguely registering the famous masterpieces as he walked by them? Or, can we simply study these Asian religions and philosophies from an apologetic or missiological standpoint, as 'rival systems' which are known *a priori* to be 'false' but which one must at least know how to refute?[8]

The unforgettable quality of his immersion in Asian thought—Asian wisdom, as he puts it—lies in the experiential and practical basis and significance of such an engagement. His emphasis and exploration have been in the area of the application of Asian wisdom in the life of the peoples of the respective cultures, the various methods and practices in meditation, and the ultimate value today. In the same article in the *Catholic World*, Merton emphasizes: 'The values hidden in Oriental thought *actually* reveal themselves *only* on the plane of spiritual *experience*, or perhaps, if you like, of aesthetic experience.'[9] (italics mine) The meaning of the 'aesthetic' in this context, should be taken in the Heideggerian sense.

Merton's involvement in the Asian religious and philosophical thought and practices started early in his life, as he records in *The Seven Storey Mountain* (1948), when he had that turning point encounter with the Hindu yogi, Brahmachari, who urged him to return to his own religious roots. An entry a year later on 24 November in *The Sign of Jonas* (1953), mentions his correspondence with an Indian in Simla about Patanjali's yoga, and of the Gethsemani visit of a Hawaiian chemist, a former Zen postulant. During his Columbia days he came across Mahatma Gandhi, and was instantly and totally fascinated and impressed by Gandhiji's philosophy and application of *ahimsa* and *satyagraha*. He avidly read books and articles relating to the Asian thought; and, we know, he continued to read keenly and extensively until his death. All this amounted to 'ventures in personal and spiritual interpretation', he notes in *The Way of Chuang Tzu* (1965), the preparation of which was started back in 1960. These 'ventures', through the passing of time, illustrate in the Chardinian and Aurobindian sense the process of complexification and amplification of his spiritual consciousness as a 'fully personalized consciousness'. In this I don't find his destiny travelling in a 'belly of a paradox'—a contradiction. On the contrary, it vivifies a definite, logical, and inevitable growth and crystalization of Merton as monk, a christian monk, and as an enlightened person.

'God speaks', writes Merton in his scintillating 'Letter to Pablo

Antonio Cuadra Concerning Giants', 'and God is to be heard not only on Sinai, not only in my own heart, but in the voice of the stranger.'[10] Surely, the Divine 'blows wherever it pleases,' if I may borrow from the Bible.

Merton entered the 'fabulous edifice' of Asian wisdom—entered 'into dialogue with all that is pure, wise, profound, and humane in every kind of culture'[11] because, to him it was an 'historical task', to apply the expression from his meditation on Father Delp in *Faith and Violence* (1968). Vatican II offered the right climate of openness and understanding, which further strengthened Merton's own dialogic and assimilative endeavours. The striking feature of this dialogue is 'no syncretism, indifferentism, the vapid and careless friendliness that accepts everything by thinking nothing'.[12] Otherwise, he wisely suggests in *Mystics and Zen Masters*, any kind of 'loose and irresponsible syncretism . . . on the basis of superficial resemblances would end in confusion'.[13] He is conscious of the differences between the christian faith and the Asian religions. Despite inconsistencies, contradictions, and differences, he is sure that such a communication between the Christian and Asian religious thought and practices is singularly enriching and essential.

'A most important aspect of this inter-faith dialogue', Merton argues is 'the special contribution that the contemplative life can bring to the dialogue, not only among Christians, but also between Christians and the ancient religions of the East, perhaps even between Christians and Marxists'.[14] Regarding the Christian and Marxist dialogue, one has to read the thoughtful and sensitive talk, 'Marxism and Monastic Perspectives', he delivered at Bangkok on the day of his death.[15]

There is another notable result of this communication, Merton reiterates in several books and articles, even in the short reviews of books on Islam, Zen, Kabir, published in *Collectanea Cisterciensia*. This sharing, he holds, is necessary in order to 'improve the quality of our own monastic life and even to help in the task of monastic renewal which has been undertaken within the Western Church'.[16] And again,

> I believe that by openness to Buddhism, to Hinduism, and to these great Asian traditions, we stand a wonderful chance of learning more about the potentiality of our own traditions, because they have gone, from the

natural point of view, so much deeper into this than we have. The combination of the natural techniques and the graces and the other things that have been manifested in Asia and the Christian liberty of the gospel should bring us all at last to that *full and transcendent* liberty which is beyond mere cultural differences and mere externals. . . .[17] (italics mine)

It will also unquestionably, Merton believes, 'renew our appreciation for our own cultural heritage. . .then it will be easier to defend that heritage, not only in Asia but in the West as well'.[18]

Finally, he writes in his letter to a Chinese priest in California: 'One of the things I would like to share with Asians is not only Christ but Asia itself. . .all the wonderful breadth and richness in the Asian traditions, which were given to China, India, Japan, Korea, Burma, etc., as natural preparations for the Coming of Christ.'[19]

Fundamentalists and dogmatists may quarrel over Merton's contention about the 'natural preparations for the Coming of Christ' in connection with the Asian traditions. But, I have no problem, nor do many in India, for that matter, in respecting Merton for his belief and hope, and appreciating the motive and outcome of the dialogue in sharing Christ, that the devout Christian, Father Louis, foresees; because the very core of his ecumenism is the 'dimension of friendship, spontaneity, and spiritual liberty'. But the breadth of his concern and commitment includes the responsibility and task of helping Asians—Asians in whose life and culture today their own wisdom is either dead or inoperative—rediscover their own fontal force. This is the extraordinary multifacetedness of Thomas Merton's involvement, understanding, and faith.

Let me now turn to yet another aspect. In the *Asian Journal* Merton remarks: 'I am convinced that communication in depth, across the lines that have hitherto divided religious and monastic traditions, is now not only possible and desirable, but most important for the destinies of twentieth-century man'.[20] Earlier in *Mystics and Zen Masters*, he warns: 'If the West continues to underestimate and to neglect the spiritual heritage of the East, it may hasten the tragedy that threatens man and his civilization.'[21]

This is exactly why Merton repeatedly uses the word 'communion' in substitution for 'dialogue' and 'communication'. It is a matter of 'sharing'—of 'walking together into contradictions and possibilities', to quote his perceptive article on his poet-friend Louis Zukofsky, and to grasp 'the common religious aspirations of humankind', and fulfill 'its groping for transcendent experience'—mystical, prophetic, contemplative, or metaphysical—as Merton asserts in *Contemplation in a World of Action*.[22]

Merton strikes a prophetic note in his *Asian Journal*: 'We are witnessing the growth of a truly universal consciousness in the modern world'. It is a 'consciousness of transcendent freedom and vision'.[23] In the same paragraph, he indicates that we are growing 'toward the full maturity of universal man'. In this respect, he sounds identical with Rabindranath Tagore's concept of the 'universal man', and with the Indian mystic-poet contemplative Aurobindo's vision of the 'new man' and the new consciousness—'the supramental consciousness'.

To return to Merton, the imperative task for the modern man, particularly the contemplative and all those he describes as 'marginal' persons, is to 'recover the original unity'. This 'lived unity', as he phrases it in 'Ecumenism and Renewal', is attained through self-transformation and transendence—'to be everywhere in it [the world] by hiddenness and compassion', to cite his Preface to the Japanese edition of *The Seven Storey Mountain*. Merton felt as a Christian, a monk, a hermit, and a responsible person of this age, that it was his calling to affirm, achieve, and generate this unity—'*to be part* of this inter-relatedness', he stresses by italics in the *Asian Journal*.

Brother Patrick Hart, Merton's secretary and my cherished friend, points out in *Thomas Merton/Monk*, that Merton 'like St Paul...was convinced that he must "become all things to all men"'.[24] He knew this would be possible only by the realization of self-transformation and self-transcendence, wherein lies the true and ultimate identity. These motifs of unity, identity, self-transformation and self-transcendence are powerful and recurrent in all of Merton's writings—prose and poetry, secular and spiritual.

Let me quote two revealing passages from Merton: this is from *Conjectures of a Guilty Bystander*:

> If I can unite in myself the thought and the devotion of Eastern and Western Christendom, the Greek and the Latin Fathers, the Russians with the Spanish mystics, I can prepare in myself the union of divided Christians. From that secret and unspoken unity in myself can eventually come a visible and manifest unity of all Christians.[25]

Again from the same book:

> If I affirm myself as a Catholic merely by denying all that is Muslim, Jewish, Protestant, Hindu, Buddhist, etc., in the end I will find that there is not much left for me to affirm as a Catholic: and certainly no breath of the Spirit with which to affirm it.[26]

This brings us to another major and vital component—dimension—in Merton's 'communion' with the Asian wisdom—both in thought and practice. It is the personal one. Thomas Merton was a contemplative, a monk. '. . . I am a monk of Gethsemani and intend to remain one all my days . . .' he insists in one of his last letters to Brother Patrick Hart. It was his conviction that for monastic growth it is essential to re-examine one's own self from time to time, and to expand. In the posthumously published book, *The Monastic Journey* (1977), edited by Brother Patrick, Merton says a monk today could not 'live entirely unrelated to the rest of the world'.[27] The contemplative is not one 'who has fiery visions of the cherubim carrying God on their winged chariot'. Instead, he is 'a man of prayer and of praise',[28] who has a 'certain openness to the world and a *genuine participation* in its *anguish*'.[29] (my italics) This openness and genuine participation, Merton assures us, 'would help to safeguard the sincerity of a commitment to contemplation'. In *The Power and Meaning of Love* (1976) he observes: 'One of the first essentials of the interior solitude . . . is the actualization of faith in which a man takes responsibility for his own inner life.'[30]

The eclectic, searching, and expansive Merton engaged himself in a special way in our time's moral issues, aesthetic tastes, and spiritual questions. In whatever he thought, uttered, and did (from photography to zen), he displayed a true sense of engagement. In his 'Notes' for a paper to have been delivered at Calcutta in October, 1968, Merton submits:

I speak as a Western monk who is pre-eminently concerned with his own monastic calling and dedication. I have left my monastery to come here not just as a research scholar or even as an author (which I also happen to be). I come as a pilgrim who is anxious to obtain not just information, not just 'facts' about other monastic traditions, but to drink from ancient sources of monastic vision and experience. I seek not only to learn more (quantitatively) about religion and about monastic life, but to become a better and more enlightened monk (qualitatively) myself.[31]

The urge for greater enlightenment, deeper spiritual consciousness —for self-transcendence, in a word—thrust him deeper into Asian wisdom, and he journeyed to the East.

Through his various readings of the Asian wisdom, he absorbed some of the key ideas and concepts which can be detected in his poetry; as, for instance, in 'Freedom as Experience' from the volume *Figures for an Apocalypse* (1947). Reminiscent of the seventeenth-century English mystic-poet John Donne's holy sonnet 'Three-Personed God', the poem combines in ideas and imagery the lyrics of the Indian mystic poets Chandidas, Mirabai, and Kabir—Kabir he admired and quoted enthusiastically in his writings. Let me quote some of the lines from 'Freedom as Experience':

> When, as the captive of Your own invincible consent,
>
> Locked in that strength we stay and stay
> And cannot go away
> For You have given us our liberty.
>
> Imprisoned in the fortunes of Your adamant
> We can no longer move, for we are free.[32]

If the first line reminds us of Mirabai, the last two lines are identical with those of Chandidas' lyric, 'I am your prisoner, Lord, in you I am free'. 'The perfect act is empty. Who can see it? Me who forgets form. . . . Everything: i.e. nothing.'[33] And in sections 84, 'Infinite Zero' resonates with the Vedantic and Buddhist experience of *sunyata* and fullness, while the line 'Fire is emptiness and fullness'[34] from 'The Legacy of Herakleitos' could very well be from the Buddha's Fire Sermon, or from the Upanishads—'Holy Fire of the Brahman, full and eternal'. Sophia in 'Hagia Sophia' unites the Hindu idea of the Divine Mother, in whom *prakrit* and *purusha* are harmonized, who is Kali, Durga, Saraswati, Brahma, and Vishnu in one—Light, Love, and Wisdom. She is the way to immortality: 'asoto ma sadgamaya; tamaso ma jyotirgamya; mrutyosa amrutya (from untruth to the truth, from darkness to light, from mortality to immortality)'. Later poems like 'Kandy Express' and 'Five breaths pray in me'[35] reflect the quintessential experience of objects and feelings distilled of imagistic exhuberance—the quality one finds in Zen poetry.

Merton, with his existential and dialectic bent of mind, reached a point in all his readings when he felt the urge to take a leap, a plunge into direct experience. It is necessary to note his persistent experiential approach—'to rise above . . . all dialectical reasoning in order to seize the truth by a pure and direct experience'.[36] *The Asian Journal* is an absorbing document demonstrating his keen sensitivity, perceptiveness, humility, and understanding—his phenomenal quality to relate, 'to connect' (Forster). His admiration for the Dalai Lama in India is genuine and enormous. His encounters with Buddhist and Tibetan monks, equally 'extraordinary', to use his own word, convinced him that they have 'a deeper attainment and certitude' with regard to 'the depth of spiritual experience, than the Catholic contemplatives'.[37] True, Indian wisdom—Buddhism, Hinduism, Jainism, and the various ancient philosophical schools—drew Merton to the subcontinent. But, there was also another powerful reason. It was Mahatma Gandhi.

Merton's admiration and reverence for Gandhiji is evident from his many writings on Gandhi. It would not be inaccurate to suggest that Merton's appreciation and understanding of Gandhiji's ideas, philosophy, and course of action formed the inspiration and basis for the book, *Faith and Violence* (1968). He also edited a book entitled, *Gandhi on Non-Violence* (1965). In the introductory essay, 'Gandhi and the One-Eyed Giant', to *Gandhi on Non-Violence*, he comments:

> Gandhi took upon himself the evil of India, not in a spirit of masochism or with the spiritual frivolity of self-punishment that believes itself to have a magic efficacy over sin. . .

He did not seek to reproach and confound others with the spectacle of his own penitence for their sin. He wanted them to recognize from his example that they could learn to bear and overcome the evil that was in them if they were willing to do so.[38]

Merton shows his usual insight as he continues:

Gandhi's symbolic acts (which were meaningful as symbols only because they marked his own flesh with the stamp of acute reality) were aimed at three kinds of liberation. First, he wanted to deliver Indian religious wisdom from the sclerosis and blindness into which it had sunk by reason of the gross injustices of a system which had become untrue to itself. Second, he wanted to liberate the untouchables, the *Harijan*, not only from political and economic oppression, but from the incubus of their own self-hate and their despair. And, finally, he wished to liberate the oppressors themselves from their blind and hopeless dependence on the system which kept things as they were, and which consequently enslaved everybody both spiritually and materially.[39]

Merton finds incredible breadth, integrity, and unity in the Gandhian concept of *ahimsa* and *satyagraha*. For Gandhiji, '*Ahimsa* is the Supreme Law',[40] and it 'implies...complete self-purification'. The non-violent revolution, according to Gandhi, 'is a programme of transformation of relationships', and 'Where there is *ahimsa* there is Truth and Truth is God'. This 'intensely active, purifying, inward force', Gandhi insists, is grounded in *satyagraha*—complete adherence to truth or 'soul-force', which is undergirded by the power of love: 'the sword of the *satyagrahi* in love' and the 'root of *satyagraha* is in prayer'. (II–62) Paul Ricouer makes a telling point that 'nonviolence was for Gandhi but one fragment in a total spiritual system which included truth, poverty, justice, chastity, patience, intrepidity, contempt for death, meditation, etc.', and 'It is this force which, in an exceptional historical experience, unites and epitomizes the end and the means'.[41]

The entire thrust of the Gandhian way is toward self-transformation, transcendence, and identification, which Merton held fast to be the indisputable, essential, and ultimate state of being for *homo sapiens*. In his introduction to *Gandhi on Non-Violence*, he illustrates the Gandhian way with innumerable parallels from the christian tradition, while fully recognizing its hindu *dharma* basis, and concludes: 'The awakening of the Indian mind in Gandhi was not simply the awakening of a distinctly Hindu form of "interior life." . . . It was for the entire world. Hence Gandhi's message was valid for India and for himself in so far as it represented the awakening of a new world.'[42]

In the Gandhian way, Merton discovers the inter-penetration of the personal history, the secular history, and the sacred history, and, 'that all history is ultimately sacred'. It is this belief that demanded of him, as a monk, far deeper and purer personhood. In *Conjectures of a Guilty Bystander* he acknowledges: 'My being is given me not simply as an arbitrary and inscrutable affliction, but as a source of joy, growth, life, creativity, and fulfillment.'[43] For this fuller growth, creativity, and fulfillment, he gravitated deeper toward the Asian religious thought and practices.

Through the years, his early misconceptions, very few in number, about the Oriental religions were modified, e.g., his understanding of the notion of *Karma*, and his estimation of the Oriental mysticism, found in his early book, *The Ascent to Truth* (1951). Even in this book, he is sympathetic, and finds affinities between the Catholic and Hindu faiths, for instance, novice/superior and guru/disciple relationship. He imbibed and integrated in his life fundamental ideas of the Asian wisdom, even practised techniques of meditation and contemplation. The integration Merton attained is as remarkable as his insights into the core of the Asian wisdom—Buddhism, Taoism, Tantra, Zen, and Hinduism, although the last did not as such dominate his attention. The intuitions and conclusions he formulated in his studies of the Asian religious thought, traditions, and practices are, as he clarifies in his Preface to *Mystics and Zen Masters*, 'practical rather than speculative'. The following passage from *The Asian Journal* illustrates my idea of the charismatic integration of perception and experience in Merton:

> Everything I think or do enters into the construction of a mandala. It is the balancing of experience over the void, not the censorship of experience. And no duality of experience—void. Experience is full because it is inexhaustible void. It is not mine. It is 'uninterrupted exchange'. It is dance. Five mudras. The dancing god embrace and penetrates the

Mother. They are one motion, one silence. They are Word. Utterance and return. 'Myself.' No-self. The self is merely a locus in which the dance of the universe is aware of itself as complete from beginning to end—and returning to the void. Gladly. Praising, giving thanks, with all beings. Christ light—spirit—grace—gift. (Boddhicitta).[44]

Both in its style and content, this is a mind-blowing passage, rather a mind-soul-expanding passage. Merton has not only blended into a total wholeness the quintessential ideas of Buddhism and Vedanta thought—sunyata, non-duality, self-transcendence—and of the Hindu concept of the 'cosmic dance' in its eternality with that of the christian mystic experience of grace and Christ-identification, but he has appropraited the entire realization as his epiphanic experience. An experience in total integration of the immanent and the transcendent, the *kenotic* seeing—Absolute Seeing, 'perception' in Husserl's and Merleau Ponty's sense—which is to understand, to receive, to love, and to give in complete surrender and compassion. Merton further explains the dance in *New Seeds of Contemplation* (1961):

the Lord plays and diverts Himself in the garden of His creation, and if we could let go of our own obsession with what we think is the meaning of it all, we might be able to hear Him call and follow Him in His mysterious, cosmic dance. We do not have to go very far to catch echoes of that game, and of that dancing. When we are alone on a starlit night; when by chance we see the migrating birds in autumn descending on a grove of junipers to rest and eat; when we see children in a moment when they are really children; when we know love in our own heart; or when, like the Japanese poet Basho we hear an old frog land in a quiet pond with a solitary splash—at such times the awakening, the turning inside out of all values, the "newness," the emptiness and the purity of vision that make themselves evident, provide a glimpse of the cosmic dance.[45]

He strikes a crescendo note of heightened mystical awareness: 'For the world and time are the dance of the Lord in emptiness.'[46] This is the 'lila' the Vedantic tradition celebrates—the Absolute, *purushottama* (the Supreme Person), the Brahman, the omniscient and omnipotent One, who creates, sustains, and redeems the creation for 'nothing else than sport', as Ramanuja says in his Commentary on the *Vedanta Sutras*, and out of his gracious love and joy. For, as Bhrigu realizes in *Taittriya Upanishad*, 'Brahman is

Joy; from Joy all beings have come, by Joy they all live, and unto Joy they all return'. *Katha Upanishad* affirms that the Brahman, Spirit, can only be experienced in this life. According to Aurobindo in *The Life Divine*: 'The Brahman, the Absolute is the Spirit, the Self-possessing Time, the Lord of Nature, creator and continent of the cosmos and immanent in all existences, the Soul from whom all souls derive and to whom they are drawn . . . ' (Bk 2, II).

'The awakening, the turning inside out of all values, the "newness", the emptiness and the purity of vision', Merton talks about, is exactly what happens to Arjuna in the *Bhagavad Gita* when Krishna reveals his *viswarupa*—the Cosmic Self. Arjuna refuses to fight, refuses to fulfill his duties and responsiblities according to his *varna*, debates with Lord Krishna, the Supreme Incarnate, holding on to his own values. Krishna, Arjuna's companion and friend, explodes the fallacy of Arjuna's logic, and out of his own grace, love, and abundance, lets Arjuna, and only he in the entire scripture of the *Mahabharata*, glimpse the indescribable and inexhaustible richness of His being. Arjuna after this vision is a transformed being, and it happens magically and miraculously in a moment's total surrender. He is in union with the Cosmic Player.

Merton in his short but illuminating essay on 'The Significance of the *Bhagavad Gita*' in *The Asian Journal* returns to the 'cosmic dance', and explicates on this particular episode of Krishna's revealed *viswarupa* and Arjuna's transformation: 'Once we live in awareness of the cosmic dance and move in time with the Dancer, our life attains its true dimension.'[47] Arjuna surrenders totally to the will and wisdom of Krishna; Krishna, out of his absolute love, grace, and trust in his friend, whose charioteer he is, elevates the relationship from a dialogue to integration and unity. Arjuna thus attains the pure consciousness of Being, in which the subject as such 'disappears'. At this moment, Merton goes on to say, one 'encounters him not as Being but as Freedom and Love.'[48] Arjuna's transformation is both epistemic and ontological, because his 'true self comes to full maturity in emptiness and solitude'. Merton's incarnational mysticism and his 'sacramental contemplation', embodying, emptying, and surrendering of one's own self to God—'the pure Being, this is to say He is the pure and infinite Act of total Reality'[49]—are subsumed in Arjuna's overwhelming experience of the beatific vision. 'I am what I am', says the Bible, and the Upanishad says '*tat twam asi*—That Thou Art'.

Let me turn to Merton's incredible experience with the Buddha rock-statues in Polonnaruwa in Sri Lanka. Clearly the experience is epiphanic—'flash of mighty intuition by which multiplicity is suddenly comprehended as basically one—penetrated through and through by the logos, the divine fire,' as he describes it in 'Herekleitos the Obscure'.[50] This ordinary encounter becomes a moment of liberation for Merton, because he 'pierced through the surface and . . . got beyond the shadow and the disguise. . . . Looking at these figures I was suddenly, almost forcibly, jerked clean out of the habitual, half-tied vision of things, and an inner clearness, clarity, as if exploding from the rocks themselves, became evident and obvious. . . . All problems are resolved and everything is clear, simply because what matters is clear. The rock, all matter, all life, is charged with dharmakaya. . . everything is emptiness and everything is compassion. I don't know when in my life I have ever had such a sense of beauty and spiritual validity running together in one aesthetic illumination. Surely, with Mahabalipuram [India] and Polonnaruwa my Asian pilgrimage has come clear and purified itself. . . clear, pure, complete.'[51]

The Ascent to Truth, The Sign of Jonas, New Seeds of Contemplation, Conjectures of a Guilty Bystander, Zen and the Birds of Appetite, or *The Asian Journal*—in fact, the major corpus of his writings are embedded in the central idea, experience, and vision of the Asian wisdom—a passionate striving toward 'the direct intuition of reality',[52] which is 'awakening, enlightenment and the amazing grasp by which love gains certitude of God's creative and dynamic intervention in our daily life', as Merton adds to his definition of contemplation in *New Seeds of Contemplation*. This contemplation, he proceeds to explain, 'is carried away by Him into His own realm, His own mystery and His own freedom'[53] so fully conveyed in the lives of Arjuna, Gandhi, and Aurobindo; and there is such a curious closeness between Merton and Aurobindo, the two radical mystics of this century, both of whom had gone past all formalistic, legalistic, doctrinal discipline and structures of their own culture and forged a unique integration. Merton's affinities with the *advaita vedantin* Ramanuja and the Madhyamika Buddhist Nagarjuna are considerable and significant. If his methodology of contemplation as delineated in *New Seeds of Contemplation*, for example, is similar to that of Ramanuja, his concept of the ultimate 'mystery of Being' corresponds to that of Nagarjuna—'All is concord indeed for one who to *sunyata* conforms', and Nagarjuna asserts that the 'mystery of *sunyata*' reveals in 'silence', and is cognized in mystical intuition—Merton's 'sacramental contemplation'.

Merton's entire religious and spiritual life, it seems to me, epitomizes the Hindu *sadhana*, the process of balancing theory and practice and the attainment of perfection (*siddhi*), since both in the buddhist and hindu thought truth and knowledge are 'precious by virtue of its soteriological functions', as Mircea Eliade suggests in *Yoga: Immortality and Freedom.* (1958)[54] *Sadhana* is experience—'To know God is to experience God', say the Upanishads. Furthermore, Merton's concept of 'liturgy', with its incarnational, mystical, and practical signification, vibrates with the same kind of dynamics one finds in the Vedic experience of *upasana*—worship, prayer—a supreme moment of celebration and transcendence.

Merton's journey to the East, his immersion in the Asian wisdom, and his integration of the christian and non-christian spiritual and mystical thought and practices unfold his deepest 'contemplation and eschatological aspirations'. Even his death carries its own symbolism and appropriateness: a death by water and fire, and during a spiritual dialogue and in the incontrovertible and inexplicable mystery of the Divine Will.

'To sing', Merton declares, 'one song in many voices.' And 'all notes in their perfect distinctness are yet blended in one'.[55] I have indicated earlier that Merton believed mankind today is on the verge of another 'Apostolic Age' that would celebrate 'the living spiritual mystery of all peoples'. Despite fear, hate, despair, and violence that eviscerates our world and age, Merton eschatologizes about the great event of 'Parousia' that 'will not destroy human history but fulfill it'.[56] This is what Gandhiji envisioned as 'Ramrajya'—the Divine Reign—and Aurobindo as the 'New Age'—'the descent of the supramental consciousness'—of the immanence of the Transcendent, which is Shiva's 'cosmic dance' of creation and fulfillment. Merton alludes to it in *Gandhi and Non-Violence*. 'Water of life', Merton extols in *Raids on the Unspeakable* (1966). 'Dance in it'—dance in innocence and wholeness. To that stage of evolution, that great symphony and dance, we have a commitment. So, the Vedas exhort us: 'Let every eye see Good; let every being be Good; let our minds apprehend alike. . . . Common be our intention; common be our wishes of the heart; common our thoughts, so that there is unity.'

Finally, Father Thomas Merton offered the special closing prayer at the First Spiritual Summit Conference in Calcutta in October of 1968:

> Oh God, we are one with You. You have made us one with You. You have taught us that if we are open to one another, You dwell in us. . . . Oh God, in accepting one another wholeheartedly, fully, completely, we accept You, and we thank You, and we adore You, and we love You with our whole being, because our being is in Your being, our spirit is rooted in Your spirit. Fill us then with love, and let us be bound together with love as we go our diverse ways, united in this one spirit which makes You present in the world, and which makes You witness to the ultimate reality that is love. Love has overcome. Love is victorious. Amen.[57]

NOTES

1. *The Collected Poems of Thomas Merton* (New York: New Directions) p. 151.
2. *Ibid.*, p. 245.
3. *Ibid.*, p. 122.
4. *The Asian Journal of Thomas Merton* (New York: New Directions) p. 4–5.
5. *Collected Poems* p. 245.
6. *Ibid.*, p. 222.
7. *The Way of Chuang Tzu* (New York: New Directions) p. 10.
8. Thomas Merton, 'Christian Culture Needs Oriental Wisdom', *The Catholic World* (May, 1962) p. 182.
9. *Ibid.*, p. 78.
10. *Collected Poems*, p. 384.
11. *Catholic World*, p. 72.
12. *Conjectures of a Guilty Bystander* (New York: Doubleday) p. 129.
13. *Mystics and Zen Masters* (New York: Farrar Straus & Giroux) p. 207.
14. *Ibid.*, p. 203.

14. *Ibid.*, p. 203.
15. *Asian Journal*, see appendix.
16. *Ibid.*, p. 313.
17. *Ibid.*, p. 343.
18. *Mystics and Zen Masters*, p. 46.
19. *Seeds of Destruction*, (New York: Farrar Straus & Giroux) p. 287.
20. *Asian Journal*, p. 313.
21. *Mystics and Zen Masters*, p. 46.
22. *Contemplation in a World of Action*, (New York: Doubleday) p. 200.
23. *Asian Journal*, p. 317.
 24. Brother Patrick Hart (ed.) *Thomas Merton/Monk* (Doubleday Image) p. 212.
25. *Conjectures of a Guilty Bystander*, p. 12.
26. *Ibid.*, p. 129.
27. *The Monastic Journey*, edited by Brother Patrick Hart (Doubleday Image) p. 35.
28. *Ibid.*, p. 8.
29. *Mystics and Zen Masters*, p. 204.
30. *The Power and Meaning of Love*, (London: Burns Oates) p. 46 (British edition of *Seeds of Destruction*).
31. *Asian Journal*, pp. 312–313.
32. *Collected Poems*, pp. 186–187.
33. *Ibid.*, p. 421.
34. *Ibid.*, p. 771.
35. *Ibid.*, p. 785.
36. *The Waters of Siloe*, (New York: Harcourt Brace) p. xxvii.
37. *Asian Journal*, p. 124.
38. *Gandhi on Non-Violence*, (New York: New Directions) p. 16.
39. *Ibid.*, p. 16.
40. Gandhi, *Non-Violence in Peace and War*, Vol. I, p. 172.
41. Paul Ricouer, *History and Truth*, pp. 230–231.
42. *Gandhi on Non Viloence*, p. 5.
43. *Conjectures of a Guilty Bystander*, p. 201.
44. *Asian Journal*, p. 68.
45. *New Seeds of Contemplation*, (New York: New Directions) pp. 296–297.
46. *Ibid.*, p. 297.
47. *Asian Journal*, p. 350.
48. *Zen and the Birds of Appetite*, (New Directions) p. 25.
49. *Conjectures of a Guilty Bystander*, p. 201.
50. *The Behavior of Titans*, p. 84.
51. *Asian Journal*, p. 236.
52. *Mystics and Zen Masters*, p. 203.
53. *New Seeds of Contemplation*, p. 5.
54. Eliade, M., *Yoga: Immortality and Freedom*, p. 4.
55. *Asian Journal*, p. vii.
56. *The Living Bread*, (Farrar Straus & Giroux) p. 152.
57. *Asian Journal*, p. 318.

The Place of Silence in
Thomas Merton's Life and Thought

John F. Teahan

John F. Teahan received his degrees in history from Fordham University and Yale University, and in Religious Studies from Princeton. His doctoral dissertation at Princeton was on 'The Mysticism of Thomas Merton: Contemplation as a Way of Life'. He has since published articles in such journals as The Journal of Religion, Thought, Church History, *and* The American Benedictine Review, *and book reviews in* Religious Studies Review, Choice, *and* Studia Mystica. *Dr Teahan currently teaches in the religion department at Wheaton College, Norton, Massachusetts. An earlier version of this essay was given at the Merton Commemoration at Columbia University in November 1978.*

CAN SCHOLARLY ANALYSIS hope to lure silence into language, to convince it to speak? Faced with silence, are we not perhaps condemned to be silent? Is it possible to say anything intelligible about a dimension that is by definition set over against language? How might we adjudicate between meaningful and vacuous expressions of silence? Need we ourselves experience the depths of silence in order to understand the quiet and stillness of the texts and symbols we seek to interpret? Such questions naturally arise from a critical encounter with religious silence, and they return to plague any effort at understanding and formulation. While this article—an exploration of the role of silence in Thomas Merton's life and thought—is not an exercise in the methodological analysis of silence, it is well to raise these questions at the outset, not because we can hope to answer all of them, but because they point to the intrinsically problematical, we might even say 'intractable', character of silence.

More a suggestive than systematic thinker and writer, Merton generally evokes rather than analyzes the meaning he found in silence. One result of Merton's approach is that he leaves certain logical and epistemological issues unanswered or unaddressed. A happier consequence is that his often compelling writings may enable us to value silence more and also stimulate us to appreciate difficulties involved in the attempt to understand it. This article, while chiefly attempting to clarify and systematize the many texts where he treats this subject, will also address some critical issues about Merton's expression of silence and about the phenomenon in general.

Religious silence, first of all, is to be understood in a positive manner; it is not the ordinary speechlessness caused by perplexity, unwillingness to communicate, or simple lack of interest. Different types and levels of silence appear throughout the history of religions. Speaking broadly, but basing our generalizations on evidence from Catholic monasticism and mysticism, Orthodox hesychasm, the Society of Friends, Sufism, Upanishadic Hinduism, classical Toaism, and some schools of Māhāyana Buddhism, we may delineate at least three types of silence: public, ascetical, and meditational. The public, or ritual, use of silence is perhaps the form familiar to most of us. As employed in the Catholic Mass, Quaker meeting, ancient Jewish temple rites, or Buddhist ashram ceremonies, silence facilitates solemnity, reverence, recollection, and a sense of mystery. Ritual quiet provides the most striking antithesis possible to the sound of music, song, sermon, and vocal prayer, thus enhancing the participant's involvement in the ritual as a whole.

Another type of silence might be called ascetical. The deliberate practice of 'keeping silent', refraining from unnecessary speech, is customarily though not exclusively observed by many who live in monasteries or similar groupings of religious men and women who regard elimination of everyday chatter as a necessary component of their renunciation. The ascetic's silence should foster patience, equanimity, charity, and detachment from those assumptions and values of the world deemed inimical to his way of life. The attempt to rescue physical quiet from verbal overload is normally considered a means to the more important goal of calming interior consciousness, an important prerequisite for many forms of mystical experience.

A final type of religious silence is associated with the practice of meditation. Not all meditation is silent; some mediators chant, dance, and contemplate elaborate images with an increase in ecstatic intensity. But most meditators follow a different route, characteristically seeking quiet, sometimes solitary places, contemplating simple images and ideas or none at all, and reducing stimulation and physical movement rather than intensifying them. The silence of meditation directs attention away from everyday ratiocinative and emotional turbulence, fosters inner calm, and thus makes the meditator more aware of his innermost self.

I call these ritualistic, ascetical, and meditative forms of silence 'types', thereby intending to underscore their empirical character. Anyone can observe, for example, intervals of silence in a worship service, monks observing the rule of silence in monasteries, and the quiet ambience of a Zen meditation hall. What I call 'levels', on the other hand, are not so easily accessible to the observer, although psychological studies of meditation have discerned different levels of alpha wave activity by using EEG measurements. Despite the many stages of psychophysiological activity measured by psychologists and often postulated, albeit in different frameworks and vocabularies, by contemplatives themselves, we can readily distinguish two levels of silence:

'Shallow' silence is characterized by tranquility and passivity. Cognitive discriminations are minimal or non-existent, normal desires are forgotten, and ordinarily powerful emotions are pacified. This condition, in which one maintains awareness of ordinary identity and individuality, frequently occurs during successful meditation practice.

In 'deep' silence, on the other hand, a person temporarily transcends awareness of the self as he becomes absorbed by the all-encompassing silence of a mystical experience. We need not list here the many other subjective features commonly characterizing such episodes, but only wish to note that many mystical narratives postulate deep silence as an essential feature of union with God, enlightenment, harmony with nature, and so forth. Mystical experience is thus often called 'silent' because the mystic claims he has become immersed in the depths of a silence greater than the self and because of the subsequent difficulties he may have when attempting to talk about the experience. The claim, regularly found in much mystical literature, that the experience is ineffable, appears in part to be an almost predictable consequence of having entered this deep silence. It is by no means a simple task to use words when attempting to describe this all-pervading quiet, and art and religious symbols may express it more effectively than language. While wordless deep silence is seen as an end in itself, and may be regarded as the goal and perfection of the types of silence already discussed, a common mystical tenet holds that one who has entered the silence must in turn use it to comprehend and relate back to the world of sound, language, and everyday concerns. Sound and silence need each other, for neither could truly exist without its counterpart. When, in Christianity, God is portrayed as Silence, he is also usually understood as Word. The ineffable and utterly transcendent Buddhist *Dharmakāya* is also manifested as *Nirmānakāya*, taking shape in the world of matter, form, sensation, and language.

Much interest has focused on Thomas Merton since his death in 1968. This appears popularly in the increasingly large sales of his books, their translation into twenty-three foreign languages, and his strong appeal as an exemplar for much contemporary religious searching. Merton's concerns were not exclusively 'religious' in any narrow sense of the word, and this factor also accounts for his accessibility; his commitment to eradicating social injustice and to fostering aesthetic creativity, for example, are only two of the many other elements in his legacy that have proved attractive. Scholarly interest in Merton has also been extensive. Two major symposia, at Columbia University and at the University of British Columbia, were held during the tenth anniversary of his death, articles and books about him and his ideas are being published with increasing frequency, and two professional bibliographies of his writings have appeared. Merton is well on his way to becoming recognized as a major religious voice of the present century, though more critical study of his relation to others similarly established needs to be pursued if we are to evaluate accurately his contribution and stature.

Given the immense number of Merton's works, both published and unpublished, it might initially seem odd to claim that silence has an important role in his life and thought. Is not writing, after all, a way of speaking and thus inimical to the cultivation of silence? But Merton also belonged to a monastic order traditionally committed to the observance of silence and he was a deeply introspective man, passionately dedicated to searching for a reality that transcends both sound and word. This monastic commitment and search for the transcendent were constant factors throughout his adult life. This article examines the critical way in which silence affected them, and also discusses Merton's theory about silence in its dialectical, metaphysical, and mystical dimensions, delineating the most important influences on his thought and raising questions about the way silence and paradox affected his writings and concept of authorship. The conclusion suggests ways in which the findings presented here might be situated in the broader context of twentieth-century philosophy, literature, and religious thought.

Merton's youthful autobiography and all but one of his four published journals reveal his need for and love of silence. His mother was a Quaker, and Merton reacted favorably to the silence of a Quaker meeting he visited in 1935, soon after his return to the United States from schooling in England. He was also moved by the liturgical silence at the first Catholic Mass he attended, only a few months before his conversion in 1938. Describing his first visit to the Abbey of Gethsemani, Merton wrote that the silence 'enfolded me, spoke to me, and spoke louder and more eloquently than any voice'.[1] A section deleted from his autobiography, but published shortly thereafter as an article, attests to the continuing power of this silence in his interior life. Entitled 'First Christmas at Gethsemani', it describes a moving experience of 1941 in which silence played a major role.[2] But Merton's early quest for silence was not limited to religious contexts: the autobiography mentions many solitary walks and silent musings in the woods and his early poetry often associates silence simply with the beauty of nature.

The Sign of Jonas, his published journal from 1946 to 1952, continued these themes. In this work Merton often reflected on the purifying effect of the ascetical silence he felt necessary to cleanse his soul. *The Sign of Jonas* reveals much more about Merton's growing need for silence than the earlier autobiography. A May 1949 entry, for example, notes that:

> In my prayer and all my interior life, such as it is, I am concerned with the need for a greater and more complete interior silence: an interior secrecy that amounts to not thinking about myself. Silence about my prayer, about the development of my interior life is becoming an absolute necessity, so that I am beginning to believe I should stop writing about contemplation altogether, except perhaps in the most general terms.[3]

Conjectures of a Guilty Bystander,[4] excerpted from journals and notebooks kept between 1956 and 1965, also treats silence, especially in the context of meditations on nature and religion. On the whole, however, this work is less personally revealing than its predecessor. Merton had not abandoned the search for silence, as *The Asian Journal of Thomas Merton*, edited by others after his death, clearly reveals. In addition to characteristic reflections about the silence in nature, this journal attests to Merton's continuing quest for silence in his inner life. On retreat in the Himalayas in November of 1968 he wrote about his 'need for a couple of days of silence', noting on the following day that 'I appreciate the quiet more than I can say. This quiet, with time to read, study, meditate, and *not talk to anyone*, is something essential in my life'.[5] The most significant interior experience (which Merton called an 'aesthetic illumination' rather than a 'mystical' or 'religious' one) recorded in *The Asian Journal* occurred in Sri Lanka. There, before the massive rock sculptures of Buddha and Ananda at Polonnaruwa, Merton was overwhelmed by the silence manifested in their knowing faces, a silence of pure emptiness and spiritual equilibrium.[6]

Merton's attraction to silence, evident before his conversion, continued until his death. This attraction consistently manifests itself not only in his reflections about meditation, nature, and religious experience, but also in his more theoretical discussions of silence and its relation to language and to God.

The most important influences on Merton's theory of silence are christian—particularly monastic and mystical writers. He had long admired the earliest christian monks and hermits, the Desert Fathers of the fourth century, for their intellectual humility and abstention from theological argumentation. Merton was also struck by the importance that John Cassian, who disseminated the sayings of the Desert Fathers in Europe, and St Benedict, the father of Western monasticism, had assigned to silence in their writings. An even earlier figure, the first century St Ignatius of Antioch, had speculated about the relationship between the silence of God and the Christian's contact with it. His ideas helped shape Merton's theory about the dialectical interplay between divine Silence and the Word of God. A cluster of medieval Cistercians, most notably St Bernard, William of St Thierry, Adam of Perseigne, and Guerric of Igny provide yet another major source. Merton was a careful student of his Order's theological tradition. He gave considerable attention to the place these Cistercians assigned to silence in fraternal charity, to their distinction between interior and exterior silence, and to their understanding of God as the wellspring of that silence in which the soul perfects its union with him. Despite the major impact of St John of the Cross on Merton, and the importance of silence in the Spanish mystic's writings,[7] it is surprising that Merton only rarely drew explicitly from him. But it is probable that Merton assimilated the Carmelite's teachings on silence and simply did not discuss them in his writings.[8] Also influential is Max Picard, the twentieth century Swiss philosopher, whom Merton credited as the inspiration for many ideas expressed in *Thoughts in Solitude*, a work that frequently discusses silence.[9] Picard's influence is most evident in Merton's formulation of a dialectical relation between silence and ordinary language, a theme that had relatively limited importance for Merton. Finally, we should not overlook Merton's attraction to Zen Buddhism and classical Taoism. Although he did not appropriate the Eastern regard for silence as deeply as christian contributions, the last decade of his life evidenced a growing appreciation for the practice and theory of silence in the East.

Merton always insisted on the importance of silence understood simply as the absence of sound. He usually called this 'exterior' or 'external' silence, and it is homologous to what we have earlier termed 'ascetical' and 'public' types of silence. But he also believed that a truly serious search for silence should seek more than the mere cessation of sound and noise. His earliest writings contrasted this exterior silence with 'interior' silence, the stilling of thoughts, desires, and judgments. Interior silence, which may appear in what we have called 'shallow' and 'deep' senses, is the goal to which exterior silence should lead, though the former cannot be obtained without cultivating the latter. He repeated this distinction in subsequent works, maintaining that exterior silence is necessary, yet insisting that interior silence is more valuable. Merton identified interior silence with the positive 'emptiness' of the 'true' or 'real' self. Partially constituted by this silent emptiness, which serves to narrow the distance between man and God, the true self has ceased thirsting after praise, reward, and fame. Interior silence in its deepest form is 'the positive rest of the mind in truth',[10] and Merton's most evocative descriptions of it are invariably mystical. During mystical experience, he wrote in 1948, 'an immense depth of pure silence expands within' as one achieves unity, simplicity, and freedom in God.[11] A rare autobiographical description of a mystical experience in his published writings, 'First Christmas at Gethsemani' cited above, describes the role of interior silence as a preparatory agency leading to union with Christ and as a constituent of that union itself.[12]

A leading feature in Merton's theory, and one that frequently appears in much of the literature about silence, is the dialectic he discerned between silence on the one hand, and sound, speech, language, and the divine Word on the other.[13] He often drew attention to the alternation between sound and silence in monastic liturgy, suggesting that chant leads readily to the silence of God. An early discussion of preaching, one of the few references to this topic in Merton's large corpus, develops the idea of a dialectic of silence and speech. Claiming that the 'only' reason to speak is to confess faith in God's glory, Merton further observes that 'preaching the word of God implies silence. If preaching is not born of silence, it is a waste of time.'[14] This preaching should, in turn, enable the auditor to return to the silence from which it emerges.

Under the influence of Max Picard, Merton extended this dialectic to incorporate the relationship between silence and language in general. Believing that we often distort reality by attending to words rather than the things they signify, Merton argued that language is effective only when it springs from silent appreciation of things in themselves. Everything that exists contains an irreducible center of silence, which Merton identified as its ground in God. 'There is in all visible things an invisible fecundity, a dimmed light, a meek namelessness, a hidden wholeness', he wrote in his most moving prose poem. 'There is in all things an inexhaustible sweetness and purity, a silence that is the fount of action and joy.'[15]

Merton thus saw a necessary interaction between language and silence, maintaining that:

> A man cannot understand the true value of silence unless he has a real respect for the validity of language: for the reality which is expressible in language is found, face to face and without medium, in silence. Nor would we find this reality in itself, that is to say in its own silence, unless we were first brought there by language.[16]

This shows that Merton was not categorically or irrationally hostile to language *per se*. He respected the necessary role of language in shaping and refining religious faith, for without shared linguistic assumptions, symbols, and metaphors no corporate dimension would be possible in religion. He also criticized the political, bureaucratic, and commercial debasement of everyday language. Those who show contempt for clarity and truth by promulgating captious, ambiguous, and deceptive jargon threaten the body politic because they corrupt the language that should promote

honest interchange and stimulate critical insight.[17] And Merton
certainly recognized that without solicitude for language no poetry
of any lasting power and beauty can come forth. Nonetheless, the
proper use of language in all its diverse forms first requires silent
reflection on reality to spark the active attention necessary for
words to come alive. The words should lead back, as Merton
claimed happens in all good poetry, 'into the silence where nothing can be said'.[18]

It is surprising—and significant—that Merton never postulated a
dialectic of silence and theological discourse. He wrote *The Ascent
to Truth*, the most theologically technical of all his works, when he
was most favorably inclined toward speculative reason. But even
this early book underscored the danger inherent in attempting to
describe God, admitting in the conclusion that 'silence is better
than speech'.[19] Merton was always more disposed to posit the
ultimate ineffability of God than to engage in technical theological
speculation about him. 'If these men say little about God', he
wrote approvingly about the early Desert Fathers and their refusal
to engage in the numerous theological disputes of their age, 'it is
because they know that when one has been close to His dwelling,
silence makes more sense than a lot of words.'[20]

Although Merton posited no interaction between the theological enterprise and silence, he did discern an intimate relationship
between silence and the Word of God. 'As silence is to speech so
the Father is to the Son', he wrote in notes for a course given at
Gethesemani Abbey. '*To hear and possess the silence of the Father* is
the real objective of reception of the Word.'[21] This idea, appropriated largely from St Ignatius of Antioch, is a leading theme in
Merton's speculation about the nature of silence. In the first century, Ignatius had identified God with silence in order to convey
divine transcendence and incomprehensibility. The deepest recesses of the soul share this silence, and one can apprehend, through a
silent 'hearing' of the Word, that which is inapprehensible by any
other means.[22] Though Ignatius did not develop these ideas extensively or systematically, they entranced Merton. Writing for a
Japanese audience in 1966, he described Christianity as a religion
of the Word that is Love. 'But we sometimes forget', he went on,

'that the Word emerges first of all from silence. When there is no silence, then the One Word which God speaks is not truly heard as Love.'[23] Merton characteristically stressed two features about this dialectic between silence and the Word: the Word is uttered 'silently' by God, and it must be received in silence by those who 'hear' it.

This dialectic has a soteriological function in Merton's thought; he often wrote about the need to respond to the Word. But when the response itself is silent one enters the mystical dimension, and Merton often described the highest degree of union with God as occurring in absolute silence.[24] So also did he see silence as an ontological attribute of the person thus transformed. 'When the soul of the monk has arrived at perfect union with the will of Christ', Merton noted in a commentary on Adam of Perseigne, 'it rests in the interior silence of a pure heart in which Christ is present.'[25] Merton's postulation of a dialectical process between silence and the Word of God is no dry christological speculation: it signals the mystic's reconstitution in the divine likeness itself. Uttered silently by God, the Word is received in the soul's deep silence; perfect reception of the Word then becomes a silent union with God through Christ.

References to the silence of God abound in Merton's writings. His early autobiography describes the soul's contemplative absorption 'in the immense and fruitful silence of God'.[26] A journal entry for 1947 expresses his longing for God's 'deep silence'.[27] Later passages discuss the presence of God's silence in monastic life and in nature. A list of divine attributes, appearing in *Conjectures of a Guilty Bystander,* called God 'the Silent'; an article published in the same year as the book similarly identified God with 'endless silence'.[28] Thus, it is not surprising that Merton portrayed the culmination of the mystical quest as union between a silent soul and a silent God. The highest form of silence then becomes 'the mystical repose of the contemplative in the divine silence, the presence of God'.[29] Exterior silence of the tongue, fostering interior silence in the soul, thus leads to mystical participation in the divine silence of God himself. In the vocabulary suggested at the beginning of this essay, ascetical silence induces the shallow silence of ordinary meditation from which one passes to the deep silence pervading the mystical union.

Despite his sincere belief in the dialectical reciprocity between silence and language, the brunt of Merton's religious emphasis leads beyond words and speech. 'Even the best answers', he wrote in 1966, 'are not final. They point to something further which cannot be embodied in a verbal ground.'[30] He refused to posit a dialectic of silence and theology because he saw propositions, concepts, and doctrinal formulations as the superstructure of christian faith, indeed of all religions. Words may impart information but can never in themselves effect spiritual insight and transformation. With a highly apophatic understanding of God, moreover, Merton tenaciously guards divine mystery and ineffability. God can best be known by 'unknowing', by a 'learned ignorance' that reaches him through silence and love.[31] The union of the contemplative with God is always dark and unfathomable. One's deepest identity—in Merton's vocabulary the 'true self'—can never be exhaustively articulated, and those who presumptuously believe they can reduce the true self to scientific laws 'tamper with it and in some ways destroy it'.[32]

Merton's respect for the inviolabilty of this silent self extends even further: those who truly wish to live in the silence of God must finally renounce the desire to explain or even to justify their unusual call to others. This theme appears frequently in Merton's writings about the monastic life. The monk, to be sure, begins his novitiate with a rudimentary conceptual understanding of his vocation. As he grows more fully into that vocation, however, his insight deepens as he comes to see that concepts cannot adequately explain his silent way. Monks, and all others in contact with their silent selves, are 'too much a part of the mystery of silence to be able to formulate an apologetic for their own lives'.[33] So their innermost recesses remain hidden, obscure, veiled, and unspoken. And yet, in the paradoxical spirit so characteristic of his writings about monasticism and contemplation, Merton did indeed offer many arguments, among the most convincing put forth in modern times, for the validity and authenticity of monastic life. His point

was simply that no apologetic can ever sufficiently account for it
and that reasoning cannot hope to plumb the hidden recesses in
which true identity subsists.

An author who wishes to introduce others to this dark dimension of the self must employ language, but words often mislead
and logic may fail to discern signs along the path. It is not surprising then that Merton's writings about silence often employ paradoxical constructions and metaphors. In 1956 Merton writes that
God is 'heard' when 'we realize that we do not know the sound of
His voice';[34] the more this silent wisdom manifests itself, the more
hidden it remains. Wisdom's perfect song, in the Mystical Body,
resonates with voices in which 'music and silence are one'.[35] Ten
years later, Merton's paradoxes show the influence of Eastern
thought. He writes of a 'silence in which the Hearer is No-Hearer'
and of the God whose speech is so quiet that 'to our way of thinking His speech is no speech' at all.[36] Merton's attraction to Zen
Buddhism and Mādhyamika philosophy stems, to a significant degree, from his appreciation of the value they assign to silence and
their contravention of ordinary language. He similarly delighted in
the paradoxes of the classical Taoist texts. But his most stunning
paradox about silence is thoroughly christian, and it turns on his
conviction that God the Father, as Silence, utters his Son, as
Word, to effect the silent transformation of all who will hear:

> We listen to the Word of God, spoken or sung, in order to hear it again in
> silence: not repeated *in* silence, but repeated *as* silence. Silence is the very
> presence of the Word, in which the naked Word itself speaks without its
> exterior covering of sound. This is the mark of the contemplative: not that
> he merely turns aside to the Word from silence, but that he recognizes the
> Word more intimately and more really when it is naked, soundless, and
> present only in the form of silence.[37]

Here we see the inversion of Merton's usual postulation that the
Word relates dialectically to its origin in the Father, for he now
shows that the Word, in its most mystical manifestation, is as
soundless as its source. While the contemplative does not reject
the message of Christ, spoken in the gospel and manifested in tradition, his closest union with Christ transcends such verbalization
and form; it rests in the silent Word that grasps the soul in quiet

embrace. This remarkable passage shows what great importance Merton gave to silence, and is perhaps the best example of his use of paradox to convey it. It also serves as additional evidence for our thesis that Merton viewed silence as the the deepest manifestation of God's mystical presence and thus as a most appropriate symbol for that which transcends exact expression and distinct idea.

Students of mysticism have devoted much attention to paradox, usually defined as a self-contradictory proposition. Robert Hoffman expresses a conventional philosophical position when he argues that mystical paradoxes do not describe anything; no valid knowledge claims can be derived from them. For Hoffman, paradox functions to evoke and to suggest mystical experience to others, but it cannot communicate any truths about the experience.[38] William Johnston, an historian of christian and buddhist mysticism, concurs with Hoffman's position that paradox functions evocatively. But Johnston differs when he argues that paradox transcends rather than contradicts reason, and that paradox often makes non-literal or symbolic sense.[39] Indologist Fritz Staal's recent study of mysticism notes that mystical paradoxes are usually only apparent: they may be reduced to noncontradictory formulations when we recognize that their terms often function ambiguously.[40] Philosopher Louis Dupré, on the other hand, claims that paradox can never be reduced to ordinary language, although ordinary language is necessary for paradox to have meaning.[41] W. T. Stace, whose influential though much controverted *Mysticism and Philosophy* devotes an entire chapter to paradox, concluded that paradox accurately describes mystical experience because the experience *per se* is self-contradictory. No straight-forward propositions are, in principle, capable of describing the experience because the rules of logic fail to apply to it. Stace further examines two other interpretations of paradox not discussed in the treatments surveyed so far. According to these alternative theories (which he rejects): (1) paradox results from the mystic's unintentional misdescription of his experience, and (2) paradox is an intentional rhetorical device used to convey an idea in a dramatic way that would otherwise be impossible.[42] Finally, Galen Pletcher, while agreeing with Stace that paradox is central to mysticism, suggests that mystics may have discovered that our ordinary conceptual system is defective, and their reliance on paradox may thus be a fault of the system rather than a deficiency in their description. Pletcher raises the possibility that a more adequate conceptual system might be found that would permit coherent descriptions of mystical experience.[43]

Some of these theories illuminate Merton's paradoxes about silence. We should recognize that his paradoxes are not, on the surface at least, descriptions of his *own* mystical experiences. But Merton employed these paradoxes primarily to evoke a condition— union of the soul with God in and through silence—that is inescapably mystical, and they have therefore a mystical intent. We should also note that Merton's paradoxes are not always self-contradictory. He could, for example, describe 'hearing' God as not 'knowing' God's voice.

Merton's writings furnish ample evidence for I. T. Ramsey's thesis that many different kinds of paradox exist.[44] A prolific and powerful writer, Merton occasionally used paradox to evoke the experience of silence in particularly striking ways; this, of course, was principally a rhetorical use of paradox. But he also intended that some of his paradoxes be understood only in apparent, or nonliteral, senses. (Recall the above quotation at note 36 where he writes that God's speech is not speech 'to our way of thinking'.) Nevertheless, most of his paradoxes about silence express his conviction that silence and its opposite (as sound, language, or the Word of God) may on occasion be indissolubly united. Thus he claimed that the attempt to make precise differentiations between the two must fail. Stace's suggestion that paradox is self-contradictory because the experience it attempts to describe is self-contradictory would seem most applicable in such cases. And we see that when Merton could not distinguish, or chose not to distinguish, silence from its opposite he expressed this paradoxically. In sum, Merton's paradoxes about silence take three forms: (1) rhetorical devices, (2) apparent contradictions, and (3) definite self-contradictions equating silence and non-silence. God must speak if man is to respond. But this speech in its most profound manifestation is divine silence. Man's response, even if initially expressed in words, must strive to appropriate the silence that is God. This, for Merton, ultimately has more than metaphorical signficance; it is an integral part of his mystical ontology. Bernard Williams has suggested that the religious paradox is often 'the essence of what is to be believed'.[45] Merton's paradoxes convey the essence of his belief about silence, and paradox has a critical place in his life and writings.

Merton held firmly to the position that paradox permeates mystical experience and, like Stace, believed that paradox cannot be eliminated from mysticism. 'In mysticism opposites tend to meet and coincide, for the realm of spiritual experience is no longer the realm of strict logic in which A and not-A are irreconcilably set apart and opposed.'[46] His personally revealing Preface to Thomas McDonnell's 1962 anthology of his writings discussed the simultaneous insecurity and peace he had discerned in the paradoxy of his own life. Merton saw the confusion, contradiction, even despair, generated by his own wrestling with paradox as an occasion for renewal and liberation.[47] He did not glorify paradox or resort to it in order to mystify; he simply tried to elicit appreciation for a necessary component of mysticism and, in his view, of life in general, so alien to an exclusively analytical orientation.

One of the most paradoxical modes of life, according to Merton, is solitude, for the hermit lives apart from others yet should somehow communicate his love for them through the witness of his life. The solitary way is usually a silent one, and Merton was seriously attracted to a life of complete solitude as early as 1946. His attempts to transfer from the cenobitical Cistercians to various eremitical Orders failed, but he was finally allowed in 1965 to live as a hermit on the grounds of Gethsemani Abbey. Correspondence from the early 1950s reveals that Merton naturally linked the hermit life to a decrease, possibly even an end to writing for publication. Letters to the benedictine scholar Jean Leclercq show that Merton feared his growing literary reputation might 'corrupt' the simplicity and obscurity he had originally sought in the monastery. 'I have stopped writing', he wrote to Leclercq in 1955, 'and that is a big relief. I intend to renounce it for good, if I can live in solitude.'[48] A posthumously published essay from the 1960s, 'Project for a Hermitage', resumes this idea, though in a less categorical way, in suggesting that a writer-hermit could continue to publish but that his themes should be spiritual rather than topical and that he should write 'at a reduced tempo'.[49] It is difficult not to interpret this advice as self-referential, though Merton's overall production did anything but decline in the final eremetical stage of his life.

Merton's ambivalence about writing ran deeper. Peter Kountz has carefully delineated the intense difficulties Merton experienced in attempting to reconcile his literary ambitions with his understanding of monastic profession in general. Concentrating on Merton's life prior to 1952, Kountz shows that Merton, who was attracted to the monastery partly by the hope that he would no longer be allowed to write, was distressed at the unexpected popularity caused by the success of *The Seven Storey Mountain*, published in 1948. As a result, Merton 'became wary of committing himself to any more writing for fear of completely losing his contemplative life and spirit and the desire for solitude'.[50] After the success of this book Merton stopped composing poems and experienced extended writing-blocks while working on *The Ascent to Truth*, a study of mysticism published in 1951.

Though Merton recovered from this particular episode (one in which his suffering was compounded by other factors not related to writing), conflicts between his vocation as a writer and his self-understanding as a monk persisted throughout his life. He recognized the value his works had for many readers: Merton had given monasticism and contemplation greater visibility than any previous American author; his criticism of war and racism had also established him as an important voice of the radical Catholic left. Merton knew that he was temperamentally impelled to write, that his life would have been intolerable without pen and paper. At various times throughout his career, furthermore, he found ascetical value in writing itself: 'when a thought is done with, let go of it. When something has been written, publish it, and go on to something else.'[51] Yet Merton did not always go on to other things. Some of his articles and books were extensively revised, he persisted in trying to publish a lengthy manuscript about art that friendly critics thought lacked merit, and in 1967 drew up a graph evaluating his own books. This is hardly a literary asceticism, not quite the letting go 'of my idea of myself'[52] Merton sincerely hoped his writing would encourage. Correspondence with his editor, Naomi Burton Stone, as late as 1968 reveals a disturbing need to get as much into print as quickly as he could.[53] Merton did not lack insight about the debilitating effects of this. Still-unpublished manuscripts and correspondence reveal disgust with his lust to write and publish because he correctly saw his attachment to these worldly preoccupations as a danger to his contemplative ideals. Had Merton been able to channel his writing according to his own suggestions outlined in 'Project for a Hermitage', writing less about fewer themes, he would have come closer to exemplifying the exterior silence he always considered the necessary counterpart of interior silence, and his authorship might have reflected more convincingly the primacy he accorded to silence. Never, to be sure, did he call for absolute silence, for an end to writing. But it appears that Merton did not manage to reconcile his massive literary production with the importance he always ascribed to interior silence. Interior silence, after all, presupposes that one has quieted many of the judgments and distinctions necessary for discursive exposition. While this conflict undoubtedly produced a creative tension leading to works of lasting value, it also shows a real inconsistency between his writing activity and his ideal of the silent life. This inconsistency does not detract from Merton's significance, but it does raise a problem about the place of silence in his life as opposed to the expression of silence in his theory. This problem may be inherent in the nature of silence itself, and in the difficulties of those who explore and write about it.

Space prevents me from exploring in depth the relationship between Merton's understanding of silence and other contemporary reflections about it, but I wish to offer a few suggestions in this direction. Much twentieth-century religious thought exhibits a deep concern for the nature and value of silence. Catholics Karl Rahner, Walter Ong, and Raimundo Panikkar have reflected on the ways in which God manifests a silent presence and how human utterance relates to it. Radical religious thinkers, like Simone Weil and

Thomas J. J. Altizer, have also stressed silence in their writings: Weil in accounts of her mystical experience; and Altizer in his Hegelian exploration of the dialectical relation between silence and speech.[54] Writers such as these recognize the creative potentiality of silence while trusting in the ability of language to wrest meaning from it. Their insights may be especially valuable today both for those who incorporate silence in their religious practice and for professional theologians who seek to transform the often dry and technical character of their discipline through greater openness to the mystery that silence conveys.

Concerned about dangers inherent in the 'temptation' to silence, while still respecting its power, literary critic Susan Sontag interprets the attraction to silence in modern literature and art as a consequence of the devaluation of language, of the assumption that language is not only inadequate but also corrupt. George Steiner shares Sontag's distress about the debasement of language and takes an even stronger stand against the recourse to silence in art. It is worth remarking, especially in the context of the present essay, that both Steiner and Sontag are aware of the positive mystical and religious value attributed to silence but neither explores this dimension thoroughly.[55] More important than the critics are those novelists and poets who have explicitly dealt with silence. Henry Miller, Samuel Beckett, Nikos Kazantzakis, Elie Wiesel, Rainer Maria Rilke, and T. S. Eliot are among the many who demonstate a sustained interest in the metaphysical character of silence. Exhibiting a more positive attitude than Sontag and Steiner, these authors have realized that silence beckons modern man when he listens to his innermost depths, that true awareness of the self and its place in the world may be limited without silent reflection and reflecting on silence.

An interest in silence also exhibits itself in contemporary philosophy. Martin Heidegger and Ludwig Wittgenstein (both of whom Merton read, though their influence on his thinking was minimal) discuss silence: Heidegger in his meditations on poetry and the concept of authenticity; Wittgenstein in his early attempts to fix the limits of valid discourse. For Heidegger, silence is both the voice of conscience recalling the authentic man to himself and the one unspoken 'poem' that shows itself as the forever unattainable goal of every genuine poetic statement. To the Wittgenstein of the *Tractatus*, the limits of our language disclose the limits of our world, but since 'the sense of the world must lie outside the world' (6.41), that is, beyond language, silence is the dimension wherein the value and meaning of the world speak to us.[56]

It would be a challenging task to exposit, clarify, and analyze these many religious, literary, and philosophical reflections on silence and to situate Merton in the larger framework that would emerge from this kind of project. Merton expresses two themes appearing in much of the literature about silence: he postulates a dialectic of silence and language; and he highlights the healing, redemptive, and regenerating power of silence. Merton's interpretation of silence does, of course, encompass far more than these considerations. But only when a study of the sort suggested here is carried out will we be able to situate Merton in a broader comparative framework and thus begin to understand his significance for our times.

Distressed by the deafening ideological, commerical, and polemical clamor of contemporary civilization, many important thinkers are understandably attracted to silence. Their reflections, like Merton's, are also more evocative and suggestive than logical and systematic. But there are problems with this approach because the desire to know silence does not satisfy the desire to know about it. Merton fails to consider many legitimate questions about silence that more analytical critics might raise. For example: Can anything substantive be known about silence itself, not merely about its effects? Is silence objectively the same for all or is it necessarily experienced and understood subjectively according to different cultural, religious, and psychological expectations? That the religious, philosophical, and literary figures surveyed above also fail to address questions like these may tell us something important about silence and the attempt to entice it into language. Perhaps, after all, listening to silence is more fruitful than dissecting it.

Perhaps not entirely. Harold Nemerov, in his essay 'Speaking Silence', gently argues that 'the first move of the understanding ought to be the silent contemplation of what is'.[57] Merton certainly helps in this, for his writings move us beyond his words to contemplate silence itself and what it might reveal. Nemerov also suggests, however, that 'the deeper purpose of silence is to produce the silence of understanding, the consent between speech and its object'[58] that should arise after reflecting on any truly significant text. Whether Merton and others enable us to recognize this correspondence between silence and speech seems to me the critical issue which those who write about silence must address; for how do we find the words to match and convey our intuitions about silence when silence has no words to give? How do we validate and convey our encounters with silence in conversation with others who wish to do the same for us?

Whatever the outcome of our quest, it is not improbable that Merton's treatment of silence may come to be recognized as a pivotal contemporary expression. His concomitant dedication to solitude introduces a more traditional theme. The present century has given far more attention to silence than to solitude. When we think of solitude, negative images—the loneliness of estrangement from others, the alienation caused by self-deception—usually come to mind. The conjunction of silence and solitude as a liberating force is one of the oldest elements in Western spirituality, but no other twentieth-century writer conveys the power of this linkage more consistently, thoroughly, and cogently than Merton. I stress the conjunction, for silence in Merton's life and thought cannot fully be understood without appreciating the corresponding place of solitude, and the intimate relation between them is one of the most striking themes in his work. Considered as preparatory disciplines, these two practices are basic to his understanding of the contemporary way: living a silent and solitary life, the contemplative can learn to unmask illusion and discover his true identity. But Merton understood silence and solitude as far more than ascetical practices. Above all, his writings illuminate their metaphysical and mystical significance, the God who embodies them, and the person who unites with the silence and solitude of God himself. This religious vision may prove to be one of Merton's more lasting gifts to those—believers and non-believers alike—who even dimly suspect that the silence and solitude we all must confront may occasion grace more than desolation.[59]

112 *John F. Teahan*

NOTES

1. *The Seven Storey Mountain* (New York, 1948) p. 321. See also p. 323. For references to the Quaker meeting and the Catholic Mass, see pp. 115 and 210.

2. 'First Christmas at Gethesemani', *Catholic World* 170 (December 1949) 166-173.

3. (New York, 1953) p. 192. For other discussions of silence in this journal, see pp. 47-48, 77, 96-98, 141, 159-160, 165-166, 257-258, 264, 288, 318, 337.

4. (Garden City, New York, 1966).

5. *The Asian Journal of Thomas Merton*, ed. from his original notebooks by Naomi Burton, Brother Patrick Hart and James Laughlin (New York, 1973) pp. 150 and 158. Merton's description of silence in nature may be found on p. 78. See also 'Day of a Stranger', *Hudson Review* 20 (Summer 1967) 211-218, for an account of his experience in the hermitage at Gethsemani. On p. 215 he writes that 'one might say I had decided to marry the silence of the forest'.

6. For this account, see *The Asian Journal*, pp. 230-236.

7. See Richard P. Hardy, ' "Silencio Divino": A Sanjuanist Study', *Eglise et Théologie* 7 (May 1976) 219-233.

8. Merton did, at least, recognize the centrality of silence in St John's asceticism and mysticism. See *Disputed Questions* (New York, 1960) p. 216.

9. See the Author's Note to *Thoughts in Solitude* (Garden City, New York, 1968; orig. pub. 1968).

10. *No Man Is an Island* (New York, 1957; orig. pub. 1955) p. 225.

11. 'The Gift of Understanding', *The Tiger's Eye* 6 (December 1948) 43.

12. See 'First Christmas at Gethsemani'.

13. My use of the word 'dialectic' in this essay is not intended in a technical philosophical sense, as the word is often employed in studies of Plato, Aristotle, Kant, Hegel, and Marx. By 'dialectic' I mean a creative interaction between two elements usually considered to be in opposition. Compare *Webster's Third New International Dictionary of the English Language, Unabridged* (Springfield, Massachusetts, 1963) p. 623, entry 5.

14. *The Sign of Jonas*, pp. 266-267.

15. The poem is 'Hagia Sophia', in *Emblems of a Season of Fury* (New York, 1963) pp. 61-69.

16. *Thoughts in Solitude*, p. 110.

17. See especially 'War and the Crisis of Language', in *Thomas Merton on Peace*, ed. with an introduction by Gordon C. Zahn (New York, 1971) pp. 234-247. Reissued as *The Nonviolent Alternative* by Farrar, Straus & Giroux.

18. *Raids on the Unspeakable* (New York, 1966) p. 160.

19. *The Ascent to Truth* (New York, 1951) p. 316. See also pp. 105-106.

20. *The Wisdom of the Desert: Sayings From the Desert Fathers of the Fourth Century* (New York, 1960) p. 14.

21. 'Ascetical and Mystical Theology: An Introduction to Christian Mysticism', unpublished mimeograph, 1961, p. 16. This, and all unpublished material I shall cite, may be consulted at the Thomas Merton Studies Center, Bellarmine College, Louisville, Kentucky.

22. On silence in Ignatius, see Virginia Corwin, *St Ignatius and Christianity in Antioch* (New Haven, 1960) pp. 119-130, and Henry Chadwick, 'The Silence of Bishops in Ignatius', *Harvard Theological Review* 43 (1950) 169-172.

23. 'Love and Solitude', *The Critic* 25 (October-November 1966) 33, rpt. in *Love and Living*, Edited by Naomi Burton Stone & Brother Patrick Hart (New York, 1979).

24. See, for example, *What is Contemplation?* (Holy Cross, Indiana, 1948) p. 20; *Seeds of Contemplation* (Norfolk, Connecticut, 1949) p. 187; *Seasons of Celebration* (New York, 1965) p. 213; *The Silent Life* (New York, 1959; orig. pub. 1957) p. 44; 'St. Peter Damian and the Medieval Monk', *Jubilee* 8 (August 1960) 42.

25. 'Christian Freedom and Monastic Formation', *The American Benedictine Review* 13 (September 1962) 312.

26. *The Seven Storey Mountain*, p. 415.

27. *The Sign of Jonas*, p. 47.

28. *Conjectures of a Guilty Bystander*, p. 154, and 'Love and Solitude', p. 34, rpt. in *Love and Living* (New York, 1979).

29. 'St. Peter Damian and the Medieval Monk', p. 42.

30. *Contemplation in a World of Action* (Garden City, New York, 1973; orig. pub. 1971) p. 170.

31. On Merton's apophaticism (use of negative theology and the symbolism of darkness and emptiness), see my 'A Dark and Empty Way: Thomas Merton and the Apophatic Tradition', *The Journal of Religion* 58 (July 1978) 263-287.

32. 'Creative Silence', *The Baptist Student* 48 (February 1969) 20, rpt. in *Love and Living* (New York, 1979).

33. *Seasons of Celebration*, p. 211.

34. *Silence in Heaven: A Book of the Monastic Life* (New York, 1956) p. 21.

35. *Ibid.*, p. 25.

36. 'Love and Solitude', pp. 31 and 33; rpt. in *Love and Living* (New York, 1979).

37. 'Prayer as Worship and Experience', unpublished setting copy, 1963, pp. 122-123.

38. See 'Logic, Meaning, and Mystical Intuition', *Philosophical Studies* 11 (October 1960) 65-70.

39. See *The Still Point: Reflections on Zen and Christian Mysticism* (New York, 1970) chap. 5.

40. See *Exploring Mysticism: A Methodological Essay* (Berkeley, 1975) pp. 5, 25-26, and 63.

41. See *The Other Dimension: A Search for the Meaning of Religious Attitudes* (Garden City, New York, 1971) pp. 215-221.

42. See *Mysticism and Philosophy* (London, 1960) chap. 5.

43. See 'Mysticism, Contradiction and Ineffability', *American Philosophical Quarterly* 3 (July 1973) 201-211.

44. See 'Paradox in Religion', in *New Essays in Religious Language* ed. Dallas M. High (New York, 1969) chap. 7.

45. 'Tertullian's Paradox', in *New Essays in Philosophical Theology*, ed. Anthony Flew and Alasdair MacIntyre (New York, 1964) p. 192.

46. *Mystics and Zen Masters* (New York, 1969; orig. pub. 1967) p. 139.

47. See *A Thomas Merton Reader*, ed. Thomas P. McDonnell (Garden City, New York, 1974; orig. pub. 1962).

48. Thomas Merton to Jean Leclercq, 3 June 1955, quoted in Jean Leclercq, 'Merton and History', in *Thomas Merton: Prophet in the Belly of a Paradox*, ed. Gerald Twomey (New York, 1978) p. 221. See also Merton's unpublished 22 January 1953 letter to Barnabas Ahern for an earlier indication of similar sentiments.

49. *The Monastic Journey*, ed. Brother Patrick Hart (Mission, Kansas, 1977) p. 140.

50. ' "The Seven Storey Mountain" of Thomas Merton', *Thought* 49 (September 1974) 260. See also Dennis Q. McInerny, *Thomas Merton: The Man and His Work* (Washington, 1974) chap. 2, esp. pp. 13-14 on Merton and the Promethean conception of writing.

51. *A Thomas Merton Reader*, p. 16. See also 'Todo y Nada: Writing and Contemplation', *Renascence* 2 (Spring 1950) 87-101.

52. *A Thomas Merton Reader*, p. 17.

53. See Thomas Merton to Naomi Burton Stone, 19 January 1968.

54. See Karl Rahner, *Encounters with Silence*, trans. James M. Demske (Paramus and New York, 1960); Walter J. Ong. *The Presence of the Word: Some Prolegomena for Cultural and Religious History* (New York, 1970); Raimundo Panikkar, *El silencio del Dios* (Madrid, 1970); Simone Weil, *Waiting for God*, trans. Emma Crauford (New York, 1973); Thomas J. J. Altizer, *The Self-Embodiment of God* (New York, 1977).

55. See Susan Sontag, 'The Aesthetics of Silence', in *Styles of Radical Will* (New York, 1970) pp. 3-34, and George Steiner, *Language and Silence: Essays on Language, Literature and the Inhuman* (New York, 1976).

56. See Martin Heidegger, *Poetry, Language and Thought*, trans. Albert Hofstadter (New York, 1971); and *On the Way to Language*, trans. Peter D. Hertz (New York, 1971); Karsten Harries, 'Language and Silence: Heidegger's Dialogue with Georg Trakl', *Boundary 2*, 4 (1976) 495-511. For one interpretation of Wittgenstein on silence, and for provo-

cative suggestions about religious silence, see Charles H. Long, 'Silence and Signification: A Note on Religion and Modernity', in *Myths and Symbols: Studies in Honor of Mircea Eliade*, ed. Joseph M. Kitagawa and Charles H. Long (Chicago and London, 1969) pp. 141-150. I wish to thank Roger Kimball for his assistance with the formulation of this paragraph.
57. In *Figures of Thought: Speculations on the Meaning of Poetry and Other Essays* (Boston, 1978) p. 114.
58. *Ibid.*
59. I intend to substantiate these necessarily sketchy and proleptic observations about solitude in a companion piece to the present article.

A Critical View of Solitude in Merton's Life and Thought

Chalmers MacCormick

Chalmers MacCormick, Professor of Religion at Wells College, did his graduate work at the University of Tübingen and Harvard University. His doctoral work at Harvard was in the History and Philosophy of Religion. He currently teaches the History of Religions with chief attention on Hinduism, Buddhism, Mysticism, and Religion in America. His previous Merton scholarship includes the universally acclaimed essay on 'The Zen Catholicism of Thomas Merton' which appeared in the Journal of Ecumenical Studies *in 1972. His current research focuses on Marriage and Contemplation. His contribution to this volume was originally presented at the Merton Commemoration at Columbia University.*

> If you seek a heavenly light
> I, Solitude, am your professor![1]

'I HAVE ONLY one desire and that is the desire for solitude', wrote Thomas Merton on 13 December 1946. Nearly three years later, he again wrote, 'everything in me cries out for solitude and for God alone'. Although both of these statements come from *The Sign of Jonas*[2] and therefore typify what has come to be referred to as 'the early Merton', in fact they express what he continued to desire, and even crave, throughout his adult life. As

Brother Patrick Hart has written: Merton's search for greater solitude was so continuous that we may regard it as 'something of a leitmotif' in all his writings, his journals especially.[3]

In an essay entitled 'The Solitary', Sister Thérèse Lentfoehr traces the chronological development of Merton's notion of solitude, which she proposes as 'the key for understanding' him.[4] It is unnecessary to retrace here what is already traced so well there. What follows, therefore, while it does not disregard the chronological development, does not stress it. Rather, it presupposes that Merton's best writing on solitude, from whatever period, constitutes essentially a whole. A division of his life and thought into the 'early' and not-yet-mature, on the one hand, and the 'later' and 'mature', on the other, though not without meaning and value, runs the risk of exaggeration. The two halves of Merton's monastic development (if such they were) cannot be separated off, or even radically distinguished from each other. More was continuous than just the search. Continuous, too, were the main drift of Merton's thinking and the shape, if not the scope, of his self-understanding.

His germinal self-understanding is indicated in one of his earliest published passages. Reflecting back in *The Seven Storey Mountain* on his debate with himself about which religious Order to join (the year was 1939, the Order briefly being considered the Jesuits), he wrote:

> They would probably have found me a great misfit. What I needed was the solitude to expand in breadth and depth and to be simplified out under the gaze of God more or less the way a plant spreads out its leaves in the sun. That meant that I needed a Rule that was almost entirely aimed at detaching me from the world and uniting me with God, not a Rule made to fight for God in the world. But I did not find out all that in one day.[5]

There is so much that is apt here. No doubt he *would* have been a misfit as a Jesuit. And how true the 'I did not find out all that in one day'. Especially apt is Merton's comparison of himself with a plant that spreads out its leaves in the sun. For a plant is organically continuous at all stages of its development: there is increase and differentiation, but the plant remains identifiably the same; a rose does not grow into a geranium or even another rose; the same rose simply becomes bigger and fuller, and it opens out more. So it was with Merton. He expanded in breadth and depth; he 'simplified out under the gaze of God'.

Just before waking on Christmas morning 1949, he had a dream which, while it does not prove the underlying unity and continuity of his growth in solitude, nevertheless, in a minor way does symbolize it. Elements in the dream correspond to his wish, expressed in the last few months of his life, to have a hermitage either in Alaska or in the Redwood forests of northern California. What he dreamt was that he was driving to a new foundation the Trappists were to make 'on the Pacific coast, somewhere in the Northwest'. In three different churches in three different towns on the way he was going to say three Masses, each of which 'would be a big step nearer to some inexpressible happiness in union with God.' He concludes his journal entry with this comment: 'The way I felt about where I was going, in the dream, makes me think of a few dreams I had about going away to be a Carthusian—which is all over now.'[6]

But of course the Carthusian dream, except in the most literal sense, was *not* 'all over'. It persisted. It did not, however, materialize. The earthly solitude Merton wished for eluded him. And something eludes us, too: a complete understanding of what he thought about solitude.

There is more than one reason for this. A minor one is that he did not express himself wholly consistently; a more fundamental one is that his notion is inherently complex and subtle: it is a rich, variegated, and paradoxical combination of many characteristics and values, such as loneliness, hiddenness, anonymity, rejection, secrecy, emptiness, poverty, egolessness, detachment, freedom, 'utter otherness',[7] and, above all, 'the undivided unity of love'.[8] As Sr Thérèse has noted, solitude has 'multiple proliferations of extension and meaning'.[9] This being so, it is hardly surprising that Merton had to make repeated efforts not only to realize true solitude in practice, but also to explain it in writing.

Furthermore, solitude is akin to silence—so akin to it that ordinary human language can but imperfectly express it. Even on a superficial level, according to Merton, the relationship between solitude and silence is close. Exterior physical solitude conduces to the experience of silence: it protects that silence. Conversely, silence protects solitude, and if silence is absent, then so too is solitude. Not surprisingly, therefore, the two words 'silence' and 'solitude' often occur together in Merton's writings. In *The Seven Storey Mountain*, he tells about his arrival at Gethsemani as a retreatant in Holy Week 1941. First the train deposited him at the station, leaving him 'in the middle of the silence and solitude of the Kentucky Hills'. That same night, he arrived at the monastery and found the whole place 'as quiet as midnight and lost in the all-absorbing silence and solitude of the fields'.[10] He was then taken to his room in the guesthouse; his reaction (reported five years later) was: 'The embrace of it, the silence! I had entered into a solitude that was an impregnable fortress. And the silence that enfolded me, spoke to me.'[11]

Silence and solitude are complementary dimensions of one reality. At the deepest level, they merge so fully as to be scarcely distinguishable. This is the level of true solitude, that 'mysterious interior solitude', as Merton once characterized contemplation, 'in which the soul is absorbed in the immense and fruitful silence of God'.[12] And it is ultimately for this reason that neither he nor we can comprehend, much less express in words, the full meaning of solitude; for as God's silence and solitude are infinite, so the full number of their meanings is indeterminate.

To realize solitude is to apprehend the solitude of God. This is a consistent, recurrent motif in Merton's writings. In *No Man is an Island*, he declares: 'we become solitaries not when we realize how alone we are, but when we sense something of the solitude of God'.[13] And in his 'Notes for a Philosophy of Solitude', he states: 'Man's loneliness is, in fact, the loneliness of God. That is why it is such a great thing for a man to discover his solitude and learn to live in it. For there he finds that he and God are one.'[14] Perhaps the most expressive statement of all is found in that time-tested, timeless work, *The Sign of Jonas*: 'True solitude is a participation in the solitariness of God—who is in all things. His solitude is not a local absence but a metaphyical transcendence. His solitude is His Being.'[15]

'His solitude is His Being.' Although this stands out as an expression of one cardinal element in Merton's metaphysics of solitude (metaphysics here being understood as primarily a configuration of insights into Reality), it does not stand alone or apart. Three other key statements about God complement and clarify it.

The first of these three is that God is 'that center Who is everywhere and whose circumference is nowhere'.[16] Like all valid metaphysical assertions, this one has major practical import. The man who has found solitude 'has advanced beyond all horizons. There are no directions left in which he can travel. This is a country whose center is everywhere and whose circumference is nowhere. You do not find it by traveling but by standing still.'[17] For a monk, this means adhering in obedience to his vow of stabililty, whereby he is 'protected against his natural restlessness' and is 'reminded that he does not need to travel across the face of the earth'; he 'remains indifferent to place and space', for 'wherever he is, he dwells in God.'[18]

The second statement is that God is a Trinity, who 'infinitely transcends every shadow of selfishness. . . . He is at once infinite solitude (one nature) and perfect society (Three Persons). One infinite Love in three subsistent relations.'[19] This implies for all of us that when we are truly solitary we are not individuals widely separated from each other, but persons deeply related to one another. 'Is each person a separate solitude of his own?', Merton asks. 'No', he answers. 'There is One Solitude in which all persons are at once together and alone.'[20] For monks (and presumably others as well) this means that there is no real conflict between being solitary and living in community. Through charity,

> the monk passes beyond the apparent conflict between solitude and communion, and finds both together in God. For the more he loves his brethren and surrenders his will to the 'common will' the more he is at liberty to be alone with God in Himself, since he rises above himself to find both himself and others in God. In the mystery of God there is both solitude and community, for God is three persons in one nature.[21]

The final key statement is that God is incarnate. The Word was made flesh in Jesus and is perpetually incarnate in the Church.

Commenting on the sixth chapter of the Gospel of St John, Merton writes:

> Jesus made no compromise with a merely worldly society. Confronted with kingship His answer was not even a word—it was rejection and solitude. But he emerged from his solitude to teach of a 'society' that was to be one flesh and one bloodstream with himself, a mystical union of all men in His Body, where solitude and the common life are realized perfectly both together at the same time.[22]

What actualizes this mystical union is, of course, the Mass. In *The Sign of Jonas* especially, Merton has a great deal to say about the significance of the Mass for the polarity-in-unity of solitude and society. Since he had recently been ordained a priest, this is not surprising. Typical statements from that time (1949-50) are: 'Solitude and society are formed and perfected in the Sacrifice of the Mass';[23] and 'nothing could be less private than the Mass. And yet it is also a perfect solitude.'[24] One such passage is doubly noteworthy, because it underscores the relationship between the Mass and solitude (while implying the social dimension of the Mass as well) and reinforces in eloquent language the truth that at the deepest level silence and solitude coalesce:

> It is in the Canon and at the words of Consecration that all solitudes come to a single focus. There the City of God is gathered together in that one Word spoken in silence. The speech of God is silence. His Word is solitude.[25]

This, perhaps one of the most timeless of Merton's utterances about silence and solitude, is in one respect also one of the most dated. Today, when the words of Consecration are no longer whispered, it is doubtful that he would express himself in just this way. Nevertheless, in the last years of his life, though in different language, he continued to stress the convergence of solitude and society in the Sacrament. There was, to be sure, a shift in emphasis and practical focus—a shift that reflects changes in his own situation. Formerly he had been savoring his newly-bestowed priesthood, now he was extolling the eremitical life. Thus, in an essay entitled 'The Cell', published in 1966, the year following his own move into the hermitage at Gethsemani, he wrote:

> There is no peace and no reality in an abstract, disincarnate gnostic soli-
> tude. St. Peter Damian insists that since the Christian hermit is hidden in
> Jesus Christ he is therefore most intimately present (*praesentissimus*) to all
> the rest of the Church. His isolation in solitude unites him more closely in
> love with all the rest of his brothers in the word. Hence there is every
> good reason for the hermit to say *Dominus vobiscum* in his office and Mass
> even though no one may be physically present. We can see here the im-
> plications of having the Blessed Sacrament reserved in the hermit's cell.[26]

God's solitude is his Being; his center is everywhere, his circumference nowhere. He is a Trinity; and he is incarnate. These
statements state and illustrate the main motifs of Merton's overall
notion of solitude. Among these motifs, one requires special emphasis—and that for two reasons: first, because (at least implicitly)
it is common to all four statements; second, and more importantly, because it is one of the most dominant, persistent, and
consistent themes in Merton's writings—the relation of solitude to
society.

'True solitude is deeply aware of the world's needs. It does not
hold the world at arm's length.'[27] We associate this outlook especially with Merton's later life, when his writings on civil rights and
the Viet Nam war drew attention to him as a social critic. But
even as he first crossed the threshold at Gethsemani, he evinced
the basic social consciousness that we find elaborated in the later
years. 'This is the center of America. I had wondered what was
holding the country together, what has been keeping the universe
from cracking in pieces and falling apart. It is places like this monastery', is a reaction he recorded in the journal he kept before
becoming a monk.[28]

The question then is not whether he did or did not always
regard the solitary life as in some sense 'social'. It *is* social—social
both because it takes place in the context of a society (the Church)
and because it benefits society-at-large. Merton was never equivo-
cal about that. The critical question is: what did he consider to be
the best balance between the life of solitude on one hand, and
social participation on the other? That is, just how much solitude,

and what kind of solitude, are necessary to the deepest, most far-reaching social commitment?

Merton's answers to this are varied and even confusing. One supposes that the variety and confusion stemmed in part from inevitable shifts in his mood and perspective, but also from his recognition that there are varieties of vocations. Not everyone is called to be a monk, but everyone is called to some species of solitude.

In what environment? Merton's answer to this fluctuates. But common to the fluctuations is the conviction that some kind of physical solitude is indispensable. Without it, true interior solitude cannot be realized. Whether it be a cell in one's monastery, a room in one's house, or a church in a city, there has to be a place to which one can withdraw in order to find both outer and inner silence. Granted that the finder of solitude is in 'a country whose center is everywhere', and that he therefore ought to be able to experience solitude wherever he is, nevertheless 'there is a mechanism for finding it that has some reference to actual space, to geography, to physical isolation from the towns and the cities of men'.[29]

This reference to isolation from towns and cities might be taken to mean that solitude cannot be truly realized there. It is well-known that Merton felt that to be so for himself. He far preferred a natural setting to an urban one—so strongly that sometimes his attraction to the former was combined with a strong aversion for the latter:

> Returning to the monastery from the hospital: cool evening, gray sky, the dark hills. Once again I get the strange sense that one has when he comes back to a place that has been chosen for him by Providence. I belong to this parcel of land with rocky rills around it, with pine trees on it.... Cities, even Louisville (which, being the city nearest to home is in some sense my city), leave me with a sense of placelessness and exile. There is an immense movement spread all over everything: the ceaseless motion of hot traffic, tired and angry people, in a complex swirl of frustration.[30]

This is perhaps the point on which we are most aware of Merton's confusion and ambivalence. There is a tension between his personal preference for life in the country and his recognition that persons can realize and express solitude anywhere, even in cities.

'In moments of silence, of meditation, of enlightenment and peace, one learns to be silent and alone everywhere. One learns to live in the atmosphere of solitude even in the midst of crowds', he states in one of his later writings,[31] thus echoing statements repeatedly made earlier.

In one of those earlier statements, he declares that the soul that has found itself by realizing true solitude 'gravitates toward the desert but does not object to remaining in the city, because it is everywhere alone'.[32] That he himself gravitated (and regravitated) toward the desert, and apparently *did* mind remaining in the city, is understandable, for he was a monk. Being one did not deliver him from vocational tension, however. At one time, the tension had been a purely monastic one: ought he or ought he not to leave the Cistercians and become a Carthusian? This dilemma persisted and, in a slightly different form, resurfaced when, late in life, he advocated the eremitical life with a devotion that, though somewhat less than exclusive, was decidedly singleminded. It was not exclusive because at least in part, he was beset by another tension: the tension between a strictly monastic vocation on the one hand, and an apostolic one on the other. 'Should not contemplatives', he asks, 'abandon their silence and solitude in order to be enlisted in the busy army of apostolic workers?' And he follows the question with the admission that 'we have often searched our own hearts and sought to resolve this question for ourselves, fearing that perhaps our call to desert solitude might be an illusion, and dreading that we might be making our silence a pretext for refusing to others a necessary service'.[33]

The pull of the apostolate was strong. This is evident not only in his exercising a quasi-apostolate by means of his writings generally, but also by what he wrote about the apostolate specifically. Especially pertinent to this side of his personality and thought is what he wrote about St Francis and the early Franciscans. Implicitly agreeing with St Thomas Aquinas that there is a vocation higher than either the active or the contemplative life, namely 'the apostolic life in which the fruits of contemplation are shared with others', he calls St Francis the 'perfect embodiment' of this: 'He was an apostle who incarnated the whole spirit and message of the Gospels most perfectly. Merely to know St Francis is to understand the Gospel, and to follow him in his true integral spirit, is to love the Gosepl in all its fullness.'[34]

Merton admired and commended St Francis and the early Franciscans. Did he also sometimes envy them, for example, because they had no formal vow of stability to restrain them and could therefore freely express their interior solitude through their activity in the world? St Francis's vocation was in part to be a hermit, but it was not limited to that: 'He frequently went off into the mountains to pray and live alone. But he never thought that he had a "vocation" to do nothing else but that. He stayed alone as long as the Spirit held him in solitude, and then let himself be led back into the towns and villages by the same Spirit.' In short, he was 'taught by the Spirit in solitude, but brought by God to the cities of men with a message to tell them.'[35] And he bequeathed this spiritual freedom to the early Franciscans, whose 'ideal could really be regarded as a return to the authentic freedom of early monasticism.'

> You could be a pilgrim, you could be a hermit, and you could be a pilgrim for a while and a hermit for a while and then a scholar for a while. Then you could go to the Muslims in North Africa and get yourself martyred if you had the grace! And so forth.[36]

In other words (mine, not Merton's), the early Franciscans had *inner* stability, which they proved by their mobility. Because they were centered in God, whose circumference is nowhere, they could travel everywhere. In this, they could be likened to a well-made ship, the proof of whose excellence is not so much how well she rides at anchor as how safely and efficiently she crosses the seas.

St Francis's vocation to solitude was one type, Merton's was another. There is, in short, more than one sort of solitude; there are many sorts, some extremely reclusive, others relatively public. Merton once wrote that 'the desert of the monk is his monastery—and his own heart. Yet in that desert he is free to encounter and love the whole world.'[37] A comprable insight has been expressed by Judith Jamison, the dancer, who said in an interview: 'The stage is for me a sanctuary. I'm a bubble of isolation, in my pure state, knowing I'm going to say something, my thing, in my way, to the whole world.'[38]

Thus, the modes and manifestations of true solitude are various. A complete list of examples would be very long indeed and, in Merton's case, would include not only fully cloistered persons (e.g. fellow Trappists), but also, I presume, *poustiniaks* like Catherine de Hueck Doherty and social activists like John Howard Griffin as well as non-Christians from the East—Mahatma Gandhi who, thanks to his discipline of silence, was solitary in the midst of massive crowds; Brahmachari, the hindu monk who first taught Merton to be indifferent to place;[39] and D. T. Suzuki, who 'stayed right where he was, in his own Zen', and bore witness to that 'silent orbiting of *Prajna* [Wisdom] which is. . .a "circle whose circumference is nowhere and whose center is everywhere."'[40]

Dom Jean Leclercq has written that Merton 'saw everything through a monk's eyes. This was both his limitation and his strength: a limitation because, after all, monastic life is not the totality of the Church or of society; other points of view are also valid. A strength, because he was a man of single purpose, a lone warrior.'[41]

Bearing in mind that a limitation is not a shortcoming, let us, for the sake of illustration, briefly consider one of those other valid points of view: marriage.

One of the respects in which Merton matured was that in his later writings he showed a greater sensitivity than he had shown earlier to the needs of the married for solitude. Previously he had, to be sure, commended marriage as a particular mode of contemplation and a high vocation,[42] but he had not yet envisaged some kind of union of this vocation with the monastic. In this very important essay on 'Ecumenism and Renewal', however, he reveals a concern, awareness, and germinal wisdom on this theme that might, had he lived longer, have developed into a major statement about solitude and marriage. (This may seem improbable, but it is not unimaginable.)[43] He wrote:

Why could there not be monasteries, with a nucleus of permanently dedicated monks, to which others come temporarily for two or three years, for periods of training or for retreat (as for instance in Zen Buddhist monasticism)? Why could not married people participate temporarily, in some way, in monastic life?[44]

And in 'Renewal and Discipline', another essay from about this time, he lamented the fact that the customs and laws of the Church provide little or no encouragement to those 'many married people who, after ten or fifteen years of married life (or longer if they are to bring up their children) would definitely like to separate and take on a different kind of life, more solitary and disciplined and perhaps in some sense monastic'.[45]

But if there is a hint of promise about this in some of Merton's later statements, on the whole there is too little, so that to those of us who are married, Merton's single-minded devotion to monastic and eremitical solitude can often be discouraging. We take little or no comfort from the assurance he proffers that even *un*cloistered persons 'like Thoreau or Emily Dickinson' can experience the kind of solitude he has in mind.[46] We are bound to ask: is there some way, a way as valid and effectual for us as the monastic way for others, that we can experience both the inner and the outer solitude that Merton so earnestly commends to us?

May those of us who are married be forgiven if at times we only half-hear Merton, for he speaks to us, it seems, only half-audibly. The reason for this lies partly in how he describes the monastery, which is often, it turns out, not a place of silence after all: there is the roaring of the D-4 Traxcavator, distraction in choir, and the noise of human ambition. But the main reason is that he knew so little about marriage. This limitation is an understandable one. After all, his parents died when he was young, and he was a monk—a combination of circumstances that could scarcely be offset by his numbering married couples (e.g. the Maritains) among his closest friends. The difference between his circumstances and ours necessarily tempers the force of his challenge to us who adhere to another mode of 'stability'. As Merton himself said (*this* we *do* hear), we are in a country whose center is everywhere and circumference nowhere; we do not find it by traveling.

These remarks are meant only to illustrate a dilemma, not to demonstrate a thesis. Nor are they supposed to suggest that Merton was wrong or even that he was only half-right. Far from it. On essentials, he was very right—so right, indeed, that he provokes us to emulate him. Less than a complete model, he remains nevertheless an excellent catalyst—a catalyst to reflection, to self-understanding, to singleness of purpose, and to purity of heart. If we could but take his best insights and infuse them into our own lives, we too would come to know that 'mysterious inner solitude in which the soul is absorbed in the immense and fruitful silence of God.'[47]

NOTES

1. The opening lines of Merton's poem 'Song: If You Seek . . .', in *Emblems of a Season of Fury*, New Directions paperback (New York, 1963) p. 38.

2. (New York, 1953) pp. 17-18, 175.

3. *The Asian Journal of Thomas Merton*, Edited by James Laughlin, Naomi Burton Stone and Brother Patrick Hart, (New York, 1973) p. xxviii.

4. *Thomas Merton, Monk*, ed. by Brother Patrick Hart; Doubleday Image edition (Garden City, N.Y., 1976) p. 64. An excellent summary of Merton's development is Richard Anthony Cashen's 'Merton the Solitary', Chapter I of Cashen's doctoral dissertation, *The Concept of Solitude in the Thought of Thomas Merton* (Institute of Spirituality, Pontifical Gregorian University, Rome, 1976). (This volume is being published by Cistercian Publications, Kalamazoo, as *Solitude in The Thought of Thomas Merton.*)

5. *The Seven Storey Mountain* (Garden City, 1951; reprint of the original 1948 edition) pp. 260-61.

6. *The Sign of Jonas*, p. 261.

7. *Disputed Questions* (New York, 1960) p. 204.

8. 'Love and Solitude' in *Love and Living*, ed. by Naomi Burton Stone and Brother Patrick Hart (New York, 1977) p. 16.

9. 'The Solitary', in *Thomas Merton, Monk* (see n. 4).

10. P. 320.

11. P. 321.

12. *The Seven Storey Mountain*, p. 415.

13. (New York, 1955) p. 228.

14. *Disputed Questions*, p. 190.

15. P. 269.

16. As rendered in *The Seven Storey Mountain*, p. 225. See also *Zen and the Birds of Appetite* (New York, 1968) p. 24, where Merton refers to God as 'the one center of all, which is "everywhere and nowhere"'.

17. *New Seeds of Contemplation* (New York, 1961) p. 81 (no change from the original *Seeds of Contemplation*).

18. *The Monastic Journey*, ed. by Brother Patrick Hart (Kansas City, 1977) p. 67.

19. *New Seeds of Contemplation*, p. 68.

20. 'Love and Solitude,' in *Love and Living*, p. 17.

21. *The Monastic Journey*, p. 69.

22. *The Sign of Jonas*, p. 219.

23. *Ibid.*, p. 269.

24. *Ibid.*, p. 287.
25. *Ibid.*, p. 267.
26. *Contemplation in a World of Action* (London, 1971) p. 258.
27. *Conjectures of a Guilty Bystander*, Image Books edition (Garden City, N.Y., 1968) p. 19.
28. *The Secular Journal* (New York, 1959) p. 183; compare *The Seven Storey Mountain*, p. 325.
29. *New Seeds of Contemplation*, p. 81 (no change from the original *Seeds*).
30. *Conjectures of a Guilty Bystander*, p. 257.
31. 'Love and Solitude', in *Love and Living*, p. 21.
32. *No Man is an Island*, p. 253.
33. *Contemplation in a World of Action*, p. 168.
34. *No Man is an Island*, pp. 159-60.
35. *Ibid.*, p. 162.
36. *Contemplation in a World of Action*, p. 358.
37. *Ibid.*, p. 228.
38. *Newsweek*, 10 February 1969, p. 76.
39. *The Seven Storey Mountain*, p. 195.
40. *Birds of Appetite*, p. 65.
41. *Contemplation in a World of Action*, p. xiv.
42. On marriage as a vocation, see especially *No Man Is an Island*, pp. 152-54. Merton's unfinished and therefore unpublished manuscript entitled *The Inner Experience* devotes seven pages to 'Contemplative Life in the World'; of these, three pages specifically concern marriage. William Shannon, author of *Thomas Merton's Dark Path: The Inner Experience of a Contemplative* and a scholar who has made a special study of *The Inner Experience*, holds that this material may date from as early as the early fifties and in any case from no later than 1959.
43. Merton concludes the above-noted section of *The Inner Experience* by remarking that what the christian layman most needs 'is a contemplative spirituality centered on the mystery of marriage. The development of such a spirituality is very necessary and much to be desired'. However, he does not indicate how, if at all, he himself would contribute to such a development.
44. Published in 1968; *Contemplation in a World of Action*, p. 192.
45. *Ibid.*, p. 108.
46. *Disputed Questions*, p. 177.
47. In an excellent paper entitled 'Merton on the Lifestyle of the Lay Contemplative: Explicit Statements and Refracted Light', Kenneth C. Russell observes that while lay contemplatives can indeed recognize themselves in Merton's writings, they are chiefly enriched when Merton's focus is on the eremitical life rather than when it is on marriage (hence the 'refracted light' of the title). See Tape = 35 of The Thomas Merton Symposium held in Vancouver, B.C., 11-13 May 1978.
   A striking instance of Merton's catalytic effect on lay couples is the Families of St Benedict in New Hope, Kentucky—a contemplative community of families participating together in liturgy and sharing voluntary poverty. See Marylee Mitcham, *An Accidental Monk: Her Domestic Search for God* (Cincinnati, Ohio, 1976).

'Pieces of the Mosaic, Earth': Thomas Merton and the Christ

George Kilcourse

George Kilcourse is Assistant Professor of Theology at Bellarmine College in Louisville, Kentucky, and a priest of the Archdiocese. He has contributed reviews of Merton's works as well as scholarly studies on Merton to various journals and has conducted Merton workshops and participated in a number of Merton conferences throughout the country, drawing attention in particular to Merton's poetry corpus. His doctoral dissertation from Fordham University (1974) was entitled: '"Incarnation" As the Integrating Principle in Thomas Merton's Spirituality and Poetry'. Father Kilcourse serves as Research Director for the Archdiocesan Office of Ecumenical Affairs and edits The Ark, *an ecumenical bulletin published quarterly by the Thomas Merton Studies Center of Bellarmine College.*

THAT A SYMPOSIUM on Thomas Merton would turn to 'The Christ' for its center of gravity is hardly surprising. The Cistercian monk-poet had seemingly anticipated this focus of his spirituality fifteen years ago when he recapitulated his contribution for the dedication of the Thomas Merton Studies Center at Bellarmine College:

> Whatever I have written, I think all can be reduced in the end to this one root truth: that God calls human persons to union with Himself and with one another in Christ . . . . [1]

A shelf of books and several hundred articles, reviews, and thousands of letters later, the chronicle of that Merton literature traces the pilgrimage of Merton's encounter with and reflections on the Christ. My purpose is to offer some systematic reading of that image and understanding of Merton's christocentric spirituality. Certain peaks and definite christological veins define Merton's reflections on the Christ. My observations will attempt to identify and to systematize that christological vision.

In one sense, what I will attempt in this exploration-survey does not afford any 'new' insights. Benedictine Jean Leclercq reminds and encourages us in that conviction, even while nominating Merton be mentioned 'with the Fathers of the Early Church and those of the Middle Ages'. 'Not only, as do all Christians, did he live the same mystery as they did, but he lives and expresses it in the same way.' His humanism, Leclercq ventures, just as the Fathers', 'drew from the culture of their own times in order to make it a part of their inner experience'.[2] Rather, what endures in this legacy of Merton's monastic instincts and spirituality is the *experience* of Christ as the center of his extraordinary reflections for a contemporary and transitional epoch.

We might venture to style this paper a 'revisionist' scrutiny of Merton's christological thought. Indeed, we find familiar and orthodox formulas, the anticipated signposts and vernacular through which he engaged contemporary theological ferment. But having termed the character of this investigation 'revisionist', one wonders: Is it already incumbent upon us to re-focus the Merton portrait? I think so. For the hagiographers and image-artificers already have set about sculpting a towering figure of the twentieth century's most famous monk. And, much to Merton's chagrin—though he appeared more and more resigned to the inevitable—that is expected, even necessary, for a figure of reliable yet creative transition in a world of turmoil. It is when we examine the features of that likeness to Merton that inquiry begins. Is the Thomas Merton which much of the literature presents recognizable? What about the contours and gestures, the posture attributed to Merton by his image-makers?

A staggering interdisciplinary task remains ahead in systematizing and integrating the multi-faceted personality of Thomas Merton. I like to image the integral Mertonian vision as something like the six vantage-points or faces of a cube: Monk, Mystic, Poet, Social Critic, Theologian, and Ecumenist. From each of those at-times scattered Merton enthusiasms, the mystery of Christ radiates.

The project of systematizing and correlating Merton's work remains complicated by his eclectic habit. He was by nature spontaneous, addressing questions and discussions as an *essayist*. Readers need only examine the genesis of his books—collections of essays, articles quilted together 'topically' and (at times) loosely fashioned into a single volume. Likewise, the *journal* style remained a tool implanted from his early French and British habitat. While the immediacy of a personal, autobiographical dimension remains the power of Merton's writing, much 'occasional' Merton grates uncomfortably against the larger, especially later, spirituality. Theology as 'story', we hear loudly today, is the reliable method. Witness the entrance of Merton to notoriety in the modern version of Augustine's *Confessions*, his *The Seven Storey Mountain*. And yet even the hazards and limits of this essayist-journalist-autobiographer tradition caught up with Merton.

'Perspective' and 'context' remain keys in our approach to Merton. Let us label it formally the hermeneutical task we bring to Merton's work. He voiced this very concern in a 1967 interview, being willing, for example, to 'accept *The Seven Storey Mountain* as a point of departure', but more anxious to 'depart from it and keep moving'.

> I left the book behind many years ago. Certainly it was a book I had to write, and it says a great deal of what I have to say; but if I had to write it over again, it would be handled in a very different way, and in a different idiom. It is a youthful book, too simple, in many ways, too crude. Everything is laid out in black and white. . . . I still did not understand the real problems of the monastic life, or even of the Christian life either. And I was still dealing in a crude theology that I had learned as a novice: a clean-cut division between the natural and supernatural, God and the world, sacred and secular, with boundary lines that were supposed to be quite evident. . . . Unfortunately, the book was a best-seller, and has become a kind of edifying legend. . . . I am doing my best to live it down. . . . I rebel against it and maintain my basic human right *not* to be turned into a Catholic myth for children in parochial schools.[3]

Similarly Merton tenaciously refused to turn the humanity of God into a 'myth' (I use the word cautiously, meaning, like Merton, an unreliable rendition) for Christians. It is here, at the intersection of autobiography and theology, that Merton's consistent presentation of the Christ mystery earns its extraordinary devotional impact.

The Columbia University philosophy professor, Daniel Clark Walsh, Merton's spiritual father, captured this essential Merton in the homily he delivered at Gethsemani ten years ago (17 December, 1968) for Merton's funeral. He spoke of 'what I personally regard as his true greatness: that deep and abiding sense of God in Christ—and of God in man through Christ—of Christ in his Church—Christ in each one of us through the action of his Holy Spirit—the Christ of God who in the spirit of his love lives in the people of God—the Christ who is in us when we love and serve one another in true brotherhood—when we realize that we are not our brother's keeper but our brother's brother'.

Without detailing the pilgrimage of Merton's christological thought (and perhaps it does not warrant the formal, systematic nomenclature of a 'Christology'), I discover a continuity, richly developed, in Merton's writing about the Christ. Let us turn to the peaks and lifelines of that journey.

The Seven Storey Mountain rehearses for us his discovery of the Christ. It was his guru, Dan Walsh, who stirred the waters of Merton's new life in Christ. By dubbing Merton an 'augustinian', Walsh located Merton's larval theological mind. Thomas Merton grew enthused with the prospect of being in the spiritual company of Bonaventure, Scotus, Anselm; in the 'spiritual, mystical, voluntaristic and practical way' of spirituality as distinct from Thomas' speculative school. As an augustinian, Merton discovered that his relationship to God was in the order of pure love; as Dan Walsh compressed this tradition, it was a philosophy of the *Person*. The lineage of Merton's spirituality emerges. Under the mentorship of Étienne Gilson, Walsh had written his doctoral dissertation on Duns Scotus and his philosophy. This franciscan strain of medieval philosophy and theology became the crossroads of Merton's later reflections on the Christ. On the question of 'Why the "redemption"?', 'What is the primary reason for the Son of God becoming man?', Scotus' point of departure is radically distinct from Thomas'. For Scotus, Incarnation is *inevitable* because of love; for Thomas, Incarnation is *necessary* to redeem us.

This Scotist contribution to Christology echoes the Church's patristic thinkers—the Greek Fathers—with their intuition of the cosmic Christ. A confidence in creation, grace building on nature, stood waiting for Merton's discovery—what I call Merton's later 'raids on the tradition', his patristic research in the nineteen fifties issuing in books like *The New Man* (1961) and *New Seeds of Contemplation* (1961).

In fact, Merton's prior experience images this link with that Christology of the Greek Fathers. In nascent form he pondered, he says, 'for the first time in my life. . . Who this Person was that men called Christ'. This came during his eighteenth year, 1933, while vacationing in Rome before beginning his riotous year at Cambridge. Bored with the ruins of pagan Rome, he gravitated uncomprehendingly to the cathedrals, the churches. There he confronted the *mosaics*, those unique roman forms of art that expressed the iconic Eastern Empire traditions imaging the Christ.

> These mosaics told me more that I had ever known of the doctrines of a God of infinite power, wisdom and love. Who had yet become Man, and revealed in his Manhood the infinity of power, wisdom and love that was His Godhead. . . . I grasped them implicitly—I had to, in so far as the mind of the artist reached my own mind, and spoke to it his conception of his thought.[4]

A sermon at Corpus Christi Church while he was a Columbia student flirting with Catholicism dramatized this same mystery of Incarnation. The experience of this central christian mystery transformed Merton. He 'looked about. . . at a new world',[5] he wrote, where all was transfigured, even the ugly facades of Broadway and Columbia's environs.

At the same time, without exercising that ecumenical sensitivity he later developed, Merton rejected Huxley's philosophy because 'in discarding his family's tradition of materialism he had followed the old Protestant groove back into the heresies that make the material creation evil of itself'.[6] Merton could not tolerate such seeming suspicion of the doctrine of Incarnation.

It is at first a curious turn for an augustinian. We might expect more Platonism—but as Jean Leclercq points out, Merton had the ability of going to the essence of a passage (or author) and making it his own. The primacy of love is his legacy from Augustine. As Abbot Flavian Burns of Gethsemani pointed out in his homily at the death of Dan Walsh (who died on Augustine's feast, 28 August, 1976), one of the most often-used Augustine texts Dan shared with his students was 'God is more intimate to me than I am to myself'. Incarnation communicated the totality of that intimacy in Merton's understanding of God's love.

In his 1938 thesis on William Blake, Merton discovered the incarnational dynamic that achieves beauty. The mystic-poet looks through matter into eternity. 'Clarity' is the 'glory of form shining through matter.'[7] The route became even more directly incarnational and christological in his sortie into the poetry of G. M. Hopkins, the intended subject of his doctoral dissertation. The Scotus link, a fransciscan-bonaventurean heritage, is germane to any serious study of Hopkins. (Although we have precious little outside Merton's own poetry to trace his appreciation of Hopkins.)

Where does the Merton pilgrimate go from Columbia University? There was the brief teaching stint at St Bonaventure's, and the struggle with a career in Friendship House activity. Finally, three days after Pearl Harbor's ordeal, Merton was walking through the arch of Gethsemani Abbey. It is almost a decade before we get much of a glimpse of his life cloistered in monastic silence. And what irony greeted his autobiography—fame and celebrity shadowed him from that literary event!

The questions we pose are gathered into a focal inquiry: What had monastic experience and formation contributed to Merton's spirituality? Certainly the liturgical and communal life heightened his insight into the Christ. And the contemplative and mystical traditions were a quiet oasis where Merton drank deeply. Through the forties and well into the decade of the fifties Merton raided the christian tradition—by osmosis and absorption. When that burlap-covered volume, *Seeds of Contemplation*, appeared, 1949, the contours of a personally-adapted spirituality, an idiom, were defined.

The contemplative questions were curled into the search: Who am I? Major directions in his spirituality were announced in the ascetic journey; solitude, integrity, humility, liberty, detachment, renunciation were traced in chapters addressed to an audience 'in the world'. Monks, he claims, quest to discover their own true selves *in Christ*. This, he continues, is the only reason for entering the monastery—to experience the *mercy* of God. The dynamics of this 'transforming union' that the monk experiences are the life project of denying an illusory, false self. The action of God's love for us (the incarnate Christ) calls us to be a unique person and, in that discovery of 'who' we are *in Christ*, to give glory to him.

> You seem to be the same person and you are the same person that you have always been: in fact you are more yourself than you have ever been before. You have only just begun to exist. You feel as if you were at last fully born. All that went before was a mistake, a fumbling preparation for birth. Now you have come into your element. And yet now you have become nothing. You have sunk to the center of your own poverty.... You are free to go in and out of infinity.[8]

The motif of this declaration—new life—is one familiar in Merton, playing on the Christ-event as an 'emptying', the *kenosis* of the ancient pauline hymn in Philippians 2:5–11. In an important chapter of *Seeds of Contemplation* entitled 'Through a Glass', Merton images the cosmic existence of God's humanity in Christ. He reflects on this mystical intuition of the 'magnifying glass' of Christ's humanity concentrating the 'rays of God's light and fire to a point that sets fire to the spirit of man'.[9]

A wealth of christological themes weaves through this text. And in the next major work, *The Ascent to Truth* (1951), an harmonious chord is struck. This is a curious work in its method, scholastic theology and vocabulary. Merton attempts to juxtapose John of the Cross's mysticism and the system of Thomas Aquinas. While ponderous and at times pedantic in style, the work is significant as a defense of mysticism (of Gregory of Nyssa and John of the Cross) against popular caricatures of Gnosticism or anti-incarnational spirituality. Incarnation—God's humanity—recurs like a refrain in this study. 'God's revelation of Himself to the world in His Incarnate Word forms the heart and substance of all Christian mystical contemplation',[10] he concludes. A radical transformation of consciousness is the response to the Christ. The dramatic imagery of Merton's prose-poetry puts it: 'God must move and reveal Himself and shake the world within the soul and rise from His sleep like a giant'. The mystic is transformed 'like a bar of iron in the heat of a furnace'.[11] Humanity is not destroyed, but transfigured.

The books that issued from Merton's solitude at Gethsemani in the fifties—*The Last of the Fathers* (1954), *No Man is an Island* (1955), *Thoughts in Solitude* (1958)—return to an idiom of personal reflection, a dialogue with the reader that signaled Merton's refusal ever to return to the theological voice of scholasticism. He calls the reflections 'personal' and avows 'leaving systems to others'. (Though he continued to study comtemporary theological literature, he was uncomfortable with its academic distancing.) Marian reflections in his study of Bernard of Clairvaux, *The Last of the Fathers*, are the threshold for reflections on the Christ, but a key is discovered in the other two works: 'Person' is the recovery of my 'deepest self', recovery of identity in Christ. 'The meaning of my life', he insists in *No Man is an Island*, 'is seen, above all, in my integration in the mystery of Christ.'[12]

The incarnational motif continues in *Thoughts in Solitude* (1958). 'If we are to become spiritual, we must remain men. And if there were not evidence of this everywhere in theology, the Mystery of the Incarnation itself would be ample proof of it.'[13] For man, 'Although he is a traveller in time, he has opened his eyes, for a moment, in eternity.... Christ, the Incarnate Word, is the Book of Life in Whom we read God.'[14]

There is a subtle temptation to envision Merton, the scribe, wistfully churning out popular books of spirituality. But we must not overlook the responsibilities assumed and opportunities for learning engaged by Merton, Master of Scholastics and Master of Novices. It was this teacher's unashamed learning that was frequently reflected in his books. Much pauline reading and reflection—the cosmic Christ—grew out of the reading of French biblical literature that went into preparations for a course on Sanctity in the Epistles of Saint Paul in 1954. Perhaps most important in those resources are references he makes to the work of Hans Urs Von Balthasar's *La Liturgie Cosmique*.[15] Irenaeus and Maximus the Confessor occupy prominent roles in that study. The familiar themes of Greek Fathers—'recapitulation' and 'divinization'— forecast his next book, a pauline-dubbed *The New Man*.

As early as 1954, Thomas Merton wrote to his Columbia literature professor, Mark Van Doren, that he was working on a book about the Greek Fathers which he would entitle *Existential Communion*.[16] The genesis of *The New Man* as that intended text evidences a marked maturity in both pauline thought and the Eastern Fathers. This often overlooked volume is Merton's assimilation of rich theological material. Building on the pauline ambiguity about 'the world', he traced the existential battle between man's true (spiritual) self *in Christ,* and the false, illusory self (*agonia*). The cosmic Christ of Paul and the 'recapitulation' theories of salvation of the Eastern Church give evidence of Merton becoming steeped in their Christology. Most of all, Merton resists the Promethean mysticism—an 'error' he calls it—that takes no account of anyone but the false Self.[17]

This same christological reflection comes to bear on the work that I consider his single most significant volume for spirituality, *New Seeds of Contemplation*. Revisions from the 1949 text are almost entirely systematic reflections on the Christ. Chapters twenty-one, twenty-two, and twenty-three express much of this. An enormous Merton transition is gained in the summary chapter, 'The General Dance'. The incarnational maturation of Merton's spirituality resounds in these pages:

> The Lord made the world and made man in order that He Himself might descend into the world, that He Himself might become Man. When He regarded the world he was about to make He saw His Wisdom, as a man-child, 'playing in the world, playing before Him at all times'. And He reflected, 'my delights are to be with the children of men'.[18]

And so, he surmises: 'The presence of God in His World as its Creator depends on no one but Him. His presence in the world as man, depends, in some measure, upon men'. But he quickly adds: 'Not that we can do anything to change the mystery of the Incarnation in itself; but we are able to decide whether we ourselves, and that portion of the world which is ours, shall become *aware* of His presence, consecrated by it, and transfigured in its light'. He concludes: 'The world and time are the dance of the Lord in emptiness'. He invites us to 'cast our solemnity to the winds' and join the cosmic Christ, transforming all creation.[19]

That may sound quite dionysian—indeed! But a sobering maintenance of that optismism remained in the next transition of Merton's spirituality, early in 1960, in the Preface to *Disputed Questions* and his introduction to *The Widsom of the Desert.* The perspective was that of 'christian humanism and personalism'. Merton has grown uncomfortable with the idea of the monk as one who 'takes flight from the wicked world and turns his back on it completely in order to lose himself in antiquarian ritualism, or worse still, to delve introspectively into his own psyche'.[20]

It was in large part the drama of his correspondence with Boris Pasternak and the ordeal of the 1958 Nobel Prize in unfriendly Russia that drew Merton into the crucible of humanity in his own era. The voice of monastic protest stirred to witness. He identifies the single theme coursing through the book (a disparate collection) as the relation of the *person* to the social organization; more traditionally put, solitude vs. community. Merton resonates with the protest religious, aesthetic, and mystical of *Doctor Zhivago.* While Pasternak was not a christian apologist, Merton discovered a great affinity; Pasternak's vision is 'essentially Christian'.

> That is the trouble: the problematical quality of Pasternak's 'Christianity' lies in the fact that it is reduced to the barest and most elementary essentials: intense awareness of all cosmic and human reality as 'life in Chirst,' and the consequent plunge into love as the only dynamic and creative force which really honors this 'Life' by creating itself anew in Life's—Christ's—image.

> It was not until after the coming of Christ that time and man could breathe freely. Man does not die in a ditch like a dog—but at home in history, while the work toward the conquest of death is in full swing; he dies sharing in this work.[21]

Dehumanization—man's alienation from his history, death like the dog in the ditch—gripped Merton. In *The Wisdom of the Desert* he reappraised his monastic 'involvement' with the world. The monk is the most hospitable of men, he affirmed. He helps the world recover from its illusory, egocentric self and live 'in Christ'.

The charter for Merton's attention to the dehumanizing plague that throttled the world of the turbulent 1960s—that arena of moral crisis—was being written during the Second Vatican Council. Merton was an enthusiastic observer. In his eclipsed volume, *Redeeming the Time* (a British edition appeared in 1965; parts are printed in the 1965 American edition, *Seeds of Destruction*), Merton addressed this new attitude of the Church toward the world. *Gaudium et Spes*, the Constitution on the Church in the Modern World, he remarked, found the Church now 'prepared to recognize that the secular world in its very secularity has values worthy of honour, and that men who have nothing to do with the Church and her faith may still be helping the human race to advance towards its spiritual maturity'.[22]

He analyzes Karl Rahner's notion of the 'Diaspora' Church as a moment of great choice and affirmation by the Christian world. And in what seems to be one of the 'Copernican revolutions' Rahner discusses, Merton himself began to consider 'Grace' outside the scholastic categories of 'obedential potency'. He summarizes an old consideration: 'Christian anthropology is not yet fully clear about the person, since what belongs to the whole Christian person has traditionally been ascribed to the *soul* (part of the person only) and to grace. The Christian theology of grace needs to be reviewed in the light of a new and deeper metaphysic of the person and of love.'[23] That was the *process* in Merton's own thought. He suggests that 'so personalistic is the humanism' of Vatican II that the Constitution on the Church in the Modern World might be renamed 'The Human Person in the Modern World'. 'It sees the meaning both of the human person and of the whole family of man in the light of the Incarnation.'[24]

Little wonder that by the time of his next important book, *Raids on the Unspeakable* (1966) he confessed in a lyrical prologue that 'I love you the best'. A citation from Gabriel Marcel inscribed as a frontespiece to the volume is piercing in its clarity: 'Today the first and perhaps the only duty of the philosopher is to defend man against himself: to defend against that extraordinary temptation toward inhumanity to which—almost without being aware of it—so many human beings today have yielded.' Quoting Berdyaev in the prologue to the book, he speaks of eschatology not as an invitation to 'escape to a private heaven: it is a call to transfigure the evil and stricken world'—the good world where Christ dwelled and is still present among us. So comes the patristic tone of his appeal: 'Guard the image of man for it is the image of God'.[25]

The fully-human had become the arena of God's humanity in Christ. Merton's protest against dehumanization—whether in the searing impact of his 'Letters to a White Liberal' in *Seeds of Destruction* (1965) where he addressed the American race war, or on Vietnam in the same pages or the essays of *Faith and Violence* (1968)—flowed from his incarnational spirituality. This experience of the Christ as God's transforming humanity, revealing to us the fullness of our human condition (suffering and glory), plunged Merton into social criticism.

In an extraordinary essay in *Raids on the Unspeakable*, Merton concentrates a magnificent reflection on the Christ. In a rare, poignant, consciously-eschatological theology, he speaks of the opposition between the secular anxieties that tend toward a hope for a violent end; and an eschatology that is 'revealed fulfillment'.[26]

'When the perfect and ultimate message, the joy which is *The Great Joy,* explodes silently upon the world, there is no longer any room for sadness.' 'All things,' Merton says, 'are transfigured' in the coming of the Word. He deepens this examination of Incarnation. In Christ, the 'fulness of time' comes to the world. And it is necessary that there be no room at the inn—'there had to be some other place. In fact, the inn was the last place in the world for the birth of the Lord.' This scene of Christ's birth is amid the 'time of the Crowd', mass man. The Word is spoken amid a 'display of power, *hubris*,' the census, the amassing of humanity (the whole world) for registration, numbering, 'identification'. For what purpose, Merton asks? Taxation and military conscription in the empire.

It was therefore impossible that the Word should lose Himself by being born into shapeless and passive mass. He had indeed emptied Himself, taken the form of God's servant, man. But he did not empty Himself to the point of being mass man, faceless man. It was therefore right that there should be no room for him in a crowd that had been called together as an eschatological sign. His being born outside that crowd is even more of a sign. That there is no room for Him is a sign of the end.[27]

To a world of rumor and noise, the bazaar of census, the kerygma of 'Good News' came in poverty. 'Christ comes uninvited,' Merton records. Resisting the 'demonic' temptation, Merton speaks of true eschatology as not 'end' but 'final beginning, the definitive birth into a new creation. It is not the last gasp of exhausted possibilities but the first taste of all that is beyond conceiving as actual.'

He ends with a question: 'But can we believe it?'[28] We must search for his answer in the legacy of his last years of ecumenical dialogue and poetic experiment.

In the arena of social criticism Merton's voice questioned old patterns: that the pious layman *endured* 'in a good way' by living a simulated monastic life 'in the world'; that baroque *external* monasticism had dissolved in favor of the monk as a 'marginal man', in dialogue and conversation with the world.

In the newly-embraced diaspora Church Merton set about reworking his spirituality. Perhaps nowhere was his reappraisal more manifest than in his ecumenical explorations. While we cannot venture into his asian studies here, I do find that his dialogue with theologians of other christian traditions matured his own devotional reflections on the Christ. He was a long way from the *Mountain's* dogmatism (one writer recently termed that early Merton as 'bigoted') to his interaction with other christological thought. It is no coincidence that he could quote approvingly from Karl Barth, 'Tell me how it stands with your Christology and I shall tell you who you are'.[29]

In *Conjectures of a Guilty Bystander,* a collection of journal pages from the late 1950s and early 1960s, Merton offers not a book 'of professional ecumenism', but a personal 'version of the world' in the 1960s. There is transparency and unsystematized flow to Merton's thought. In *Redeeming the Time* Merton refined his monastic renewal: monasticism is not arrogantly to bring the world to submit 'to the feet of Christ in his traditional and familiar aspect (the Christ painted on wood and covered with gold in the sanctuaries)'. Rather, Merton notes, it is monasticism 'which hopes the living Christ will reveal himself in these meek ikons of flesh and blood hidden in the world, solitary and humble men of prayer'.[30] The monk himself had come to embody what Merton had first glimpsed in those ancient mosaics—iconic presence, a hopeful sign of transformation.

The overture to *Conjectures* Merton entitled 'Barth's Dream'. An anecdote there about a dream Barth had of Mozart's reply to his Protestantism belongs to some of Merton's most memorable pages. Mozart's accusations against a Protestantism 'all in the head' captures both Barth and the Gethsemani monk. Barth is, Merton summarizes, 'Unconsciously seeking to awaken, perhaps, the Sophianic Mozart in himself, the central Wisdom that comes in tune with the divine and cosmic music and is saved by love.'[31] Incarnation is paramount in Barth's own theology. Reflecting on Barth's 1931 Christmas sermon, Merton delights in what he discovers. He identified with Barth's affirmation that the Light born at Bethlehem is 'certainly *the most unprincipled reality one can imagine*'. The solidarity between both writers is forged in Barth's query: 'Is perhaps an unconditional faith in all sorts of principles not the typically German form of unbelief?' He agreed with Barth's insistence on the character of revelation: Incarnation is an act of *gratuity*, not to be explained by reason, but to be responded to in faith as 'gift'. So also he admired Barth's earlier work on Anselm, *Fides Quaerens Intellectum*. The mystery of the Cross, Merton concurs, takes its meaning not in terms of blood vengeance but the mystery of *love* united with justice. Interest in Anselm's *Cur Deus Homo* sparked Merton's enthusiasm; as Merton points out, his medieval favorite, Duns Scotus, 'is in many ways a disciple and interpreter of Anselm'.[32]

The affinity for Barth's work is rooted in this rich terrain. Certainly the 1956 work, *The Humanity of God* by Barth, drew upon the depths of a common vision. Barth elected to speak of the 'humanity' of God and not his 'divinity'. For Barth, God's relative-qualities—omniscience and power—can be sacrificed. Two absolute qualities, the absolute *authority* of God and the *love and freedom* of the God, are maintained when God presides over the whole creation in humility. In the incarnation we see the freedom and love of God that permits him in all humility to be for us 'God for a second time', as Barth would phrase it.

Merton tempered his reading of Barth by noting his disagreement without specifying details. They would certainly include an uncomfortableness with Barth's Calvinism, his conviction that the finite is ultimately incapable of the infinite. In this sense, Barth's Neo-Orthodoxy confronted Merton's more thoroughly incarnational confidence. The image is used of Barth's Christology that it depicts the incarnation as a 'tangent', not penetrating the human condition, but merely contacting or intersecting with the circumference of humanity. Nevertheless, the primacy of God's Word in love, God's humanity, riveted Merton's attention.

If Barth was a discovery for Merton, the work of Dietrich Bonhoeffer was a revelation. While Barth would speak of the transformation of persons 'in faith' by *religious* categories, Bonhoeffer addressed the transformation of the world in *human* categories. His appraisal of the human was far more confident than Barth's. Merton's optimism thrives in the dialogue:

> The news that God has become man strikes at the very heart of an age in which the good and the wicked regard either scorn for man or the idolization of man as the highest attainable wisdom.[33]

'Christendom,' Merton said, 'must recognize the "embarrassing truth" of the world into whose history the revelation of God as man broke through profoundly modifying all human structures and cultural developments'.[34] Quoting Bonhoeffer, he repeats: 'the humanity He accepted was, and remains, in all truth, *our* humanity'. False spiritualism takes us on an escalator to unworldliness; Bonhoeffer orients us back to a true christian 'worldliness'. The Christian choice is 'simply a complete, trusting and abandoned consent to the "yes" of God in Christ'.[35] Bonhoeffer's 'worldliness' Merton locates as God's presence 'in the world *in man*', an elementary New Testament teaching from 1 Corinthians 3:17.[36] Merton returns to Pope John XXIII's *Pacem in Terris* and its anthropocentric focus, man 'sanctified in the Incarnation'. The great threat, re-

sisted and reversed by Bonhoeffer Merton insists, comes from a reversal of the meaning of incarnation: 'Man's refusal of himself'.[37]

The Bonhoeffer dialogue ignites new dimensions of conscience
in Merton's monastic protest. I consider the re-evaluation it pro-
voked one of Merton's more searching final ordeals. His reading
notes on Bonhoeffer date from the time of his retirement to the
hermitage at Gethsemani, August 1965. It is beautifully ironic that
his struggle with Bonhoeffer's 'worldliness' should coincide with
his hermitic nativity. The main text from Bonhoeffer he was reading at this juncture was the *Ethics*. In the midst of refining a sense
of 'social responsibility', Merton unearthed Bonhoeffer's accusation that 'medieval monasticism' is a misunderstanding 'escape'
from this world. I consider that the title for this volume, while
perhaps already in Merton's imagination, owes much to Merton's
wrestling with the challenging thought of the imprisoned German
Lutheran pastor. A notebook selection dated October 1965, explains the aptness of a repentant, converted 'monk', a guilty bystander, who comes to embrace the world ever more boldly. He
entitles the lengthy excursus 'My place in the world'. 'Obviously
in my early writings I said things about "the world" that had a
gnostic or manichaean flavor about them.' He goes on to say that
he no longer accepts such statements, but there is in the tradition a
basis for them—the 'negative view' of 'the world' that balances the
positive in the New Testament. He further specifies his 'anti-
worldliness' as that of genuine medieval monasticism, not the reac-
tionary stance of Pius IX's 'Syllabus of Errors': 'I think my writing
is split in two categories as regards this question. "The world"
seen in terms of nature, of manual work, of literature, culture,
Asian philosophy etc. etc. is fully *accepted*. Also "man" in his
historic reality. What is not accepted—the world in its contemporary confusions.' At this point Merton admits to not having
faced the technocracy and the crises of contemporary culture with
anything but pessimism. Perhaps his own harshest critic, he continues: 'There may be some truth in my pessimism, but the pessimism itself has an evil root, and instead of getting the root out I have
been cultivating it in the name of "spirituality" or what you will.
This is no longer honest. My task is to come to terms *completely*

with the world in which I live and of which I am a *part*, because this is the world redeemed by Christ—even the world of Auschwitz.' There cannot be a compromise with Auschwitz, Hiroshima, or Southern racism, he insists. But, on the other hand, 'they too must be "redeemed". The great task of redemption is in *America* which imagines itself Christian! That is why I am here, and must stay here.'[38]

No longer relying on the 'God of the gaps', as Bonhoeffer termed this inadequate theological legacy, Merton turned his appreciation of the German revisionist of secularity to the project of contemporary radical theologians, the American 'God is dead' idiom. His appraisal of it bears on his reflections on the Christ. While J. A. T. Robinson (author of the controversial *Honest to God*) and his disciples won praise from Merton for their apt diagnosis of 'diaspora' Christianity, he judged the movement as theologically lamed. Essays in *Faith and Violence* endorse their diagnosis of the contemporary impasse of faith without subscribing to their claim to be descendents loyal to Bonhoeffer. It was the 'absolute religious kenoticism' by which Christianity is even *emptied* of God that halted Merton. He scolded the radical theologians for what he dubbed 'the death of history', and therefore the loss of biblical eschatology, and he found them stopping at the Cross. God does not rise again 'to resume his former transcendence,' Merton surmised. 'He remains only as immanent, empty, and hidden in man and in the world.'[39] Merton found Thomas Altizer's *The New Apocalypse* redeeming radical theology by relying on William Blake's work. No surprise that Merton's own appreciation of Blake would produce some common bond! However, in summation, we must ask whether Merton's reading of the directions of radical theology and its Christ was reliable? The subsequent work of Robinson, especially this New Testament scholar's *The Human Face of God,* presents a Christology of God's 'Man for us' that resonates strongly with Merton's own reflections on the Christ. Indeed, we must face the prospect of Merton's failure to appreciate the directions of The Radical Theology Movement. What this contemporary theological enterprise searched to express, he suggested, was already familiar in the traditions of apophatic mysticism (a 'knowing by unknowing'). Their narrow response risked failing to come to grips with deeper currents and christological developments in the 'God is Dead' school.

In this same light we evaluate Merton's somewhat terse and limited reading of Pierre Teilhard de Chardin. It is surprising that while Merton and Teilhard are grounded in the Christology of the Greek Fathers (a transfigured creation), they never entirely converge. Merton's hesitant and half-hearted recommendation of Teilhard, at least, disappoints. His familiarity with Teilhard seems limited. An unpublished review article of *The Divine Milieu* as well as a record of his reading of deLubac's *The Religion of Pierre Teilhard de Chardin* are major resources. Though he would applaud Teilhard as 'the symbol of the new Catholic outlook upon the modern world' and praise him as the one who 'can speak the language of contemporary man without totally compromising his faith in God and in Christ',[40] Merton's aversion to the system of science aroused a marked hesitation which smacks of the Barthian aversion to 'principled reality', undermining the *gratuity* of an incarnational God. Yet Merton could gravitate to an enthused appreciation of Teilhard: Teilhard's perspectives are Paul's 'recapulation of all things in Christ', the cosmic Christ:

> The radiant focus of all reality is not only the Divine Being, but God Incarnate, Jesus Christ. The Spirit of man exists for Christ. But material things exist for man in Christ. Not . . . (as) obstacles. . . . He gave Himself to us in matter sanctified and sacramentalized. . . . (This is the) sublimely eucharistic heart of the spirituality of Teilhard. . . . The mystical Christ (and not merely) The Risen Lord dwelling in heaven.[41]

In his commentary on Albert Camus' *The Plague* Merton ventured his most direct critique of Teilhard. While we remember that in Bangkok Merton would acknowledge the Marxists' enthusiasm for Teilhard and his great contribution, Merton had resisted the scientist's alleged devotion to a mystique, a system. Camus, he said, had also protested the sacrifice of man in his present condition to the lure of an ideology attracting him to some 'future'. Teilhard, he judged, opts for 'an optimism which tends to look at existential evil and suffering through the small end of the telescope',[42] unable to anguish with Camus over the murder of an innocent child, but able to glory over the new atomic-powered bomb without pausing over its human toll. Perhaps as revisionists appraise Merton on Teilhard, they will want to search for more convergence between these two poets of twentieth-century christological reflections. Indeed, Merton's hesitation about Teilhard will seem hard to defend.

Our panorama of Merton's ecumenical dialogue on the Christ demands a cursory glance at an intergral partner, the Greek Orthodox tradition. A student of the Greek Fathers, Merton did research and showed enthusiasm for contemporary Orthodox spirituality. Bulgakov, Meyendorff, and Schmemann are prominent in his reading. Alexander Schmemann's *Sacraments and Orthodoxy* captures the essence of the tradition in Merton's late readings. He reviews the book and announces it as 'my legacy' to the novices as he retired to the hermitage in August 1965. In that book, he saw 'life as "cosmic liturgy,"'... man as restored by the Incarnation to his place in that liturgy so that with Christ and in Christ he resumes his proper office as high priest in a world that is essentially liturgical and eucharistic.'[43]

Most notable is Merton's appreciation of the transformation that lies central to the Orthodox tradition: again, it is the sense of the icon as mediating God's humanity. It is here that Merton expresses one of his most direct reflections on the cross as integral to the paschal mystery. Christianity often appears, Merton quoted Schmemann, 'to preach that if men will try hard enough to live Christian lives the crucifixion can somehow be reversed'. We cannot, however, evade or ignore death, or neutralize the force of the Cross. The victory of Resurrection is *through* the humility of the Cross—God's humanity—which declares Christ's presence *in the world* as risen Lord. This is a distinct affirmation of the secularists' great truth which Orthodoxy renews.

The voice of Merton's protest resounds most powerfully a Christic consciousness in the much-neglected poetry of this talented Trappist. To turn to his poetry we observe the familiar thesis of Romano Guardini that artistic imagination precedes theological reflection by a decade, even a generation.[44] Merton's meditation on the incarnate Christ exercised a profound influence through his poetry, also 'Word become flesh'.

The regeneration of Christianity finds a loyal ally in poetry. Merton's own confidence in the humanistic art strengthened as he matured. He gained momentum as a poet. There is a development from what George Woodcock styles the 'poetry of the choir' to the 'poetry of the desert'. Each is etched with that 'sacramental realism' (as Nathan Scott likes to term the quality of the religious imagination) which radiates a transfigured humanity.[45] In one of his early poems, 'Song for Our Lady of Cobre', Merton remarked how the inspired lyric set him on a path of similar poems for several years.[46]

This is a kinetic poem, flowing with motion, almost choreography. Meditating on the black madonna of Cuba, the virgin of devotion, its simple transition from 'black...white' urges a rhythmic meditation. There is, in technical terms, great immaturity in this poem's reliance on simile ('like' recurs throughout the poem). But the cosmology of the poem, reflected in a 'ring of stars', points to the Christ-event as transforming the earth. This is signalled in the 'pieces of the mosaic, earth' getting up and flying away 'like birds'. Although the poem is naïve in its expression, the confidence in transformation and the very apt image of the mosaic's intricate pattern draws our memories back to those mosaics in which Merton discovered the Christ.

Images of transformation inhabit Merton's poems. But always the dynamic is that of incarnation, the full *humanization* of persons and the earth process. Creation is worthy of God's Christ. Indeed, in this strategy Merton reflects much of what Kierkegaard rehearses as God's 'journey toward us', a most apt revelation of the fully human. Perhaps Merton's most famous poem, 'For My Brother, Reported Missing in Action, 1943', thrives on such metaphors (not the simpler similes) of transformation. The humility of God on the cross of suffering and death embodies this fully incarnational dynamic in John-Paul's death and Merton's transformed consciousness.

The currents of the New Criticism as a literary charter merged happily with Merton's incarnational consciousness. Interestingly,

Merton's first published book review in the New York papers was of John Crowe Ransom's *The World's Body*.[47] There prospered a confidence in the poem as a 'verbal icon' (as William K. Wimsatt captured the sense of this critical theory in his book of that same title). Perhaps the finest example of that success in Merton's short poems arrives in 'Night-Flowering Cactus', a poem Merton's friend Bob Lax has dubbed 'his spiritual autobiography'. The landscape of 'desert' dominates the geography of the early monastic centuries. It declares the 'marginality' of the monk. But more, its poverty, aridity, and isolation are the environs for the dynamic of transformation. So the first stanza of the poem images the protean hiddenness of the cactus' identity. There is a sacramental quality in this cactus' quiet praise, lifting its 'sudden eucharist' out of 'the earth's unfathomable joy'. The images of void, poverty, 'virginal thirst' are in harmony with the 'world's body', which is mosaic-like in its intricacy and wholeness. The quality of 'mystery' (*sacramentum*) is simultaneously to reveal and to conceal. So the yawning 'white cavern without explanation' becomes the silent bell in the next stanza. The echo of contemplative union with God transforms. Quietly, silently, isolated in the solitude of the desert, the cactus flower ('bell', too) blossoms. In the emptiness and barrenness of the desert, the 'impeccable' humanity of this personified cactus offers its poignant beauty. From darkness and solitude, the fragrance of the flower lures. The 'bird. . . flies' from the mosaic of the desert's earthen tones, reminiscent of those icon–painting techniques, using only earth's elements, pure, unadulterated elements like the egg and natural pigments. They are transfigured in the corona of gold. The fully human figures are transformed into a third dimension of spirituality by the affirmation of earth. In later poems I judge that Merton was even more successful in similar mosaics of earth.

The articulateness of Merton's own critical measure of other poets afford us unique insight about his poetic project. And in a review of the work of musicologist-poet Louis Zukofsky he has offered one of his most enlightening and revealing statements. He opens 'Paradise Bugged': 'All really valid poetry (poetry that is fully alive, and asserts its reality by its power to generate imaginative life) is a kind of recovery of paradise. Not that the poet comes up with a report that he, an unusual man, has found his own way back into Eden; but the living line and the generative association, the new sound, the music, the structure, are somehow grounded in a renewal of vision and hearing so that he who reads and understands recognizes that here is a new start, a new creation. Here the world gets another chance. . .another start in life, in hope, in imagination.'[48]

It is this mythic vocation of the poet that Merton discovers in his own monastic identity. There is a kindred religious dimension in the poet's work. An article in 1968 on 'Symbolism: Communication or Communion?'[49] testifies to this ability of the symbolic imagination to contain 'in itself a structure which awakens our consciousness to a new awareness of the inner meaning of life and of reality itself'. This Zen-mindfulness is an attention to things in their identity. It dissolves illusion. Symbols are 'in themselves religious realities in their own right', Merton said, 'especially when their nature is sacramental'.

He delighted in the speech of Zukofsky's many children, 'a paradise speech' that addresses things 'familiarly' because it is not alien and 'anticipates nothing but joy'. Merton described Zukofsky as his 'favorite Franciscan'. The 'paradise ear' must hear Zukofsky's poems. 'In fact they cannot be heard except against the vast background of silence and warmth. . . . His poems do not make sense except as part of the whole creation that exists precisely for love, for free, for nothing, unnecessary.'[50]

There is not time to explore the change in Merton's poetics when he announced they were 'on vacation' with *Cables to the Ace* and *The Geography of Lograire*. Suffice it to say that he continued to probe and meditate on the fully human and the sacramental quality of life. The idiom changes abruptly into 'antipoetry', which Merton employed as a tool to shock, cajole, and 'feedback' static to the culture, parodying its deprivation and advertising jargon. It became a matter of salvaging the word, piece by piece, so that 'Language itself [would] get another chance'. Merton referred to both these works as 'mosaics'—once again this more than coincidental image offers the integral but complex detail of the human factor. The chronicles of dehumanization recorded in the cantos of *Lograire* are an odyssey of the world's spiritual consciousness, portrayed with searing compassion. They witness to Merton's tenacious confidence in the humanity of God and his protest against the heresy of Docetism wherever he found the mystery of Incarnation compromised. Indeed, these last testaments, the lengthy poems, are his most problematical but sustained imaginative ventures on the Christ. That transformation of consciousness catalyzed by the poet's imaginative construct presents anew the Christ mystery.

As Merton himself remarked in summarizing Zukofsky's poetry, 'The real subject of the poem',—all his poetry—'is . . . an anticipation that is aware of itself as a question.' The poet shares the reality 'of that question. . . in a way. . . in which it cannot provoke any answer that would appear to dispose of it. So we never go onto the next question. Each poem is very much the same question, but brand new', a venture back to ultimate questions.

This conviction Merton wrote into his poem, 'Elias—Variations on a Theme'. Let us end with its meditation, a suggestion that the cosmic Christ, firstborn of all creation, is that recurrent mystery for the spiritual pilgrimage.

> Here the bird abides
> And sings on top of the forgotten
> Storm. The ground is warm.
> He sings no particular message.
> His hymn has one pattern, no more planned,
> No less perfectly planned
> And no more arbitrary
> Than the pattern in the seed, the salt,
> The snow, the cell, the drop of rain.
>
> . . . .
>
> The free man is not alone as busy men are
> But as birds are. The free man sings
> Alone as universes do. Built
> Upon his own inscrutable pattern
> Clean unmistakable, not invented by himself alone
> Or for himself, but for the universe also.
>
> (iv. 11. 1–13; 21–36)

NOTES

I wish to thank my colleague, the Reverend Eugene L. Zoeller of the faculty of Bellarmine College, for his suggestions and very helpful criticisms during the course of my study and the composition of this essay.

1. 'Concerning the Collection in the Bellarmine College Library—A Statement, November 18, 1963', *Bulletin of The Merton Studies Center*, I (1971) p. 3.
2. Introduction to *Contemplation in a World of Action*, ed. Naomi Burton (Garden City, N.Y.: Doubleday, 1971) p. 18.
3. Thomas McDonnell, 'An Interview With Thomas Merton', *Motive* 27 (October, 1967) pp. 32–33.
4. *The Seven Storey Mountain* (New York: Harcourt, Brace, 1948) pp. 107–10.
5. *Ibid.*, pp. 210–11.
6. *Ibid.*, p. 85.
7. 'Nature and Art in William Blake: An Essay in Interpretation', Department of English and Comparative Literature, Columbia University, February, 1939, pp. 81–82.
8. *The Seven Storey Mountain*, pp. 146–47.
9. *Seeds of Contemplation* (Norfolk, Conn.: New Directions, 1949) p. 91.
10. *The Ascent to Truth* (New York: Harcourt, Brace, 1951) p. 131.
11. *Ibid.*, p. 318.
12. *No Man Is An Island* (New York: Harcourt, Brace, 1955) p. xxiii.
13. *Thoughts in Solitude* (New York: Farrar, Straus and Cudahy, 1958) pp. 46–47.
14. *Ibid.*, p. 96.
15. Paris: Aubier, 1947.
16. Letter of 16 October 1954, Special MS Collections, Columbia University Library.
17. *The New Man*, (New York: Farrar, Straus and Cudahy, 1961) pp. 73–77.
18. *New Seeds of Contemplation* (New York: New Directions, 1961) p. 290.
19. *Ibid.*, pp. 296–97.
20. *Disputed Questions* (New York: Farrar, Straus and Cudahy, 1960) p. x.
21. *Ibid.*, pp. 12, 66.
22. *Redeeming the Time* (London: Burns & Oates, 1966) p. 12.
23. *Ibid.*, pp. 56.
24. *Ibid.*, p. 64.
25. *Raids on the Unspeakable* (New York: New Directions, 1966) p. 6.
26. 'The Time of The End Is the Time of No Room', *Ibid.*, p. 65.
27. *Ibid.*, p. 68. Previous exerpts appear on pp. 65–68.
28. *Ibid.*, pp. 72, 75.
29. *Dogmatics in Outline* (New York: Harper & Row, 1959) p. 66.
30. *Redeeming the Time*, p. 117.
31. *Conjectures of a Guilty Bystander* (Garden City, N.Y.: Doubleday, 1966) p. 3.
32. 'St. Anselm and His Argument', *American Benedictine Review* 17 (1966) p. 261.
33. *Conjectures of a Guilty Bystander*, p. 50.
34. *Ibid.*, pp. 58–59.
35. *Ibid.*, p. 244.
36. *Ibid.*, p. 274.
37. *Ibid.*, pp. 289–93.
38. Working Notebook = 76 '1965—Readings, etc., August to November,' Bellarmine College MS Collection, Louisville, Kentucky.
39. *Faith and Violence: Christian Teaching and Christian Practice* (University of Notre Dame Press, 1968) p. 242.
40. *Redeeming the Time*, p. 43.
41. 'The Universe as Epiphany', unpublished manuscript, Bellarmine College MS Collection, p. 2, published in *Love and Living* (Farrar, Straus & Giroux, 1979).
42. *Albert Camus' The Plague: Introduction and Commentary*, Religious Dimensions in Literature, No. 7 (New York: The Seabury Press, 1968) pp. 39–43.

43. 'Orthodoxy and the World,' Monastic Studies 4 (1966) p. 111.

44. See, for example, Romano Guardini, *Rilke's Divino Elegies: An Interpretation,* trans. K. G. Knight (Chicago: Regnery, 1961).

45. N. Scott, *The Wild Prayer of Longing: Poetry and the Sacred* (New Haven: Yale University Press, 1971) xiii.

46. *The Collected Poems of Thomas Merton* (New York: New Directions, 1977). All the poetry is available in this volume.

47. 'Standards for Critics', *New York Herald Tribune,* 8 May 1938, p. 10.

48. 'Paradise Bugged', *Critic 25* (February-March, 1967) pp. 69–70.

49. 'Symbolism: Communication or Communion?' *New Directions in Prose and Poetry 20,* ed. J. Laughlin (New York: New Directions, 1968)

50. 'Paradise Bugged', a review of *All the Collected Short Poems, 1956–1964* of Louis Zukofsky, in *The Critic 25* (1967) 70.

The Life of Merton as Paradigm:
The View from Academe

Lawrence S. Cunningham

*Lawrence S. Cunningham is a Professor of Religion
at the Florida State University at Tallahassee, Florida. His special field of interest is religion and the humanities. He served for three years as associate director
of the Florida State University Study Center in Flor-
ence, Italy. He has published over sixty articles and reviews for a variety of publications. His books include
Brother Francis (Harper and Row, 1972) and Saint
Francis of Assisi (Twayne, 1976). He has just finished a book on The Meaning of the Saints (Harper
and Row, 1980), and is at work on a two-volume text-
book on Western Humanities which is to appear from
Holt, Rinehart and Winston in 1982. His contribution to this volume was originally given at the Columbia Merton Commemoration in November 1978.*

> *What advice do you want from me?*
> *I can tell you this: each man, today,*
> *Gets what he wants,*
> *Except that no one has discovered a*
> *really perfect*
> *Way to kill time.*
>
> Thomas Merton

THOMAS MERTON was one of the most public persons in mod-
ern American Catholicism. There is an irony in this, for
Merton travelled little after he entered monastic life in 1941.
He was never on the lecture circuit. His name was not to be found

on the rosters of the conferences, symposia, and conventions that make up an important part of the tribal rites of academics or those church-people who travel conspicuously through the ecclesiastical infrastructures. He held no visiting professorships and gave no lecture series. In fact, Merton's public *persona* was projected primarily through the publication of a series of autobiographical disclosures that began in 1948 with *Seven Storey Mountain* and ended in 1973 with the posthumous publication of *The Asian Journal*. The Merton *persona* was fleshed out further by his many other volumes of writings that ranged over a broad area of human inquiry.

Despite this vast literary outpouring, a not insignificant part of it confessional, one can still ask how Merton is to be understood as a public person. One could not call him a theologian save in the patristic sense of one who spoke experientially of God. He produced no sustained reflection on the classical *loci* of theology. Even in the area of ascetical theology it has been left to such scholars and commentators as John Higgins, Marilyn King, Raymond Bailey, Elena Malits, and Henri Nouwen to reconstruct systematically what is latent or scattered in his many books. In 1977 New Directions published *The Collected Poems* of Thomas Merton, a volume of over a thousand pages which, as Father Dan Berrigan said, one doesn't read; one climbs aboard.[1] It does no disrespect to Merton's memory to say that he was not quite a poet of the first rank: Father Berrigan is probably correct; we are hardly equipped to judge him rightly in the present.[2] Merton's criticism, belletristic and social, constitutes a fairly large body of material, yet no one would consider Merton a serious literary or social critic. He was committed to literature and to the problems of the social order (in fact, he never completely disentangled the two) but they did not constitute the poles of his horizon; such interests surged up from a wider and deeper standpoint. Curiously enough, in the halcyon days immediately after Vatican II, Merton was not—if memory serves well—one of the 'media stars' of Catholic publishing. It is instructive to look back over his bibliography for that period to find it quite restrained, especially when one remembers that any random *obiter dictum* of Küng, Rahner, *et al* could find a ready place on the fall publishing lists. While one could plausibly argue that Thomas Merton was one of the truly reforming spirits of modern Catholicism, he was not closely identified with the highly publicized reforming wing of the liberal sixties. There is no small irony in the fact that as the battlecry of relevance and engagement was sounding across the landscape of America, Merton was writing about, and living through, the ideals of detachment, silence, and the deep solitude characteristic of the eremetical life.

In the last analysis one must understand Thomas Merton as he understood himslf: as a monk. It is true that over his long monastic life Merton's understanding of what a monk was deepened and matured from an earlier, somewhat romaticized, view. He recognized that earlier view by satirizing himself as a 'man who spurned New York, spat on Chicago, and tromped on Louisville, heading for the woods with Thoreau in one pocket, John of the Cross in another, and holding the Bible open to the Apocalypse'.[3] His mature notion of the monk was far more generous and compassionate: '. . . a marginal person who withdraws deliberately to the margin of society with a view of deepening fundamental human experience.'[4]

The notion of marginality was crucial for Merton's understanding of the monastic life. It was his persistent pursuit of that ideal which, paradoxically enough, brought him from the hiddenness of the cloister into the public eye. His desire to render more precise the 'marginality' of the monk was expressed in his idea that the monk is, in a very real sense of the term, 'irrelevant'. How ironical to read in his essays of the sixties (later published in *Contemplation in a World of Action*) about 'irrelevancy' when the *Zeitgeist* was loaded with cries for the opposite. For Merton, *Zeitgeist* notwithstanding, 'the monk is not defined by his task; his usefulness. In a certain sense he is supposed to be "useless" because his mission is not to do this or that job but to be a man of God'.[5] It is from this peculiar perspective of being at the margin that would provide the monk the opportunity for getting a sense of the deepest meaning of life. In such a life of irrelevancy the true relevancy (if one can be permitted such an oxymoronic turn of phrase) becomes apparent. Such a life 'will be in some sense critical of the world, of its routines, its confusions, and its sometimes tragic failures to provide other men with lives that are fully sane and human'.[6] Father John Eudes Bamberger summed it up perfectly when he noted that Merton never saw the contemplative life as a purely private affair. The life was both an affirmation and a protest because 'it is basically affirmative of the absolute value of human life, of the person who is transcendent. This view of man leads to a refusal to become involved in those actions and practices of modern society which degrade man.'[7]

This paper uses the word paradox freely in discussing Merton: the paradox of the public person who rarely ventured from his monastery; the paradox of the preacher of irrelevancy in a period that sought relevancy; the paradox of the centrality of marginality. Here is yet another paradox: Merton sought the transcendent freedom of being a spiritual person within the conservative confines of an historically-shaped religious order of the Roman Catholic church. For one who would link his style of life with the hippie, the vagrant poet, the prisoner, the rebel, or the dying person there was the puzzling fact that he lived within the confines of an historical brotherhood that bore on its back an eight-hundred year history of custom, usage, tradition, rule, literature, and, at times, encrusted prejudice. What, in short, is the logic of seeking solitude, hiddenness, quiet, and self-transcendence in an atmosphere which was described with busy metaphors like a 'spiritual powerhouse' or 'a spiritual dynamo' within which was a bustling and, presumably profitable cheese factory ('poems are naught but warmed up breeze/Dollars are made by Trappist cheeses'[8])?

That problem, a microcosm of the whole tumult of *aggiornamento* in contemporary Catholicism, was not addressed by Merton alone. It has engaged the energies, not only of the Trappists, but of every religious Order in the Catholic Church. What is instructive is that Thomas Merton not only lived within the monastic tradition of the Trappists but it was within that tradition that he deepened and matured as a monk and as a person. It is one of the persistent simplisms about Merton that he was increasingly alienated from the Trappist fraternity. He felt it necessary to correct such stories himself while at the same time defending his desire for a greater solitary life as a development of, rather than a break from, the cistercian charism. Books such as Ed Rice's *The Man in the Sycamore Tree* (1970) and defensive rejoinders to it seem to indicate that Merton had his moments of trial in the years at Gethsemani. We can only hope that the publication of the long-awaited biography will clarify such matters for those who are interested.

I have no direct knowledge of these affairs and only a limited appetite for the gossipy nature of speculations and revelations. What strikes an outsider is the abiding interest, study, research, and reflection that Merton exerted on making the treasures of monasticism available to the larger public. It is easy to be misled by the vast output of what some regard as Merton's 'esoterica' (the enigmatic volumes of poetry, the studies and translation from Eastern thought, the wide ranging essays on everything from Shaker furniture to the fiction of Albert Camus) and forget his continuous research and writing on monastic literature and monastic themes. One can point not only to early volumes like *The Waters of Siloe* or his translations of the *Verba Seniorum* but his enthusiasm for the projected *Cistercian Studies* series and his many essays and monographs on the great figures of monastic history or his pioneering work in recovering the eremetical ideas of Western monasticism. It was from the base of this rigorous study and his own lived experience that he was able to 'cross over' (I use here the suggestive ideas of Father John Dunne[9]) to the traditions of the East in order to enlarge his own monastic experience and his deep appreciation for the contemplative life. 'Passing over', writes Father Dunne, 'is a shifting of standpoint, a going over to the standpoint of another culture, another way of life, another religion. It is followed by an equal and opposite process we might call "coming back", coming back with new insight to one's own culture, one's way of life, one's own religion.'[10] Is that not, in fact, what Thomas Merton proposed in an address he prepared for a non-western audience during his last days in Thailand when he wrote:

> I speak as a western monk who is pre-eminently concerned with his own monastic calling and dedication.... I come as a pilgrim who is anxious not just about facts about the monastic traditions, but to drink from ancient sources of monastic vision and experience. I seek not only to learn

more (quantitatively) about religion and monastic life, but to become a better and more enlightened monk (qualitatively) myself.[11]

The point to be urged here is that Thomas Merton was a devoted christian monk who, at the same time, never committed himself merely to monasticism; he committed himself only to God. While Merton had many wisely instructive (and rather blunt) things to say about the reform of monastic life as he knew it in practice he never became obsessed with forms, styles, or other historically-conditioned superficialities of monastic reform. He knew the monastic tradition with complete intimacy, as Dom Jean Leclercq, the great monastic scholar, has asserted. He also knew that true monasticism need not be tied to forms or usages which have been canonized only by their longevity and staying power. His intimate understanding of, and faith in, the monastic charism permitted him, as it were, to see the limitations of monastic forms while resting content with the peculiar value of the monastic life. In fact, Father Leclercq feels that Merton had a certain prescience about the need for change in the monastic life. Leclercq writes:

> Earlier than others, he had seen, he had known without a doubt that—in monasticism as well as in everything else—many things would change. One might say everything—except the essential, except for Him who is not a thing, and the primordial encounter made with Him in love.... All the details, the outward observances, ideas, even, all these 'things' could change; but the union of man with God in Jesus Christ, for the salvation of the world would continue to be a living reality.[12]

The title of this paper promised a discussion of Merton as a 'paradigm'. The word 'paradigm' is used in the sense that Merton's life (as opposed to his 'doctrine') could serve as a model or blueprint, *mutatis mutandis*, for the lives of others. If we judge by the lively interest in Merton's legacy within contemporary monasticism itself (if one can judge from the ever increasing flow of articles about him in monastic journals), his life seems to give the monk and/or nun many hints and clues about better living in that state of life. But we are not all monks even though there is truth in Max Weber's *mot* that after the Reformation all Christians were called to be monks. But, more specifically, one must address the question of how the life of Thomas Merton might be a model or paradigm for someone who is not *formally* within the monastic tradition.

There is no need to document the fact that Thomas Merton influenced vast numbers of people in our age. It is not simply an influence on Christians, but the powerful attraction that non-christians, agnostics, revolutionaries, skeptics, and others felt in the presence of his work and his *persona*. In that sense Thomas Merton was a saint (albeit uncanonized; the *advocatus diaboli*, one suspects, will have a field day should his cause ever be introduced!) if one accepts Karl Rahner's suggestive notion that before all else saints 'are the initiators and the creative models of the holiness which happen to be right for, and is the task of, their peculiar age'.[13] Saints, in that sense, Rahner continues, 'create a new style; they prove that a certain form of life and activity is a really genuine possibility; they show experimentally that one can be a Christian even in "this" way; they make such a type of person believable as a Christian type'.[14] The saint, in short, is a paradigm.

In what sense would a monk-hermit like Merton be a paradigm or model for, say, an academic? Perhaps the closest thing to a secularized monastery in our culture is the university. More than any other large institution in our culture the university still gives recognition to 'monastic' values even though such values are more often praised than practised. The university has a long and noble historical tradition that stretches back to the time of Cîteaux and Clairvaux. It puts a great stress on the idea of cenobitic life (the community of scholars); it has its period of novitiate with successful completion of this testing period resulting in the final vows of tenure. More to the point, this community is dedicated to the search for truth. The motherhouse of all American universities (Harvard) has as its motto: *Veritas* (Truth). Akin to the model of buddhist monasticism, the university takes the young for shorter or longer periods of time to initiate them in the ways of the university while encouraging some of them to become permanent votaries within the ivy-covered walls to follow a life-long commitment of disciplined study.

The university, like the monastery, goes through its own cycle of stresses and crises. Again, like the monastery, the university is

the object of reforming impulses and enters cycles of custom, en-
nui, and plain decadence. In the contemporary period the American university has shown symptoms of the same illnesses that af-
flict the religious life. When monk-critics can ask (seriously, we
presume) if the monastic life or the contemplative life is finished,[15]
one can find academic critics raising the same questions about the
continued viability of the 'ivory tower' life of academic community. If some monasteries have been beguiled by heady economic
successes and wealthy benefactors so, also, the universities have
become camp followers of the largesse of government, industry,
and other agencies. The academic equivalent of the 'Trappist
cheese factory syndrome' is the scarcely concealed whoring after
foundations and other granting agencies that one finds in academe.
An academic reads with immediate recognition the warnings
about mindless activity in the cloister. At a 1971 symposium on
'Contemplative Community' Professor D.H. Salmon, OP warned
his audience on the discussion of community organization and
government. It would be a more grievous misunderstanding still to
believe that such discussions have any necessary connection with
contemplation.[16] Any academic, emerging from the most recent
committee on academic reorganization, collective bargaining, etc.
can only nod in weary agreement.

The larger dissatisfactions of the academy as an institution have
caused the individual professor, if he is halfway serious about his
work, episodes of deep questioning: is it possible to have faith in
the academic life? Is there an authentic collegial searching for truth?
Should we be, or better, is there hope of being more than trainers
of future corporate persons or lawyers or doctors? Are there still
values to pass on that derive from the humanistic tradition of our
past?

These questions should bother every serious academic humanist.
They become all the more acute if that academic is a believer or a
searcher after belief. One needs to be clear about what is being suggested at this point. I am not talking about being a 'religious witness' or an open (or crypto) apologist for one's religious tradition.
I am talking, however, about that basic affirmation that there is an
inner-connectedness, a deep center, if you will, to all human phe-

nomena. In short, the believer is here understood in the sense of one who posits ultimate meaning or significance to the various phenomena that passes before human scrutiny. It is that basic trust in what the late Paul Tillich has called 'the all determining ground and substance of man's spiritual life'.[17]

It is precisely at this point where the committed academic can learn from the example of Thomas Merton. Merton not only teaches how one can live, however uncomfortably, within the historical tradition of an ancient institution but, and this is far more important, how to appropriate the accumulated wisdom of that tradition into one's life and work. What impresses the monastic outsider is how Merton cut through the pretensions and encrustations of his own tradition without rancor or bitterness. Merton was never mesmerized by the epiphenomena of institutional criticism; he had a penchant for going to the heart of things. David Steindl-Rast provides a good example when he records some remarks that Merton gave at a conference to contemplative nuns in California before he left on his fateful trip to the East: 'Maybe new structures are not that necessary. Perhaps you already know what you want to do. I believe that what we want to do is pray—o.k. now pray. This is the whole doctrine of prayer in the *Rule of St Benedict*.... If a man wants to pray, let him pray.'[18]

A final point. This paper has tried so to emphasize Merton's stance within the monastic tradition as to underscore the dialectical relationship of his critique of the tradition and his desire to understand it in a new way. Beyond that, one is impressed by his wide ranging interests outside of the *loci classici* of spirituality and theology. It would be otiose to document his wide reading and writing in the areas of literature, philosophy, art, anthropology, and social criticism. What does demand recognition is that it is hard to think of another Catholic thinker in our time with such wide ranging interests and such diverse intellectual skills. Yet any fair reader of Merton would be ready to affirm that such a catholicity of reading was not the result of any dilettantish mind or the symptom of an intellectual busybody. Indeed, Merton seems to be one of the few contemporary Catholic writers who seemed to hold faith with the notion of a christian humanism. His wide ranging interests reflect that deep sense of inter-connectedness which was mentioned earlier in this presentation.

Here again Thomas Merton provides an example for the academic. With the continuing pressure to specialize and compartmentalize one's range of interest (we no longer hire a professor of, say, American Literature; we now search for a 'Melville' man) it is a sign of hope to be reminded that it is possible to range wide in the arena of human accomplishment and not lose focus. Merton insisted that some monks, of proven maturity and growth, should be capable of entering into dialogue with those persons who are interested in the inner dimensions of human growth and spiritual experience (poets, philosophers, psychiatrists) since they need to recognize in monks 'professionals like themselves who have deliberately chosen a different road and a different kind of experience, and can give some account of their choice and its fruits'.[19]

Likewise the monk should be capable of learning from those other sources of human learning that would help him 'develop the special human capacities which will enable him to experience the deepest values of the contemplative life'.[20] Merton, then, saw the task of the monk as being that of a teacher (*contemplata aliis tradere*) and a learner. All of this has direct and immediate relevance for the life of the mind.

Merton had a deep understanding of the integrity of human learning. He did not read literature for apologetical or reductionistic reasons. His reflections on the fiction and poetry of our day show a real openness to the perceptions of others who wrestled with the depth experiences of being human. Likewise, one could argue that his late-found interest in photography and calligraphy was not simply a hobby with him. It was a way of seeing and doing with deliberation (his grasp of Zen principles is apposite in this regard) and with what Simone Weil has called 'attention'. A case could be made for conceptualizing the wide-ranging reading of Merton as a deepened understanding of the exercise of *lecto divina* so that to the study of Sacred Scripture was added those creations of the human spirit which deepen the drive for what the poet Theodore Roethke has called the center which is at the heart of form.[21]

Not the least among the graces which Thomas Merton received was the power to see in the writings of poets, novelists, buddhist monks, essayists, philosophers, and scholars lines and directions which took him to the deep center of existence. One would hope that his example is not inappropriate for those who toil at analogous tasks in far different situations. It is not an easy task in this day when we worry not only about such a search but about the very language which we speak and use in its pursuit. Yet the integrity of that search was exemplified in the life of Merton and his rugged dedication to it. Thomas Merton once wrote a beautiful essay on that enigmatic figure of greek philosophy, Herakleitos. There are some words in that essay which make an apt tribute to Thomas Merton and a fitting final challenge to any academic who finds in his own work some desire for basic trust. Merton wrote:

> Divinely impatient with the wordplay and imposture of those pseudowise men who deceive others by collecting and reshuffling the current opinions, presenting old errors in new disguises, Herakleitos refused to play their pitable game. Inspired, as Plato said, by the 'more severe muses' he sought excellence, in his intuitions, at the cost of verbal clarity. He would go deep, and emerge to express his vision in oracular verses, rather than flatter the crowd by giving it what it demanded and expected of a philosopher, of a professional scholar we would say today. He would be like the 'Lord of Delphi who neither utters or hides meanings but shows us a sign'. His words would be neither expositions of doctrine nor explanations of mystery, but simply pointers, plunging towards the heart of reality: 'fingers pointing at the moon'. He knew very well that many would mistake the finger for the moon, but that was inevitable and he did not attempt to do anything about it.[22]

NOTES

1. Daniel Berrigan. 'The Seventy Times Seventy Seven Storey Mountain', *Cross Currents* (Winter, 1977/78) p. 385.

2. *Ibid.*, p. 389.

3. *Contemplation in a World of Action* (Garden City, 1973) p. 159. All quotations are from the Image paperback edition.

4. *The Asian Journal* (New York, 1973) p. 305.

5. *Ibid.*, p. 27.

6. *Ibid.*, p. 28.

7. John Eudes Bamberger, 'The Monk', in *Thomas Merton, Monk*, ed. Brother Patrick Hart (Garden City, 1976) p. 54.

8. Lines from a hitherto unpublished piece of doggerel Merton once wrote; See *Collected Poems* (New York, 1977) 799–800 for the entire poem.

9. In books such as *A Search for God in Time and Memory* (New York, 1969) and *The Way of All the Earth* (New York, 1972).

10. *The Way of All the Earth*, p. ix.

11. The entire piece is reprinted in an appendix to *Asian Journey*.

12. Jean Leclercq, 'The Evolving Monk', in *Thomas Merton, Monk*, p. 98.

13. Karl Rahner, 'The Church of the Saints', in *Theological Investigations III* (Baltimore, 1967) p. 100.

14. *Ibid.*

15. See, for example, Merton's essay 'Is the Contemplative Life Finished?' in *Contemplation in a World of Action*, pp. 343–396.

16. D. H. Salmon. 'Some Psychological Dimensions of the Contemplative Community', in *Contemplative Community*, ed. M. Basil Pennington, OCSO (Washington: Cistercian Publications, 1972) p. 331.

17. Paul Tillich. *A Theology of Culture* (New York, 1964) p. 8.

18. David Steindl-Rast. 'The Man of Prayer', in *Thomas Merton, Monk*, p. 86.

19. *Contemplation in a World of Action*, p. 213.

20. *Ibid.*, p. 213.

21. In an unpublished paper titled 'Literature as *Lectio Divina*: The Case of Thomas Merton' which I have read to various audiences (e.g., the Southeastern Section of the American Academy of Religion and The Wake Forest University Religion Dept. colloquium) I have argued this point at length.

22. Thomas Merton, 'Herakleitos the Obscure', in *A Thomas Merton Reader*, ed. Thomas McDonnell (Garden City, 1974) p. 265. The essay appeared originally in *The Behavior of Titans* (New York, 1961).

Thomas Merton and
the Tradition of
American Critical Romanticism

Dennis Q. McInerny

*Dennis Q. McInerny, a Professor of English at Brad-
ley University, did his doctoral dissertation on
'Thomas Merton and Society, a study of the man and
his thought against the background of contemporary
American culture' at the University of Minnesota in
1969. Later he published a volume based on his
research entitled,* Thomas Merton: The Man and
His Work *(Cistercian Publications, 1974). His contribution to this volume was delivered at the Merton
Commemoration at Columbia University in November 1978. Dr McInerny also contributed a paper at
the Merton Session of the Cistercian Conference held at
Western Michigan University at Kalamazoo in May
of the same year.*

S INCE HIS DEATH ten years ago a good deal has been written on
Thomas Merton. Predictably, given the fact that he was a man
possessed of an amazing diversity of talents and interests, he
has been studied from many different points of view. In this essay I
shall discuss Merton and his work within the context, and from the
point of American literature. My intention is to 'place' Merton
within that literature, to demonstrate that, whatever else he might

have been besides, he was an American writer to the core. Specifically, I want to show how Merton was in the mainstream of, and a substantial contributor to, a tradition which I choose to call American Critical Romanticism.

Up to this time not much attention has been paid to Merton as a specifically American writer. I suspect that one reason for this is the feeling that there was no need to belabor the obvious. A second reason, from the opposite point of view, was that Merton, though undoubtedly a writer, was not seen as especially American: Merton was born in Europe, he received a good portion of his education there, and it was only in his late thirties that he became a citizen of the United States. Special significance might be attached to the fact that he belonged by deliberate, adult choice to a church whose character is emphatically international, and he was as well a member of an international monastic order. Finally, this second point of view would not see in the writings themselves anything peculiarly American; one could imagine that a good number of Merton's books could just as well have been written by a twentieth-century monk living in Europe.

It shall not be my purpose to minimize the importance and significance of Thomas Merton's European 'roots', nor to ignore the fact that he was in many ways strikingly cosmopolitan, a fact which in large part explains his international and cross-cultural appeal. Least of all is it my purpose to make a case for Merton's American-ness for the sake of some kind of narrow chauvinistic end, arbitrarily forcing him into a pre-selected category. I take Merton's identity as an American writer as something which emerges naturally from his writings, once they are properly understood. I have become increasingly impressed over the years by the fact that many of the attitudes and themes found in the works of Merton are reflective of attitudes and themes which play an important part in the national literature as a whole. It is that relationship between Merton's works and the national literature upon which I want to focus. I am operating under the assumption here that no writer works in a vacuum; he works out of an identifiable literary tradition. Thomas Merton's literary tradition, though not exclusively so, was predominantly American.

I would like to emphasize that I am looking upon Merton chiefly as a literary figure, and that my analysis of him will thus necessarily be limited. I make no attempt to explain a given attitude of his from every possible point of view, but only from a literary point of view. In some cases explanations which I ignore may in the long run prove to be more important than those which, because of the peculiar focus of this study, I choose to examine. Finally, although I will focus on what Merton has in common with other American writers, I will at the same time show how he differs from them. I do not have it in mind to denigrate his uniqueness as a writer.

I would like first to reflect briefly on what I will call Merton's American consciousness. When Merton came to live permanently in this country at the age of nineteen, he was not a complete stranger to the land. He was in a sense 'coming home', returning to a country where he had received from time to time part of his elementary schooling, and which he subsequently visited. Every indication suggests that he fit very rapidly and easily into his role as an undergraduate at Columbia University. In a conversation we had some ten years ago, Father Daniel Walsh, who taught Merton at Columbia, told me that young Tom was very much 'one of the boys' on campus. There appeared to be nothing remarkably foreign about him. The facility with which he worked himself into the culture can be attributed, I would suggest, to a deep-seated affinity he had for it. There is no evidence I am aware of that he was making a conscious attempt to 'be American' at the time, or that he thought anything about the implications of changing his citizenship.

But things had altered by 1951, when he was preparing for his naturalization exam, which he talks about in *The Sign of Jonas*. Apparently, he was initially prepared to take the whole matter somewhat casually. Then, in the entry for 28 February, we read the following: 'Suddenly realized that this business of citizenship raises a moral question. Impossible to take it as mere formality. Either it means something or it doesn't. There is more to this than a problem of semantics.'[1] 'Either it means something or it doesn't.' The statement is highly indicative of Merton's character; here was a man who was throughout his life primarily concerned with meaning. His vivid consciousness of the event and its implications caused him to seek out the special meaning of his becoming an American. Later in that year, 1951, on 23 June, the day after he became a citizen, he was writing in the journal that he could not kid himself into believing that it was 'as important a step as religious profession or taking the habit'.² Even so, he had prayed over the matter, and on the night before taking the oath of allegiance, looking out over the hills of Kentucky, he realized that this was going to be 'his' country. 'It was a bit disturbing to find that I was suddenly discovering America in 1951 when it was supposed to have been discovered for me by Columbus in 1492.'³

One of the 'meanings' of his becoming an American, which he could not have foreseen at the time he changed his citizenship, became evident in the following decade. By this time much had changed in the country. The relatively benign fifties had given way to the rambunctious sixties, in which criticism of the U.S. government and, more broadly, of anything American was almost *de rigueur* for the intellectuals and writers among whom Merton enjoyed considerable prestige. Merton had always been a critic of American culture to the degree that it mirrored a decadence which he believed to be endemic to Western civilization as a whole, but even so it would be difficult to imagine him saying in the late sixties what he had said in the early fifties: 'Why do half the people in America seem to think it is a moral weakness to admit that they owe America something—and perhaps everything? And that the country is worth loving?'⁴ His criticism of America in the sixties was poignant and pungent; often he is more than half apologetic for the country. And there were times when, by appealing to his identity as a monk or a poet, he seemed to want to dissociate himself from America, to transcend his citizenship through one or another of these identities. This new attitude is not without ambivalence, and in a telling instance, recorded in *Conjectures of a Guilty Bystander*, he laid claim explicitly to his American citizenship and makes a meditation upon it.

> It suddenly dawned on me that the anti-Americanism in the world today is a hatred as deep and lasting and as all-inclusive as anti-Semitism. And just about as rational. I see now that I must understand myself in the light

of hatred. To identify myself completely with this country is like accepting
the fact of a hidden Jewish grandfather in Nazi Germany. My European
background gives me a protective coloring, no doubt. I am, as it were, a
Jew with blond hair and blue eyes. But no, I remain a citizen of a hated nation, and no excuses will serve. I know for a fact that this does have some
influence on the way my books are received in some places in Europe.[5]

There was a general American consciousness, but more directly
related to our discussion there was Merton's knowledge of American literature, a knowledge which made up in liveliness what it
lacked in comprehensiveness.

He knew best specific writers: T. S. Eliot, Emily Dickinson, and
Henry David Thoreau. These are the three that he mentions most
often, not insignificantly, for all three are religious writers and two
of them, Thoreau and Eliot, were dedicated moralists. Merton
was a religious writer in a way more serious than were Thoreau
and Dickinson, and at least as serious as was Eliot; as a moralist he
outdid the three of them. He had evidently been reading Eliot
since his days at Columbia, and perhaps even before. I cannot say
with certainty when he was first introduced to Emily Dickinson,
but in a journal entry made in the spring of 1949 he speaks of her
as the 'one person in the world—Emily—with my own aspirations, though in a different way. I wish I had Emily's good sense.'[6]
One can surmise that what Merton meant by their shared aspirations was simply the fact that they both yearned for the infinite,
for God. But what follows that is enigmatic. Certainly Emily
Dickinson's unorthodox orthodoxy could not be considered compatible with Merton's temperament (if that is indeed what he is
referring to by the phrase 'a different way'), but what he meant by
her 'good sense' I don't know.

In an unpublished letter written to a correspondent in California, Merton claims that he admires Thoreau tremendously. He
goes on to say that Thoreau 'is one of the only reasons why I felt
justified in becoming an American citizen. He and Emily Dickinson. . .'.[7] Another reference is made to Thoreau in an article entitled 'Day of a Stranger', which appeared in *The Hudson Review*.
In this article Merton claims that he is being 'accused of living in
the woods like Thoreau instead of living in the desert like St. John

the Baptist'.[8] He responds to this accusation by saying that he is not trying to live 'like anybody'. I cite these references to Thoreau especially because subsequently I will show that Merton had much in common with that nineteenth-century thinker and writer. Whether or not Merton was consciously modeling himself after Thoreau in any serious way is not at issue, and frankly I do not think that this was the case. What is significant is that, by reflecting ideas that predominated in the American literature of the second quarter of the last century, when American Critical Romanticism came into being, he was showing himself to be part of that tradition. It is now time that I explain what I mean by that tradition.

American Critical Romanticism is a tradition whithin American literature which saw its inception in the second quarter of the nineteenth century. It held sway throughout the course of that century, although in a steadily diminishing way, and has survived into this century, even to the present day—through the influence of writers like Thomas Merton. By using the term 'Romanticism' I mean simply to establish two broad facts about the tradition in question: 1. American literature came fully into its own during the second quarter of the nineteenth century, at a time when the Romantic Movement still dominated Western literature. The tradition of which I speak, then, besides being for all practical purposes as old as serious American literature itself, is 'Romantic' simply by dint of taking its distinguishing hue from the literary 'climate of opinion' which dominated at the time of its coming-to-be; 2. I mean to suggest by the word 'Romantic' that the tradition is characterized importantly by what F. O. Matthiessen called the 'optative mood'. Put very simply, I am saying that to be a Romantic is to be prevalently optimistic.

By 'Critical', I mean to suggest both the broader meaning of the term, that is, a systematic, analytic approach to experience, and also the narrower, popular meaning of the term, that is, a negative, fault-finding attitude.

American Critical Romanticism is a tradition which is marked by sharp awareness of the American scene. The Critical Romantics are conscious of their identity as Americans, and this makes them alternately happy and uncertain. They see great moral and artistic potential in the country; they are impressed by the raw energy of its youthfulness and envision the manifold ways in which it could be channelled to good uses. But at the same time they see a tendency in that energy to direct itself to less than edifying ends. In this sense, American Critical Romanticism might be described as a kind of worried optimism.

The two principal representatives of the tradition at its inception were Ralph Waldo Emerson and Henry David Thoreau. Like theirs, Merton's writings are characterized by the 'optative mood'. This is by no means to suggest that there is not a strong, even at times predominant, element of pessimism in Merton's writings, but it is a pessimism which is balanced, and in a sense, identified, by the presence of an underlying optimism. To say that Merton was an optimist as were Emerson and Thoreau is not to say that the quality of his optimism was in every important respect identical to theirs; as a matter of fact, it was not. The source of Emerson and Thoreau's optimism was different from Merton's.

The optimism of Emerson and Thoreau, as was the case with most nineteenth-century Romantics, was founded ultimately on a faith in human perfectibility. Though the Romantics had repudiated the eighteenth-century brand of optimism, which was based on what that century considered to be the virtually boundless potential of human reason, their own optimism was equally man-centered. If the Romantics mistrusted reason, they saw in the realm of man's pure and spontaneous emotions the locale for those energies which would one day eliminate the world's ills and pave the way for a Utopian tomorrow. The foundation of the Romantics' optimism is perhaps the best explanation for its tentativeness. Emerson and Thoreau seemed to have been spared any thoroughgoing disillusionment in their lifetimes, but contemporaries like Hawthorne and Melville, looking deeply into the human heart, were never to find there any reason to be encouraged about the human condition or about human prospects. On a larger scale, as the nineteenth century progressed, the optative mood very definitely lost its potency as Romanticism gave way to Realism and its step-child Naturalism. American literature eventually came to reflect a loss of faith in man as the center of the world's drama and especially as the controller of his own destiny, be it good or bad. Man was demoted from being 'the captain of his soul' to being a beleaguered deckhand on a rudderless vessel buffeted about on a stormy sea.

Merton's optimism, by way of contrast to that of the early Romantics, was based upon christian hope, which made it at once more interesting, more durable, and—paradoxically—more subject to the onslaughts of real despair. Because his optimism was not founded upon any human capability, either rational or emotional, for bringing about some kind of apotheosis for the race as a whole, there was nothing which men could do by way of stupidity or even all-out evil that was capable of undermining his optimisim. Nonetheless, he had to wrestle with the exasperating 'absence of God' in the face of human activity. I am operating under the assumption here that, for the man of faith, the virtue of hope *is* a virtue only by reason of the fact that it stands always in militant opposition to despair. Hope is the response, the alternative, to despair. The theological virtues aside, Merton's perhaps temperamental pessimism was not so much the result of his suffering chagrin over man's not living up to his 'true human potential', as it was a reaction to man's unwillingness to respond positively to the salvific grace of God.

Having made the major generalizations, I turn now to the attempt to specify the ways in which Merton is in the tradition of American Critical Romanticism. I see no better alternative to listing and discussing those attitudes and themes which Merton's works share with those of other representatives of the tradition. It is admittedly a somewhat mechanical procedure, but I will try to go about it in as unmechanical a way as possible. For all its limitations, it does have the good effect of quickly isolating the specific evidence upon which my thesis is based.

There are six themes which I wish to call special attention to; I do not claim that there are not more, but these, I think, are the most important. They are: (1) individualism; (2) living life deliberately; (3) prophetism *vis à vis* American culture; (4) place; (5) anti-technology; (6) anti-government.

(1) 'Trust thyself: every heart vibrates to that iron string', Ralph

Waldo Emerson proclaimed in his essay 'Self-Reliance', and thereby provided a rallying cry for his generation of American writers, and indeed for generations extending to our present day. Individualism was to become the central tenet of the Romantic movement in this country. It was posited upon the firm faith that the single person was central, that everything was ultimately reducible to him because everything initially proceeded from him. If individualism and its corollary self-reliance tended to remain primarily theoretical truths for Emerson, his disciple Thoreau put them to the practical test by attempting to pattern his life after them. His residence at Walden Pond, for example, was an experiment in self-reliance.

Merton too was committed to individualism, and in his hermitage at Gethsemani we have a rough analogue to Thoreau's Walden Pond, but, just as Merton's optimism was qualitatively different from that of the earlier Romantics, so too was his individualism. One might be tempted to argue that Merton, as a monk, simply did not believe in self-reliance, that for him the individual possesses whatever nobility he has precisely to the extent that he relies on God. Such a conclusion would be deceptive. Certainly it is true that Merton was no advocate of a simplistic approach to the subject. He did not believe that an individual's worth was to be found exclusively in terms of himself, nor that the individual was able to ameliorate his moral condition simply by asserting himself and drawing upon hitherto untapped inner resources. But, for that matter, neither Emerson nor Thoreau thought thus simplistically. To the extent that they were Transcendentalists, they believed that the individual's worth derived from the fact that he was part of the One, the Over-Soul, which informed and encompassed everything that existed. But one of the traits of Transcendentalism was its indefiniteness, and because the One or the Over-Soul is no where clearly specified or specifiable, it eventually and unavoidably assumes the blurred contours of a huge, fuzzy abstraction; and what the individual is relying on in being self-reliant is not so much a truth of his being linking him with Being as a pseudo-truth cutting him off from his sources of spiritual sustenance. The self-reliance Merton advocated was synonymous with God-reliance.

He maintained that God was to be encountered in the very center of one's being, in what he called the True Self. Because God is the ground of the individual's being, the True Self, to be reliant on that self is to participate in the most perfect sort of prayer; it is to rely on God. Of course, Merton was always alert to the danger of an individual's becoming deceived by a commitment to his empirical or false self. Any reliance upon the empirical self was bound to prove retrogressive.

Perhaps the most concrete index of Merton's individualism is to be found in his lifelong love for solitude. It is one of the paradoxes of his life that though he belonged to a cenobitic monastic order his natural inclinations, seemingly dating to his earliest days as a monk, were toward eremitism. Unfortunately, Merton never expounded upon his reasons for liking Henry David Thoreau, as he did with writers like William Blake and Robert Lowell. Had he done so, I cannot help but think that he would have given no little time to the chapter in Thoreau's *Walden* entitled 'Solitude'. By comparing Thoreau's views on the subject with those of Merton, as expressed in a book like *Thoughts in Solitude*, we get a distinct sense that we are dealing here with 'kindred spirits'. Merton's attraction to solitude, and the reasons he delineates for its values are founded on explicitly theological premises, and in this respect he differs from Thoreau. But the very fact that there is no explicit theological orientation in Thoreau does not preclude the possibility of there being an implied one. In his chapter on solitude Thoreau remarks that 'there can be no very black melancholy to him who lives in the midst of nature and has his senses still'.[9] I can easily imagine Merton incorporating an insight of this sort into his notions of contemplative prayer. If Thoreau went off to the woods so that he could be alone and thus better commune with Nature, so too the monk seeks solitude, if only a solitude he can find in his own soul, so that he can there encounter that ineffable Reality upon which his very existence is established and within which he is immersed.

Thoreau made it a point to argue that solitude was by no means synonymous with loneliness. He admitted that he loved to be alone, and that he 'never found the companion that was so companionable as solitude'.[10] But if to be alone was not necessarily to be lonely, the converse was also true. He argued that collectivity was not the same as community. Throughout Thoreau's ruminations is implied the notion that the individual must first discover himself as an individual, which can be done only in solitude. When this self-discovery has taken place, and the individual is a true individual, then he is able properly to function in and contribute to a community. These are the very ideas which Merton attempted to further in his own discussions of solitude. Reading him on the subject, one quickly learns how cognizant Merton was that, in advocating the value of solitude in a culture which was almost totally committed to a vapid togetherness, he was fighting a difficult battle. His intention was to counter what he considered the shallow notion that the only way in which christian charity can be expressed is through a gregarious activism. Merton shared the Thoreauvian imagination by exploring the insight that, especially in our highly industrialized, urbanized societies where anonymity is paramount, there is little solace in sheer collectivity. Merton knew the 'lonely crowd' first hand, in a way which never could have been the case for Thoreau. The type of paradox which Merton saw in solitude could be seen by others, he knew well enough, only through the eyes of faith. The paradox lay in the hermit's desire to live by himself so he could find himself, and his deeper desire to lose himself in God. The paradox consisted in the fact that the hermit severed himself physically from other human beings, not out of an antipathy for men, but rather out of a love for them. The hermit is guided by the conviction that, just as the collective experience is no guarantee of community, so solitude is not identical with spiritual isolation. Looked at positively, he sees solitude as a means of binding himself in spirit with the whole of humankind. It is not escapism, but an affirmation of a reality higher than that which can be encompassed by sociology.

(2) Thoreau claimed that he went to the woods because he wanted 'to live deliberately, to front only the essential facts of life . . .'. [11] What he meant was that he wanted to live life in earnest, with full consciousness, with a seriousness which was commensurate with the nature and import of the enterprise. There

was nothing at all automatic in this; to be physically alive did not imply that one was morally alive, and, for Thoreau, most men 'lived lives of quiet desparation', never once during the course of their sojourn waking up to the 'essential facts', the deepest meanings, of their existences. This is a theme which is to be found throughout Merton's works, but is especially evident in the later ones when, under the influence of Oriental thought, he stressed the importance of avoiding abstractions and concentrating on the concrete—the concrete situation, the concrete person. His gloss on the statement of Thoreau quoted above is interesting: 'I suppose he means he did not intend to be resigned to anything like a compromise with life'.[12] Merton was convinced that he lived in a world and a culture which were centrally characterized by evasion and delusion. Contemporary Western man was in flight, a massive madcap flight from God, from self, from his fellow man. And at the same time he was caught up in a serious delusion, for while in fact in flight from the deepest realities, he fondly believed himself to be concerned with nothing else but those realities. Contemporary man, for example, prides himself on a knowledge of himself, of his species, which he thinks no previous generation even came close to possessing. But, for Merton, this knowledge is a false knowledge; it is a knowledge of the empirical self, an abstraction, rather than of the True Self, the essence of human identity. Everything in contemporary society seems to work toward the perpetuation of this delusion, for we live in a world which is aroar with noise, a world which seems to be conspiring constantly to distract man from himself. Contemporary man is stimulated to the point of satiation. As the stimulation becomes so intense and so pervasive that he is rendered morally numb, values are shuffled, shift positions, and eventually are reduced to a single, bloodless common denominator. The ubiquitous media cover all, and they trivialize everything they touch; by a process of relentless reductionism they depress everything to the level of bland inanity. The 'news' which we think it so important to 'keep up with' is often little more than glorified gossip. On this Merton and Thoreau were in perfect agreement.

In a world in which there is much activity one might conclude that one is in the thick of significant life. Merton would argue otherwise. Look closely at the activity and you will note its frenetic quality. It is the activity of a people who are in despair, who use activity as a means of maintaining a distance between their consciousness and a reality which they do not want to face. The name he gave such activity was 'activism', and he regarded it as one of the most pernicious sicknesses of our time. Nothing is more pitiable than a people who cannot be still, who are afraid of silence, who believe that at every turn and in every situation they must be 'doing' something to effect some purpose which, often arrogantly, they deem to be of the utmost importance.

The alternative to activism was clear enough to Merton. He never regarded the monastic life as intended for any but a few, but he did think that the quest of the monk should be, in its essentials, the same as that of all Christians, indeed, of all mankind. The choice of living deliberately, of confronting the essential facts of life—and for Merton this meant eventually confronting *the* essential fact of life, God—was not one which a person could expect to ignore and still hope to attain full humanness. What was contemporary, beleaguered man to do to save himself? He must, in whatever way and to whatever degree his state in life permit, withdraw himself, at least periodically, from society's distracting, life-evading noise. He must seek silence, find a pocket of peace in the midst of the turmoil, and there seek the living God.

In *Walden* Thoreau issued an invitation, indeed a challenge, to his readers to establish in their lives their personal equivalent to his sojourn into the woods, so that when they came to die they would not discover that they had never lived. Many of Merton's books— I mention off-hand *Thoughts in Solitude, No Man is an Island, The New Man,* and *Seeds of Contemplation*—were in effect invitations to his readers to adopt a monastic mentality toward the world and their experiences. He was constantly challenging them to force the issue, to face their situation nakedly, to dispose themselves for the totally transforming *metanoia*, change of heart, conversion.

A selective reading of Merton's works could lead to the conclusion that he was anti-american in his sentiments. But the same thing could be said about Emerson and Thoreau. To the degree that to be

American means to be materialistic, to believe unreservedly in expansion (for whatever is bigger is *ipso facto* better), to be enamored of the machine and any new gimmickry or gadgetry—Emerson and Thoreau were very definitely not in the mainstream of their culture. Thoreau particularly was not reflecting established opinion when he advised his countrymen to disencumber their lives, to live simply, and even to consider the value of voluntary poverty. Nonetheless, the voices of writers like Emerson and Thoreau, though not echoing the sentiments of the majority, were for that reason no less genuinely American. Their voices—to which we add Merton's—remind us that every national stereotype is limited in what it reveals, and that the picture is always more complicated, and interesting, than what a superficial perusal indicates. The Romantics were acutely conscious of American culture, with the effect, in more cases than not, that they stood in judgment of it, took a prophetic stance in relation to it. That points to the third theme which I wish to examine in this discussion.

(3) A prophet is almost by definition a loner. By publicly expressing his lack of sympathetic regard for the sacred cows of a culture he is effectively setting himself against that culture, separating himself from it. This Emerson and Thoreau did with deliberateness and verve. They knew that they did not constitute a majority, but that, for them, was a point of pride; they felt that they were arguing from a position of strength. Thoreau was convinced that 'there was little virtue in the actions of masses of men',[13] and conjectured that the majority would get around to voting for the abolition of slavery only when they were indifferent to slavery. Emerson observed in his journal that 'the mass are animal, in a stage of pupilage, and nearer the chimpanzee'.[14]

At the time when Emerson and Thoreau were writing the country was very young, and serious American literature was in its birthing period. Emerson in his 'American Scholar' address called upon Americans to sever the spiritual umbilical cord that tied them to Europe and to produce an art, a literature, a culture, which was distinctly American. In the propheticism of both Emerson and Thoreau one clearly detects that, for all they see to criticize in the country, they are incapable of escaping the general ebul-

lience of the era, an ebullience which is explained by the sheer
newness of the land and the heady sense its inhabitants had that
they were a new and improved version of the human race. The
propheticism of Emerson and Thoreau was confident. They saw
the country as young and malleable; it could be shaped, for all its
faults, into something worthy of humankind's highest ideals.

The case was not quite the same with Merton, and for the good
reason that the America he lived in was considerably different
from that of Emerson and Thoreau. The country was older but
not necessarily wiser. What in the second quarter of the nineteenth century were only tendencies had become major national
traits by Merton's day. Accordingly, his propheticism was less benign; it was often apocalyptic in its overtones. Merton felt that he
was up against a culture which for all practical purposes was
pagan. The people whose vacuous lives were formed and guided
by militarists and businessmen had hardened their hearts against
the truth of their situation. They spoke a language which no longer conveyed meaning but was a defense against meaning. Toward
the end of his life Merton's prophetic voice became more and
more astringent, especially when he was speaking through the me-
dium of poetry. The prophet relies on the vehicle of language to
convey his message, but if that vehicle is incapacitated what is the
prophet to do? Merton's decision to turn to anti-poetry was based
on his belief that once the vehicle has been sabotaged you continue
to use it, as incapacitated, as an indictment of its saboteurs.
Whether or not this is effective is a separate question. What is
clear is that the prophetic voice we hear Merton speaking toward
the end of his life could scarcely have been imagined of him as a
young monk in the late 1940s. We read in the Prologue to *Cables
to the Ace*:

> You, Reader, need no prologue. Do you think these
> Horation Odes are all about you? Far from the
> new vine to need a bundle. You are no bundle.
> Go advertize yourself.
> Why not more pictures? Why not more rhythms,
> melody, etc.? All suitable questions to be an-

swered some other time. The realm of the spirit
is two doors down the hall. There you can obtain more soul than you are ready to cope with,
Buster.
The poet has not announced these mosaics on
purpose.
Furthermore he has changed his address and
his poetics are on vacation.
He is not roaring in the old tunnel.[15]

The prophet is a prophet not only by virtue of what he says but
also by virtue of the manner in which he says it. The prophetic
style is ringing and oracular; it is eminently quotable, hence
memorable. Such observations have often been made, justifiably,
of the style of Emerson, and, to a lesser degree, of that of Thoreau.
I think the same can be said of Merton's style. His prose is capable
of taking on a soaring quality. Whatever might have been the
opinion of Evelyn Waugh on the subject, Merton's writing has
about it a compelling immediacy. He was capable of producing
sentences which are reminiscent of the products of Emerson and
Thoreau for their succinctness, their surprise, and their preemi-
nent rightness.

(4) When Thoreau remarked that he had travelled widely in
Concord, his home town, he was, albeit facetiously, making a serious point about the importance of place to human identity. He
was, like his mentor Emerson and like Emily Dickinson, the
recluse poet of Amherst, primarily a traveller of internal spaces, a
sojourner of the mind. The Romantics valued place, stability, and
often cited travel as escapism. Emerson went so far as to call
travelling a superstition. 'The soul is no traveller,' he said, and 'the
wise man stays at home . . .'. [16]

The peculiar attitude toward place taken by the Critical Romantics is reflected clearly in Merton's life and writings. In deciding to
become a monk, he seems to have brought his life to a kind of
Thoreauvian resolution. In his first twenty years he did a great
deal of travelling, almost as if he were searching for a home, a
place to settle down and plant roots, a place which would provide

a stable context within which he could properly identify himself and his life. Merton found his home at Gethsemani, in Kentucky; there he joined a monastic order and, significantly, took a vow of stability. Subsequently his travelling was to be severely restricted, in fact virtually non-existent—in one sense. In another sense, not so; he travelled widely at Gethsemani.

The American imagination has given a special twist to the importance of place by assigning a higher value to it should it lie in a westerly direction. To move west in America is to move forward. The West is the dream land, the golden land, the place which by its expansiveness and indefiniteness holds seemingly inexhaustible potential for new beginnings. The West in this country, either as a geographical fact or, more importantly, a fact of the imagination, is the perennial Promised Land. But if the West symbolizes goodness and promise, then the East is considered to be a lesser place than the West. Within the context of the American East-West tension, the movement to the wide and welcoming West often seems at the same time a move away from an East which is stagnant and stifling. These special ramifications of the theme of place are to be found in Merton's writing. In the poem called 'Three Postcards From the Monastery', Merton speaks of a turbulent, cacophonous land, the East, he has 'receded from'. He has come inland. The poem, taken as a whole, is a recounting of westward movement. But that movement is as much 'upward' as westward. The poet is claiming that when he went West to become a monk he moved into not only a different country but a better one. In the last three stanzas of the poem we get a kind of triumphal climacteric as the poet rejoices in his deliverance.

> Our lives were suddenly weaned in strange Ohio,
> (Whose towns made little love to us, in their green
>   requiems)
> Weaned from the land and atmosphere of men.
>
> Have you ever heard this music
> Sung over and over by night,
> How will we live *in loco pascuae*?

Or the assuring voices of those inward violins
Play: 'Going to Gethsemani?'

(We were begotten in the tunnels of December rain,
Born from the wombs of news and tribulation.
By night, by wakeful rosary:
Such was my birth, my resurrection from the
      freezing east,
The night we cleared you, Cincinnati, in a maze of
      lights.)[17]

(5) One of the most recurrent themes in Merton's works, especially his poetry, is that of anti-technology. It reflects not only an anti-technology attitude, but more broadly, anti-industrialization and anti-urban attitudes as well. The three are, of course, historically interconnected. Given his life-long antipathy to those things which are most characteristic of the modern age, one is tempted to suggest that Merton was a man born out of his time, more at home in the Middle Ages. But one indulges in such speculations only to be reminded that in so many other respects Merton was the quintessential modern man. His bias against technology was the result of considerably more than a cranky personality. His attitude, though reflecting a natural penchant toward Thoreauvian simplicity, was ideologically based, and there its prime significance lies. Merton was against technology because he believed that, ultimately, technology was against man. The machine had become so prevalent and powerful that it ruled the life of its creator. The master had become the slave to his own creation. He had been dehumanized by it, himself transformed into a machine.

The pattern for this type of thinking had been established in the early nineteenth century, at the time when the industrial revolution was first beginning to make its presence felt in this country. The ideas of Thoreau are especially interesting to follow in this regard. He was ambivalent toward the machine, as represented in the railroad locomotive and the power it bespoke. He was capable, on the one hand, of regarding it in a quasi-poetical light. But even as he admired he was troubled, as if he suspected that this iron horse might prove to be a Trojan one and eventually disgorge upon the land all sorts of vicious enemies. In the end he seemed to return inevitably to the notion that the machine's benefit to man is deceptive; in fact, man is subservient to the machine, and crushed by it. 'We do not ride the railroad; it rides upon us.'[18]

For Merton, a great deal of what was wrong with American culture could be explained by the social structure of this country, built almost totally around the machine. The machine lies at the heart of the troubles that beset contemporary life. And the geographical analogue for the machine, which manifests and magnifies all the machine's destructive qualities, is the city. In Merton's imagination the city serves as a comprehensive symbol of the decadence of Western civilization in general and American culture in particular. The city is the consummately unholy place. The city ultimately is unreal. Merton was surely inspired by T.S. Eliot in this, but I think Merton went beyond Eliot in seeing the city as not only dessicated, but destructive, as not merely a twilight zone inhabited by the innocuous dead, but as a pitch black hell in which demonic forces conspired to conjure up madness and despair. Finally, if the machine and the city are inextricably interlinked, so the virtue of the country, the West, lay importantly in its relative freedom of the machine. The early poems which Merton wrote about Gethsemani are pervaded by a marked pastoral tranquility. Its peace was not desecrated by the raucous noises of the city. Not for a while, at any rate. Merton was none too happy about the gradual proliferation of machines at the monastery.

The generalizations which I have made about Merton's adamant anti-technology attitude, about his intense antipathy toward the city, can be exemplified by so many of his poems and corroborated by so much of his prose that one could almost suggest a random sampling of his works to those interested in pursuing the matter. In a poem called 'Holy Communion: The City', for example, in his first book, *Thirty Poems*, published in 1944, we hear the residents of urban America speak: '. . . .we know no hills, no country rivers,/ Here in the jungles of our waterpipes and iron ladders. . . .'[19] The theme is carried through his second book, *A Man In A Divided Sea* (1946) by poems like 'Aubade-Harlem', 'Aubade-The City', and 'A Letter to My Friends'. It receives extended treatment in the poem 'Figures for an Apocalypse', contained in the book of the same title. The dire message of this poem is that it is only through the destruction of the city—'Drowned in the waters of her own, her poisoned well'[20]—that the City of God, the New Jerusalem can be established.

The picture in 'How to Enter a Big City', the lead poem in *The Strange Islands*, is composed of an oppressively bleak urban landscape. Unquestionably, the city was Merton's waste land. The poem argues that the machine-dominated city dehumanizes its inhabitants. Their lives are empty, their sensitivity toward themselves and one another destroyed. Thus the residents of the 'big city' are described:

> Everywhere there is optimism without love
> And pessimism without understanding,
> They who have new clothes, and smell of haircuts
> Cannot agree to be at peace
> With their own images, shadowing them in windows
> From store to store.[21]

In 'And So Goodbye to Cities' (*Emblems of a Season of Fury*, 1963) the poet tells us that '. . . . cities have grown old in war and fun. /The sick idea runs riot'.[22] Nor is much hope held open that the dreary situation will be improved, for 'Old machine runs loose again, /Starting another city with a new disgrace'.[23] The cycle seems to be as endless as it is depressing, and always it is the machine which is the source of the trouble. 'Let the perversity of a machine become our common study,' Merton requests with unusual resignation, in his poem, 'An Elegy for Five Old Ladies'.[24] I will end this sketchy presentation of illustrations by citing a section called 'Six Day O'Hare Telephane' which is part of Merton's lengthy anti-poem called *The Geography of Lograire*, his last published book of poems. His anti-technology, anti-urban biases were as alive as the end of his poetic career as they were at the beginning. For all the formal differences between his late and his early poetry, there is remarkable consistency in terms of thematic content. The manner may have changed in his late years, but the matter remained much the same. In *The Geography of Lograire* we read:

> Invent a name for a town
> Any town
> 'Sewage Town'.[25]

(6) The final theme which I would like to discuss in demonstrating Merton's participation in the tradition of American Critical Romanticism is the theme of anti-government, or more pointedly, anti-politics and politicians. Historically, an antagonism toward government is bound up with the primacy which the Romantics attached to individualism. Government represented collective man, and the Romantics put little trust in collective man. Thoreau, as in 'Civil Disobedience', was capable of stating his case in the extremest possible terms, when, going beyond Thomas Jefferson, he declared that 'that government is best which governs not at all'.[26] The Romantics' political philosophy was based upon the idea that the most important unit in society is the individual, both by reason of the intrinsic superiority of the individual over collective man, and also because in time individual man preceded collective man. In his essay entitled 'Politics', Emerson instructs his readers to remember that institutions are not aboriginal, 'that they are not superior to the citizen; that every one of them was once the act of a single man . . .'.[27] Later in that essay Emerson sounds a note which was to reverberate down through the course of subsequent American history and be echoed in the country's literature; it is still in the air today, and Merton heard it and played upon it. Emerson says: 'Every actual state is corrupt. Good men must not obey the laws too well. What satire on government can equal the severity of censure conveyed in the word *politic*, which now for ages has signified cunning, intimating that the State is a trick.'[28]

Merton never displayed much trust in governments of any kind. He had, understandably, an abhorrence for totalitarianism. In *The Secular Journal*, written before he entered the monastery, he shows his disdain for the fascism which had then gained the ascendancy in Italy and Germany. But at the same time he does not wax enthusiastic over the governments of Britain and the United States. What he sees is not sick countries as opposed to healthy countries, but countries in which a disease that infects all is more advanced than in others. The disease is a mindless materialism and an infatuation with power which is caused by severe spiritual anemia. And governments, far from demonstrating an ability to arrest the disease, seem only to exacerbate it. If they are not malicious in their dealings with the citizenry, they are at least dangerous by reason of their bumbling ineptitude.

Merton's suspicion of government, particularly the U.S. government, was clearly expressed during the 1960s. His opposition to the Vietnam war caused him to write several pieces on the general subjects of violence and war, which reminds us that Thoreau's opposition to the Mexican War was one of the stimuli for his writing 'Civil Disobedience'. It was not until the 1960s that Merton began to pay any kind of systematic attention to the public sphere. He came to conclude that governments, even well-intentioned democratic governments, could by their actions prove to be a threat to the physical and moral well-being even of the citizens whom it is their obligation to protect. Furthermore, he thought it the special responsibility of the monk to speak out against govenment. The monk could not pretend that he was not involved, for this would go against what Merton regarded as an important dimension of the monastic vocation: one becomes a monk not to sever himself from mankind but to bind himself more intimately to it.

There is in Merton's anti-government attitude the overriding assumption that if a government is awry it is because the culture of the country as a whole is awry. So we see a connection between this theme and that of anti-technology. 'My outlook is not purely American,' Merton wrote to an acquaintance, 'and I feel some- times disturbed by the lack of balance in the powerful civilization of this country.'[29] The 'lack of balance' is explained by the country's spiritual impoverishment, all the more obvious for the fact that it goes hand in hand with garish affluence. When he says that his outlook is not purely American I think he refers to his lack of affinity with the country's practical politics and with its popular culture. It seems that toward the end of his life Merton felt more and more alienated from political America, from this country's government, but no less from the governments of all countries and all political entities. 'I believe my vocation is essentially that of a pilgrim and an exile in life,' he continues in the letter, 'that I have no proper place in this world, but for that reason I am in some sense to be the friend and brother of people everywhere, especially those who are exiles and pilgrims like myself.'[30] But if Merton was never a political American, he was decidedly so spiritually. He was, in other words, by reasons of themes which were central to his thought and writing, well within a venerable tradition of American literature. He is numbered among the ranks of those adamant outsiders, beginning with Emerson and Thoreau, who did not skate along the surface of things. Their contributions to the national literature is substantial.

In bringing this discussion to a close, I would like to venture some generalizations about Merton's place within twentieth-century American literature. As a literary artist, Merton contributed to no fewer than five separate genres: the novel, poetry, autobiography, the essay, and the journal. Over his contribution to the novel, we need not pause for long. He apparently completed three novels before he entered the monastery in 1941. The manuscripts of two were destroyed; the third, which he called *Journal of My Escape from the Nazis*, was published posthumously in 1969 under the title *My Argument with the Gestapo.* Our interest in it today is founded primarily upon the fact that it was written by Thomas Merton, and not for its intrinsic merits. It is a clever book, but in the final analysis not an example of good fiction. After noting its flaws in *The Sign of Jonas* Merton remarks: 'But I can do nothing with it.'[31]

I have already had occasion to comment at some length on Merton's poetry.[32] Although I would modify some of my judgments, in the main my views remain the same. I continue to think that his anti-poetry is not what it is estimated to be by some, that its tone lacks the authenticity of his earlier work; further, I would even suggest that his earlier work, for all its relative conventionalism from a formal point of view, in fact displays more daring and imagination and is in some respects more experimental than the anti-poetry. I maintain my earlier expressed view that he deserves to be considered an important American poet of this century. And if I call him 'minor' it is in the understanding that the country has produced very few major poets since the death of Walt Whitman.

Merton's own habit, during his later years, of playing down *The Seven Storey Mountain* has had the effect of lessening the value of the book in some people's minds. This is unfortunate, for I think it is one of the giants of modern autobiography. Perhaps the early dust jacket blurbs that compared it to St Augustine's *Confessions* may have been exaggerated, but there is in fact a more than superficial affinity between the two works. It is written with a direct, unguarded sincerity, a fetching artlessness, which lends it a force which I do not see can ever be seriously diminished. *Cor ad cor loquitur*—that is the source of its strength and its appeal. It is a classic.

It is not only the fact that their writings reflect so many of the same themes which leads me to associate Merton with Emerson. Emerson was principally an essayist, and so was Merton. He was an essayist by temperament; that is to say, he used writing in great part as a means of exploration and discovery. He was not a stylist in the sense that he labored over his creations, polishing them until every imperfection was removed. In fact, his stated approach was to move on to a new project as soon as the current one was completed.[33] As a result there is often a rushed quality to some things which Merton wrote; we get suggestions and adumbrations, but not always a rounded-out, comprehensive exposition. This is common to the temperamental essayist. The *forte* of the essayist is that he is a seminal thinker. He is in the vanguard of writers, roaming in new territory, uncovering new mines. Merton may not always have examined an idea with studied thoroughness, but he knew a good idea when he saw one, and he was constantly coming up with ideas which were novel and exciting.

Merton was a diarist, as far as I know, for his entire career as a mature writer. Three collections of his journals have been published: *The Secular Journal, The Sign of Jonas,* and *Conjectures of a Guilty Bystander*, besides *The Asian Journal* which was edited and published following his death. It seems likely that, as was the case with Emerson and Thoreau, others of his published works were derived in whole or in part from journal writings. The aforementioned books are quite remarkable in their way, and may contain some of the best writing Merton did. In any case, I foresee him being recognized more and more for his prowess as a journal writer. Merton's tone is direct, relaxed, and conversational. He is confiding without being insinuating, and sensitive without being sentimental. His respect for the reader is a constant, as is his humor. The honesty and integrity of the man is everywhere apparent.

The fact that Merton was a keeper of journals signals just how thorough and serious a writer he was. The diarist is the inveterate writer. He writes because he wants to write, but more fundamentally because he needs to write. Writing is for him a way of realizing his experiences fully, of concretizing them. The many times that Merton himself refers to and discusses his writing in his journals is a telling index of the importance it had for him. Whatever attitude, positive or negative, he may have taken toward it at any given time, it is clear that journal writing held a prominent place in his consciousness. Merton tried to escape from writing, and failed. He was variously to decide that it was for him simply his monastic work or a penance which he was to undergo with patience and courage—part of his ascetic vocation. Eventually he came to see, I believe, that because writing often involves an encounter with self at the deepest levels, it could properly be regarded as a form of prayer. It was in that spirit that he did his best writing, and it was in that spirit, and at that level, that he ranks with literary figures of the stature of Emerson and Thoreau. They were all at bottom writer–contemplatives, a type of which this country, paradoxically, has produced no small number.

NOTES

1. Thomas Merton, *The Sign of Jonas* (New York: Harcourt, Brace & Co., 1953) pp. 320–321.
2. *Ibid.*, p. 330.
3. *Ibid.*
4. *Ibid.*, p. 321.

5. Merton, *Conjectures of a Guilty Bystander* (New York: Doubleday, 1966) p. 257.
6. *The Sign of Jonas*, p. 166.
7. 'H. M., Pacific Palisades,' in an unpublished manuscript entitled *Cold War Letters* in the Thomas Merton Studies Center, Bellarmine College, Louisville, Kentucky, p. 157.
8. Merton, 'Day of a Stranger,' *The Hudson Review*, Vol. XX, No. 2 (Summer 1967) pp. 211–212.
9. Henry David Thoreau, *Walden and Other Writings* (New York: Modern Library, 1950) p. 119.
10. *Ibid.*, p. 122.
11. *Ibid.*, p. 81.
12. *The Sign of Jonas*, p. 316.
13. Thoreau, *Walden and Other Writings*, p. 641.
14. Bliss Perry, ed., *The Heart of Emerson's Journal* (New York: Dover, 1958) p. 267.
15. Merton, *Cables to the Ace* (New York: New Directions, 1968) p. 1.
16. Ralph Waldo Emerson, 'Self-Reliance,' in Perry Miller, ed., *Major Writers of America*, Vol. I (New York: Harcourt, Brace and World, 1962) p. 519.
17. Merton, *Figures For an Apocalypse* (New York: New Directions, 1947) p. 37.
18. Thoreau, *Walden*, p. 83.
19. Merton, *A Man in the Divided Sea, Thirty Poems* (New York: New Directions, 1946) p. 132.
20. *Figures For an Apocalypse*, p. 23.
21. Merton, *The Strange Islands* (New York: New Directions, 1957) p. 19.
22. *Emblems of a Season of Fury*, p. 71.
23. *Ibid.*, p. 8.
24. *Ibid.*, p. 9.
25. Merton, *The Geography of Lograire* (New York: New Directions, 1969) p. 122.
26. Thoreau, *Walden and Other Writings*, p. 635.
27. Robert E. Spiller, ed., *Selected Essays, Lectures, and Poems of Ralph Waldo Emerson* (New York: Washington Square, 1970) p. 317.
28. *Ibid.*, p. 321.
29. Merton, 'A. A., Pakistan,' *Cold War Letters*, pp. 116–117.
30. *Ibid.*
31. *The Sign of Jonas*, p. 321.
32. Dennis Q. McInerny, *Thomas Merton: The Man and His Work* (Kalamazoo, Michigan, Cistercian Publications, 1974) p. 28 ff.
33. Merton, 'First and Last Thoughts,' Preface to, Thomas P. McDonnell, ed., *A Thomas Merton Reader* (New York: Harcourt, Brace and World, 1962) p. x.

Thomas Merton and the
Discovery of the Real Self

William H. Shannon

William H. Shannon, a priest of the diocese of Rochester, New York, did his doctoral studies at the University of Ottawa, and is currently Chairman of the Department of Religious Studies at Nazareth College, Rochester, where he regularly teaches a seminar on the writings of Thomas Merton. Monsignor Shannon is also Director of the Thomas Merton Society of Rochester. His paper on 'Thomas Merton and the Discovery of the Real Self' published here was delivered at the Merton Symposium at the Vancouver School of Theology in May 1978. Farrar, Straus and Giroux is publishing his more recent study on the writings of Thomas Merton on the subject of contemplation, entitled Thomas Merton's Dark Path: The Inner Experience of a Contemplative *(1981).*

> We shall not cease from exploration
> And the end of all our exploring
> will be to arrive where we started
> And know the place for the first time.
> T.S. Eliot, *Four Quartets*

THAT OUR SANCTITY consists in discovering our true identity is one of the central themes that weaves its way through the writings of Thomas Merton in passage after passage. Merton makes it clear that the essence of the spiritual quest is our search for our true or real self. In *Seeds of Contemplation,* one of his earliest works, Merton writes:

> For me to be a saint means to be myself. Therefore the problem of sanctity and salvation is in fact the problem of finding out who I am and discovering my true self.[1]

A necessary preliminary to the discovery of one's true self is the realization that one's true identity is not the one on the surface. Over and over again, Merton asserts that we are not what we appear to be. The exterior self, which I think myself to be and which I show to others, is not the deep inner self that alone in me is real. I must, therefore, lose myself (my exterior self) in order to find myself (my true self). But I cannot even begin to do this until I come to the realization that I am lost in the realms of unreality, as in the density of a forest out of which I must find my way.

I cannot find my way out of this maze of unreality by my own efforts. The secret of my identity is hidden, paradoxically, more in God than in myself. God alone can make me who I am.[2] God makes me who I am by identifying me with Himself. I become myself, not in separateness and isolation, but by becoming identified with Him in whom is hidden the reason and fulfillment of my existence.[3] God is present in me, not simply as my Creator, but as my 'other and true self'.[4] Since, therefore, it is God who bears in Himself the secret of my identity, I cannot hope to find myself anywhere except in God. The spiritual quest, the quest for the real self, becomes the quest for God.

It must not be thought, however, that finding God is simply a process of emptying oneself by natural means of all that is not God. A person could conceivably do this without arriving at a true knowledge of God or of himself; he could withdraw from all that is external and, in an inward movement of centering, arrive at an intuition of being which would place him on the threshold of that point where his being becomes one with the being of God. But this is not yet the experience of his real self, much less of the reality of God. Being at the threshold is not yet being in the house. One still has to cross that threshold, and he can do so only when God calls him and enables him to take that step. As Merton puts it:

As long as we experience ourselves in prayer as an 'I' standing on the threshold of the abyss of purity and emptiness that is God, waiting to 'receive something' from Him, we are still far from the most intimate and secret unitive knowledge that is pure contemplation.[5]

No natural activity, not even the desire for contemplation, can ever put us in living contact with the reality of God. Only in response to the call initiated by God himself can we really find him. In this vein, Merton writes:

If, like the mystics of the Orient, you succeed in emptying your mind of every thought and every desire, you may indeed withdraw into the center of yourself and concentrate everything within you upon the imaginary point where your life springs out of God; yet you will not really find God. No natural exercise can bring you into vital contact with Him. Unless He utters Himself in you, speaks His own name in the center of your soul, you will no more know Him than a stone knows the ground upon which it rests in its inertia.[6]

God alone can enable me to know my real self, and I can know my real self only if I know God in his inmost reality. Thus the search for my real self becomes the search for God as he is in himself. Nor are these experiences—finding God and finding myself—two distinct experiences; rather the experience is one. 'If I find Him, I find myself and if I find my true self I will find Him.'[7]

This may seem to be a simple task; in fact, it is an immensely difficult one. For knowing God as he is in himself (which is absolutely necessary if I am to know my true self) is not the same thing as knowing about God; and I have in my natural being no capacity able to be activated by my own powers that will enable me to know God as he is in his own reality. It is true that I can know something about God's existence and nature through reason, but

there is no human and rational way in which I can arrive at that contact, that possession of Him which will be the discovery of Who He really is and Who I am in Him.[8]

No one can do this by his own power; no created thing can help him to accomplish this goal. 'The only One Who can teach me to find God is God, Himself, Alone.'[9] The crucial question therefore on which our salvation and true fulfillment depend, is: how can we find the living God in *His* own reality and in that divine reality find ourselves?

The answer to this most basic question is complicated by what appear to be two forces at work in us: (1) a centrifugal force, in our natural being, as it is now constituted, that carries us away from our true identity and therefore away from God; (2) a centripedal force which is God's gift to us beyond our natural being, that draws us to return to our true self, so that we can become once again in God who we really are. The centrifugal force is the influence of original sin which draws us away from our center into regions of unreality. It propels us to build up a superficial, even illusory, ego that is ultimately without substance. The centripedal force, on the other hand, is the power of the Holy Spirit, drawing us to our center, creating a new self in us or, more correctly, uncovering the true self that in essence was there all the time, though unable to be awakened by our natural powers.

The external self,[10] therefore, is a human construct which we bring into being by our own actions, especially our habits of selfishness and our constant flights from reality. It is the 'empty' self, with a substantiality that is superficial, even fictional: the complex in me of all that is not God and, therefore, of all that is ultimately destined to disappear. It is incapable of transcendent experiences. It has a biography and a history, both of which end at death.[11]

The true self,[12] on the other hand, is the self that sleeps silently in our depths, waiting to be awakened by the power of the Spirit. It is the openness of our spirit to the call of God. It is what Merton's onetime teacher and friend, Daniel Walsh, called 'man's capacity for divinity'. It is what Merton calls 'the white-hot point of mystical receptivity'[13] present in all of us, but dormant in most of us. The true self is beyond observation and reflection. It is our own subjectivity that can never be known as an object or a thing. It has no biography or history. It simply is—in hiddenness and in God.[14]

Whereas the external self, created as it is by our own egocentric desires, is ever in the process of coming into existence (though at a superficial level of being), the true self is always there as God's call to become identified with him. It is the insistent voice of God's

Spirit telling us in the deepest ground of our being: you must be born again.

This rebirth of the Spirit, which is the awakening of the true self in us, must not be confused with the awakening of rational consciousness 'which makes a human being responsible for his actions as an individual'.[15] It is rather a deep spiritual consciousness, what Merton calls 'that insatiable diamond of spiritual awareness',[16] which takes one beyond the level of his individual ego. As Merton expresses it:

> This deep consciousness to which we are initiated by spiritual rebirth is an awareness that we are not merely our everyday selves but we are also one with One Who is beyond all human and individual self-limitation.[17]

Spiritual rebirth awakens in us that centripedal force that changes us from within and yet tells us at the same time that this change is 'a recovery of that which is deepest, most original, most personal in us'.[18] To be born again under the touch of the Spirit is 'not to become somebody else, but to become ourselves'.[19] We become ourselves through

> a continuous rebirth, in which the exterior and superficial life of the ego-self is discarded like an old snake skin and the mysterious self of the Spirit becomes more present and more active.[20]

This continuous rebirth reaches perfection when there is only love and there is no more selfishness. As Merton puts it:

> In the language of the mystics, there is no more ego-self, there is only Christ; self no longer acts; only the Spirit acts in pure Love. The perfect illumination is then the illumination of Love shining by itself. To become completely transparent and allow Love to shine by itself is the maturity of the 'New Man.'[21]

The 'New Man' is the real self.

The perfection of new birth which fully awakens our inner identity does not mean the loss of any relation to external reality. On the contrary the inner self is in contact with the world of objects, but it does not see that world in bewildering complexity, separateness, and multiplicity; nor does it see the objects in it as things to be manipulated for pleasure or profit. Instead it sees the world from a deeper and more spiritual perspective. There is a direct and immediate view of reality in which the experience of subject-object duality is destroyed. The inner self 'simply sees what it sees and does not take refuge behind a screen of conceptual prejudices or verbal distortions'.[22]

Most people achieve this perfection of new birth, which is illumination and the full awakening of the true self, only in death.[23] For the Christian striving, though often at a superficial level, to live in Christ, death becomes the ultimate affirmation of his true identity. In death he knows at last who he is, for death is understood, not as the separation of the soul from the body, but as the disappearance of the external self and, for one who is in Christ, the emergence of the real self. Thus Merton writes: 'To be saved is to return to one's inviolate and eternal reality and to live in God.'[24] The emergence of the real self in death is the discovery of our oneness not only with God but in him with others.

> We do not finally taste the full exultation of God's glory until we share His infinite gift of it by overflowing and transmitting glory all over heaven, and seeing God in all the others who are there, and knowing that He is the Life of all of us and that we are all one in Him.[25]

This side of the eschatological awakening, it is possible for us to realize our true self only in contemplation. In the experience of contemplation we are enabled to answer God's call to become one with him. In contemplation the false self recedes and the true self awakens. Contemplation is the journey from the realms of unlikeness (to God) to the realms of likeness. It is the journey from Egypt to the Promised Land. It is the return from exile to paradise. For our true state—the state in which we were intended to be—is the state in which we existed before the fall. This state Merton identifies with contemplation.[26] Indeed he saw the fall as a fall from the unity of the contemplative experience into the state of disunity and alienation in which we presently find ourselves. It is this fall from contemplation that brings into existence the fallen, alienated external self that wants to live in isolation and separateness, and that, as a self-constructed illusion, attempts to take over the functions of the inner self.

This external self is not evil; it suffers the effects of sin. It is respected by God, though it suffers from metaphysical poverty. It may be involved in the external practices of religion. It may even desire to be contemplative or to write books on contemplation. But the external self can never become truly contemplative. For contemplation is the union of myself with God and I cannot unite with God what is, in ultimate terms, an illusion.

> It is not enough to remain the same 'self', the same individual ego, with a new set of activities and a new lot of religious practices. One must be born of the Spirit Who is free, and teaches the inmost depths of the heart by taking that heart to Himself, by making Himself one with our heart, by creating for us, invisibly, a new identity; by being Himself that identity.[27]

Contemplation is possible only by going beyond the external self to the real self that is identified with God. Only then do I discover who I am. The discovery is a return to my original identity that was never fully lost. It is 'not that we discover a new unity. We recover an older unity.'[28] In contemplation I do not become something I was not; I become what I am and what I am called to be. I do not really become contemplative; I discover that in the depths of my being I am, and always have been, contemplative.

The journey into the land of contemplation is a long journey in which we have to begin where we are and go to where we should be. But the paradox of the journey is that when we arrive at our destination we discover that we were there all the time and did not know it.

> The human soul is still the image of God and no matter how far it travels away from Him into the regions of unreality, it never becomes so completely unreal that its original destiny can cease to torment it with the need to return to itself in God and become, once again, real.[29]

Again, Merton writes:

> In returning to God and to ourselves, we have to begin with what we actually are. We have to start from our alienated condition. We are prodigals in a distant country, the 'region of unlikeness,' and we must seem to

travel far in that region before we seem to reach our own land (and yet secretly we are in our own land all the time!).[30]

Merton is echoing the words of one of his favorite poets, T.S. Eliot, who wrote in Four Quartets:

> We shall not cease from exploration
> And the end of all our exploring
> Will be to arrive where we started
> And know the place for the first time.[31]

Because we have to start where we are (the state of our outer self), 'God respects that outer self and allows it to carry out the functions which our inner self cannot yet assume on its own'.[32] Hence

We have to act in our everyday life as if we were what our outer self indicates us to be. But at the same time we must remember that we are not entirely what we seem to be and that what appears to be our 'self' is soon going to disappear into nothingness.[33]

For this reason Merton calls the external self the 'smoke self': it is 'doomed to disappear as completely as smoke from a chimney'.[34] When at long last this happens, the true inner self will emerge—not so much into the light of day (for it still remains hidden) but into the light that is the being of God. For contemplation is the loss of any awareness of distance between ourselves and God.[35] It is the experience of God 'identifying a created life with His own life, so that there is nothing left of any significance but God living in God'.[36] Then the soul 'vanishes out of itself'[37] into God. It becomes incapable of reflecting upon itself as a 'self' apart from God.

When one has thus vanished into God in pure contemplation, God alone is left. 'He is the "I" Who acts there. He is the One Who loves and knows and rejoices.'[38] Our identity disappears into the identity of God,[39] and we find our rest in God—not the God who can be objectified in concepts, but the God who is above and beyond all concepts. Our union with Him is not merely a moral, much less a notional, union; rather God becomes 'One Spirit with our own soul'.[40] In coming to know God in his own reality we come to know ourselves in our own reality. This is the work in us of God's Spirit, making himself one with our heart, creating for us a new identity, indeed, in Merton's words, 'being Himself that identity'.[41]

Clearly, contemplation for Merton does not mean my finding God's identity and then my own, as if they were separate realities that I experience successively. The contemplative experience is neither a union of separate identities nor a fusion of them; on the contrary, separate identities disappear in the All Who is God.[42] In the contemplative experience 'we are emptied into Him and transformed into His joy'.[43] We find ourselves (or, what amounts to the same thing, we lose ourselves) in the All, the All that is no thing—and therefore no individual identity as we suppose such an identity to be—for, if the All were a single thing separate from all other things, it would not be the All. The goal of contemplation is to live in All, through All, for All, by him who is All.[44]

> But for me to do this I must let go my hold upon myself. I must not retain the semblance of a self which is an object or a 'thing'. I too must be no thing—and therefore no separate individual identity. And when I am no thing, I am in the All.[45]

When I find myself in the All, I find my brothers and sisters there, too. 'For the more we are united with God, the more we are united with one another.'[46] 'He is the life of all of us and we are all one in Him.'[47]

On one occasion, D.T. Suzuki, the Zen scholar whom Merton admired and corresponded with, spoke at a gathering of Christians of the christian call to unity with God. In the course of the discussion that followed his remarks, someone put the question to him: 'But what about the others?' Suzuki thought a moment and then answered: 'There are no others'. Thomas Merton would have approved of this answer. In fact, he said something quite similar in an informal talk he gave at Calcutta in October 1968. Speaking of the need of communication among monks of different religious traditions, he said:

> The deepest level of communication is not communication, but communion. It is wordless. It is beyond words, and it is beyond speech, and it is

beyond concept. Not that we discover a new unity. We discover an older unity. My dear brothers, we are already one. But we imagine that we are not. And what we have to recover is our original unity. What we have to be is what we are.[48]

The real self is the self that we are in our depths. It is not our creation, but God's. It is nothing other than the divine call at the core of our being to become one with God and in him with all others. It is the capacity for divinity, the openness to transcendence, that God creates in each one of us. It is the seed of God straining to burst the shell of the superficial self in order to activate our capacity for the divine.

The discovery of the real self is achieved (1) through death, which Merton conceives not so much as the separation of the soul from the body, but as the disappearance of the external self and the emergence of the real self, or (2) through contemplation, which is the renouncing of our 'petty selves' to find 'our true selves beyond ourselves in others and above all in Christ'.[49] Contemplation is the letting go of the false self—which is why it is a kind of death, a death that takes place during life.

The discovery of the real self is the termination of the experience of duality in our lives. It is the realization that we are one with God, with him who is All and therefore with all that is. We no longer approach God as a subject approaching an object. Our subjectivity becomes one with the subjectivity of God in Christ and in His Spirit. As Merton puts it

The gap between our spirit as subject and God as object is finally closed, and in the embrace of mystical love we know that we and He are one.[50]

NOTES

1. Thomas Merton, *Seeds of Contemplation* (New York: New Directions, 1949) p. 26.

2. *Ibid.*

3. *Ibid.*, p. 29.

4. *Ibid.*, p. 33.

5. *New Seeds of Contemplation* (New York: New Directions, 1962) p. 282.

6. *Seeds of Contemplation*, pp. 31–32.

7. *Ibid.*, p. 29.

8. *Ibid.*, p. 30.

9. *Ibid.*

10. Merton uses a variety of terms to describe the external self: the 'superficial self' (*New Seeds*, 7, 11, 16), the 'empirical self' (*New Seeds*, 7, 11, 279), the 'outward self' (*New Seeds*, 7, 21), the 'outer self' (*New Seeds*, 281), the 'shadow self' (*New Seeds*, 109), the 'smoke self' (*New Seeds*, 38), the 'contingent self' (*New Seeds*, 38), the 'imaginary self' (*New Seeds*, 57), the 'private self' (*New Seeds*, 34), the 'illusory person' (*New Seeds*, 34), the 'illusory self' (*New Seeds*, 281), the 'false self' (*New Seeds*, 21, 25, 26, 33, 34; *Zen and the Birds of Appetite*, 128), the 'practical and outward self' (*No Man Is An Island*, 221), the 'hedonistic and destructive ego' (*New Seeds*, 38), the 'petty self' (*Monastic Journey*, 40).

11. See *New Seeds of Contemplation*, p. 279; also *Zen and the Birds of Appetite*, pp. 127–128.

12. Merton uses a variety of descriptive terms: 'true self' (*New Seeds*, 31, 279: *Monastic Journey*, 40), 'inner and hidden self' (*New Seeds*, 279), 'creative, mysterious inner self' (*New Seeds*, 38), 'inner self' (*New Seeds*, 280), 'inmost self' (*New Seeds*, 282), 'real self' (*Conjectures of a Guilty Bystander*, 134), 'deepest most hidden self' (*Conjectures of a Guilty Bystander*, 166).

13. Thomas Merton, *The New Man* (London: Burns Oates, 1976) p. 147.

14. *New Seeds of Contemplation*, p. 7.

15. 'Rebirth and the New Man in Christianity,' in *Love and Living* (New York: Farrar Straus & Giroux, 1979).

16. *The New Man*, p. 147.

17. 'Rebirth and the New Man,' in *Love and Living*, p. 198.

18. *Ibid.*, p. 5.

19. *The New Man*, p. 4.

20. 'Rebirth and the New Man,' in *Love and Living*, p. 199.

21. *Ibid.*, p. 199.

22. *The Inner Experience* (unpublished) p. 16.

23. See *New Seeds of Contemplation*, p. 71.

24. *Ibid.*, p. 38.

25. *Ibid.*, pp. 65–66.

26. See *Zen and the Birds of Appetite*, pp. 116ff.

27. 'Rebirth and the New Man, ' in *Love and Living*, p. 200.

28. *The Asian Journal of Thomas Merton* (New York: New Directions) p. 308.

29. *The New Man*, p. 78.

30. *New Seeds of Contemplation*, pp. 280–281.

31. T. S. Eliot, *Four Quartets* (New York: Harvest, 1971) p. 59.

32. *New Seeds of Contemplation*, p. 281.

33. *Ibid.*

34. *Ibid.*, p. 7.

35. *Ibid.*, p. 279.

36. *Ibid.*, p. 284.

37. *Ibid.*, p. 285.

38. *Ibid.*, p. 287.

39. See *New Seeds of Contemplation*, p. 292.

40. *The New Man*, p. 79.

41. 'Rebirth and the New Man' in *Love and Living*, p. 200.

42. See *New Seeds of Contemplation*, p. 292.

43. *Ibid.*, p. 288.

44. Thomas Merton, 'Preface to the Japanese Edition of *The Seven Storey Mountain* (to be published in a collection of Merton foreign prefaces by Unicorn Press, edited with an introduction by Robert E. Daggy.
45. *Ibid.*
46. *New Seeds of Contemplation*, p. 66.
47. *Ibid.*
48. *The Asian Journal of Thomas Merton*, p. 308.
49. *The Monastic Journey*, edited by Brother Patrick Hart (Sheed Andrews & McMeel, 1977) p. 40.
50. *The Inner Experience*, p. 69.

Thomas Merton's
Glimpse of the Kingdom

James W. Douglass

James W. Douglass, well-known spokesman for peace and nonviolence, did his graduate studies at the University of Notre Dame and the Gregorian University in Rome. He helped found the Institute for Non-Violence at Notre Dame and was theological adviser to several British and American Bishops during Vatican II. He has taught at Bellarmine College in Louisville and the University of Hawaii. His books include The Nonviolent Cross (*Macmillan, 1968*) *and* Resistance and Contemplation (*Delta, 1973*). *His contribution to this volume was delivered at the Vancouver School of Theology's Merton Symposium and appears in expanded form in his new book,* Lightning East to West (*Sunburst Press, 1980*).

NONVIOLENT ACTIVISTS become overwhelmed by the world. The world of nuclear proliferation, the world of global poverty and famine, the world of imperialism and terrorism, the world with a constant undercurrent of mistrust, exploitation, and mutual violence, a violence ready to consume the earth, is a world which offers no hope to humanity. Yet that world is at the center of the consciousness of anyone concerned with justice and peace, for that is the world which needs to undergo change, or rather a radical transformation, if justice and peace are to become real. That world, which will either be transformed or destroy itself, is overwhelming to a person's consciousness. The world is too much with us in our eyes and hearts and souls, the world is too overwhelming to our consciousness and too deep in our spirits for us to see and live a way of radical transformation in our end-time. How can we even conceive of nonviolent transformation of the world in our nuclear end-time?

The seemingly hopeless question of the nonviolent transformation of so overwhelming a world suggests the need for a perspective in which the world is less with us, yet a perspective which must be just as real as nuclear stockpiles and starving children.

Thomas Merton gave us a beginning clue to such a perspective at the conclusion of one of his last works, *Mystics and Zen Masters*. He questioned there 'the Western acceptance of a "will to transform others"' in terms of one's own prophetic insight accepted as a norm of pure justice'.

> Is there not an 'optical illusion' in an eschatological spirit which, however much it may appeal to *agape*, seeks only to transform persons and social structures *from the outside?* Here we arrive at a basic principle, one might almost say an ontology of nonviolence, which requires further investigation.

Perhaps it was that further investigation into an ontology of nonviolence which Merton was engaged in when he died in Bangkok in 1968. Can we join now in such an investigation ourselves? What was Merton pointing to as that basic principle, or ontology of nonviolence, which would go beyond a 'transformation from the outside' and beyond 'one's own prophetic insight accepted as a norm of pure justice'? Is there a genuine transformation of the world possible beyond the 'optical illusion' of our 'outside' struggles? Can we perhaps understand our optical illusion critically enough to open our lives to the reality beyond it?

A second clue to a new perspective on the world comes from Thomas Merton's entry in his *Asian Journal* less than a month before his death. There Merton recounts his meeting in the Himalayas with the Tibetan Chatral Rimpoche, whom he describes as 'the greatest rimpoche I have met so far and a very impressive person'. In the conversation between the christian monk from Gethsemani and the Tibetan spiritual master, who 'looked like a vigorous old peasant in a Bhutanese jacket tied at the neck with thongs and a red woolen cap on his head,' the talk covered all sorts of ground

> but all leading back to dzogchen, the ultimate emptiness, the unity of sunyata and karuna, going 'beyond the dharmakaya' and 'beyond God' to the ultimate perfect emptiness. He said he had meditated in solitude for thirty years or more and had not attained to perfect emptiness and I said I hadn't either.
>
> The unspoken or half-spoken message of the talk was our complete understanding of each other as people who were somehow *on the edge* of great realization and knew it and were trying, somehow or other, to go out and get lost in it—and that it was a grace for us to meet one another.

We need to take seriously the belief of these two spiritual masters, from both East and West, that the deepest experience of reality is the ultimate perfect emptiness which they were on the edge of and needed to get lost in. For the nature of the supreme realization being sought by them, the ultimate perfect emptiness, is a classic description of reality from the standpoint of those few who have perceived reality from its very center. That description from the center must have something to say about our activist struggle to move the mountain of the world at the surface.

Ramana Maharshi, a great Indian sage who lived in the first half of this century, said of the relation between the world and the individual, 'As you are, so is the world'.

The ultimate perfect emptiness of reality suggests that the mountain of the world, and the struggle of the self to transform it, is in fact an illusion. The ultimate perfect emptiness suggests further that the illusion of struggling with the mountain is based on the ignorance of that ego in each of us which would like to regard itself as an identity separate from the world, as a separate identity which stands over against the objective mountain of suffering and injustice. But 'as you are, so is the world'. The mountain of the world with its overwhelming evil and suffering is not out there. In a very deep sense, that mountain is in here. The world in its deepest evil is, in fact, me.

As Thomas Merton once put it in his essay, 'Is "the World" a Problem?':

> for anyone who has seriously entered into the medieval Christian, or the Hindu, or the Buddhist conceptions of *contemptus mundi, Mara* and the *'emptiness of the world*,' it will be evident that this means not the rejection of a reality, but the unmasking of an illusion. The world as pure object is something that is not there. It is not a reality outside us for which we exist. . . . It is an extension and a projection of ourselves and of our lives, and if we attend to it respectfully, while attending also to our own freedom and our own integrity, we can learn to obey its ways and coordinate our lives with its mysterious movements. The way to find the real 'world' is not merely to measure and observe what is outside us, but to discover our own inner ground.
> For that is where the world is, first of all, in my deepest self.

Thomas Merton's and Ramana Maharshi's identification of the world with our innermost reality has been confirmed from another direction by the scientifically revolutionary worldview of modern physics. From a strictly scientific standpoint, we can clear our eyes of that habitual blindness, which defines the world as an object beyond the self, by recalling that modern physics has exploded the myth of the commonsense perception of the world as a solid, tangible mass existing by itself.

The world revealed by the modern physics of quantum theory and relativity theory recalls us to our inner spiritual world. At the atomic level the objective world ceases to exist altogether, so that modern physics confronts one ultimately with a vast emptiness outside time and space, but not far removed from the spiritual master's experience of reality as the ultimate perfect emptiness.

If we in fact live in a shadow-world of ultimate emptiness whose objective reality and conflicts are derived from our own psyche, the world is too much with us for a radically spiritual reason. As we are, so is the world because the world derives its fundamental shape and definitions from ourselves, and primarily from our ego, in a way too profound for us to grasp except in the rare case of the spiritual master's experience of reality. As we are, so is the world, in so deep-rooted a sense that the world can and will be transformed only and exactly to the extent that I undergo transformation in myself. What we know 'out there' as the most resistant evil reality to be transformed, is in reality 'in here' in its primary being.

Once we begin to see this profound interpenetration of inner and outer worlds in a oneness of reality, the insoluble enigma of the world of evil gives way to the edge of the unifying mystery of Oneness, of Love, a mystery which we cannot fully understand but which we can in fact move into with our lives and participate in to the extent of experiencing an ever-more-united world in Reality.

At this point there begins to appear the deeper significance of Jesus' teaching that the person who loses self will find it, and of Gandhi's parallel teaching that the satyagrahi, or person of truth-force, must reduce herself to zero. For it is the individual self or ego which goes about defining the world together with its evil and suffering, and it is that ego which then taking itself as a distinct reality confronts its own world of suffering with the demand that it change. Yet the prerequisite for change is, as Jesus points out, in the eye of the beholder. Or as Gandhi teaches, such change becomes possible only when the satyagrahi has so humbled herself that even the very dust could crush her. Only then, and not until then, at the point of being crushed by the dust itself, will the satyagrahi have reduced the ego-self enough to have a living glimpse of Truth, a Truth whose nonviolence can transform the world.

In another passage of his *Asian Journal*, Thomas Merton describes a transforming glimpse of Truth which opened up for him, the experience given to him in his contemplation of the great stone Buddhas at Polonnaruwa in Ceylon one week before he died:

> I am able to approach the Buddhas barefoot and undisturbed, my feet in wet grass, wet sand. Then the silence of the extraordinary faces. The great smiles. Huge and yet subtle. Filled with every possibility, questioning nothing, knowing everything, rejecting nothing, the peace not of emotional resignation but of Madhyamika, of sunyata, that has seen through every question without trying to discredit anyone or anything—*without refutation*—without establishing some other argument. For the doctrinaire, the mind that needs well-established positions, such peace, such silence, can be frightening. . . .
> Looking at these figures I was suddenly, almost forcibly, jerked clean out of the habitual, half-tied vision of things, and an inner clearness, clarity, as if exploding from the rocks themselves, became evident and obvious. . . . The thing about all this is that there is no puzzle, no problem, and really no 'mystery'. All problems are resolved and everything is clear, simply because what matters is clear. The rock, all matter, all life, is charged with dharmakaya. . . everything is emptiness and everything is compassion.

'Everything is emptiness and everything is compassion.' In our resistance to humankind's destruction, we need to live and act in that spirit of ultimate perfect emptiness and compassion if we are to experience transformation.

Along such a way, there is no us and them, no problem of evil fixed insolubly in the world in the lives of others. The truth is that there is no intentional evil or sin of which we can be certain except our own. It is thus our own sin which is the metaphysical key to the apparent sin of all—an insight with shattering political implications which is the undiscovered basis of Gandhi's vision of non-violence identifying profound personal change with a global transformation. One can make an analogy to Einstein's scientifically revolutionary formulation: Just as mass is resistance to change but in the process of change (i.e., motion) has energy, so is sin resistance to change which nevertheless can be converted into great energy for change. If I can know for certain in reality only the responsibility of my own sin, then the essence of reality involves my accepting as an extension of that insight the responsibility for all evil—turning a recognition of the radical nature and extension of sin into a new energy for revolutionary personal/social change. Our own sin can, through a responsible insight, be converted into an undiscovered energy for change. We are all one, and the person responsible for global evils, as confirmed by our own radical insight into consciousness, is not somewhere out there but right here.

As Merton and Gandhi taught (together with Dostoevsky in *The Brothers Karamazov* and, basic to them all, Jesus in the Gospels), because an experiment in this reality has to go deeply into ego-shattering truths, we seldom experience the primary truth: the responsibility of each for all through the recognition of one's own sin as fundamental to the most destructive violence and evil. Through my own sin I experience the truth that each is responsible for all, as seen in widening circles from one's own immediate situation (the first sin-barrier we refuse to acknowledge and cross) extending outward to the entire world. Without denying that evil has many external agents in the world, we find its ultimate source and responsibility comes home with startling clarity when we are finally humbled enough by reality to see simply and clearly that as we are, so is the world. At that point we become open to Merton's way of transformation, as experienced in his encounter with the Buddhas, where everything is emptiness and everything is compassion. We begin then to walk on that transforming way of ultimate perfect emptiness and compassion.

I believe that Thomas Merton's ultimate experience of Reality, and the insight emerging from it, is the foundation we need for nonviolent direct action—that 'ontology of nonviolence' for action that will transform our nuclear end-time into the kingdom of God.

Bibliography

Books by Thomas Merton

Thirty Poems, New Directions, New York, 1944
A Man in the Divided Sea, New Directions, New York, 1946
Figures for an Apocalypse, New Directions, New York, 1948
The Seven Storey Mountain, Harcourt, Brace, New York, 1948
Exile Ends in Glory, Bruce Publishing Co., Milwaukee, 1948
Seeds of Contemplation, New Directions, New York, 1949
The Waters of Siloe, Harcourt, Brace, New York, 1949
The Tears of the Blind Lions, New Directions, New York, 1949
What are These Wounds?, Bruce Publishing Co., Milwaukee, 1950
The Ascent to Truth, Harcourt, Brace, New York, 1951
The Sign of Jonas, Harcourt, Brace, New York, 1953
Bread in the Wilderness, New Directions, New York, 1953
The Last of the Fathers, Harcourt, Brace, New York, 1954
No Man Is an Island, Harcourt Brace, New York, 1955
The Living Bread, Farrar, Straus, New York, 1956
The Strange Islands, New Directions, New York, 1956
The Tower of Babel, New Directions, New York, 1957
The Silent Life, Farrar, Straus, New York, 1957
Thoughts in Solitude, Farrar, Straus, New York, 1958
The Secular Journal of Thomas Merton, Farrar, Straus, New York, 1959
Selected Poems of Thomas Merton, New Directions, New York, 1959
Spiritual Direction and Meditation, Liturgical Press, Collegeville, 1960
The Wisdom of the Desert, New Directions, New York, 1960
Disputed Questions, Farrar, Straus, New York, 1960

The Behavior of Titans, New Directions, New York, 1961
New Seeds of Contemplation, New Directions, New York, 1961
The New Man, Farrar, Straus, New York, 1961
Original Child Bomb, New Directions, New York, 1962
A Thomas Merton Reader, Harcourt, Brace, New York, 1962 (a revised paperback edition published by Doubleday Image Books)
Life and Holiness, Herder and Herder, New York, 1963
Emblems of a Season of Fury, New Directions, New York, 1963
Seeds of Destruction, Farrar, Straus, New York, 1964
The Way of Chuang Tzu, New Directions, New York, 1965
Seasons of Celebration, Farrar, Straus, 1965
Raids on the Unspeakable, New Directions, New York, 1966
Conjectures of a Guilty Bystander, Doubleday, New York, 1966
Mystics and Zen Masters, Farrar, Straus, New York, 1967
Cables to the Ace, New Directions, New York, 1968
Faith and Violence, University of Notre Dame Press, Notre Dame, 1968
Zen and the Birds of Appetite, New Directions, New York, 1969
My Argument with the Gestapo, Doubleday, New York, 1969
The Geography of Lograire, New Directions, New York, 1969
The True Solitude, Hallmark, Kansas City, 1969
The Climate of Monastic Prayer, Cistercian Publications, Kalamazoo, 1969 (also published under the title *Contemplative Prayer*, Doubleday Image)
Opening the Bible, Liturgical Press, Collegeville, Minn., 1970
A Hidden Wholeness, (Thomas Merton and John Howard Griffin) Houghton Mifflin, Boston, 1970
Contemplation in a World of Action, Doubleday, New York, 1971
Thomas Merton on Peace, McCall, New York, 1971 (reissued under the title *The Nonviolent Alternative*, Farrar, Straus & Giroux, 1980)
The Asian Journal of Thomas Merton, New Directions, New York, 1973
He Is Risen, Argus Publications, Niles, Mich., 1975
Ishi Means Man, Unicorn Press, Greensboro, N.C., 1976

The Monastic Journey, Sheed, Andrews & McMeel, Kansas City, 1977

The Collected Poems of Thomas Merton, New Directions, New York, 1977

A Catch of Anti-Letters, (Thomas Merton and Robert Lax) Sheed, Andrews and McMeel, Kansas City 1978

Love and Living, Farrar, Straus & Giroux, New York 1979

Thomas Merton on Saint Bernard, Cistercian Publications, Kalamazoo, 1980

CISTERCIAN PUBLICATIONS INC.
Kalamazoo, Michigan

Texts and Studies in the Monastic Tradition

TITLES LISTING

THE CISTERCIAN FATHERS SERIES

Temporarily out of print

†Forthcoming